NEW MEXICANS IN CAMEO AND CAMERA

❈

NEW MEXICANS IN CAMEO AND CAMERA

New Deal Documentation
of
Twentieth-Century Lives

EDITED BY MARTA WEIGLE

UNIVERSITY OF NEW MEXICO PRESS
Albuquerque

Library of Congress Cataloging in Publication Data
Main entry under title:

New Mexicans in cameo and camera.

   Bibliography: p.
   Includes index.
   1. New Mexico—Social life and customs—Sources.
2. New Mexico—Biography.   3. New Mexico—Social
conditions—Sources.   I. Weigle, Marta.
F801.N47   1985   978.9   85-8531
ISBN 0-8263-0811-2
ISBN 0-8263-0812-0 (pbk.)

Designed by Emmy Ezzell

Dedicated to
All who worked on these New Deal projects
and to
All whose lives are documented herein

CONTENTS

PREFACE

Like the rest of the nation, New Mexicans of the 1930s and early 1940s were battling the effects of prolonged drought and depression. Their heroic stories were chronicled by some two hundred artists, writers, and photographers employed by various New Deal agencies. Although somewhat constrained by official directives and criticisms, these workers produced a remarkably sensitive and powerful grass-roots picture of the neighbors they already knew and those they met in the course of their work. *New Mexicans in Cameo and Camera* is a collection of their portraits, gathered from throughout the state.

Franklin D. Roosevelt's New Deal provided acutely needed relief for Americans in the 1930s, at the same time spawning numerous programs to document both the social conditions that necessitated such federal aid and the effects of its implementation. The guides to the forty-eight states assembled by workers on the Federal Writers' Project and the over 130,000 photographs taken by members of the Historical Section of the Farm Security Administration are probably the best

known products of these documentation programs. However, except for the 1940 state guide and some of Dorothea Lange's and John Collier's FSA photographs, very few of New Mexico's wealth of New Deal documents are generally known.

Most of the photographs, life and oral histories, and descriptive accounts in this collection have been selected from Farm Security Administration photographs in the Library of Congress and New Mexico Federal Writers' Project (later, Program) files in Santa Fe and Washington, D.C. These have been supplemented by works of art produced on federal projects between 1933 and 1943, by photographs and architectural drawings from the Historic American Buildings Survey, and by a few photographs taken in El Cerrito under the auspices of the United States Department of Agriculture's Bureau of Agricultural Economics.

The five sections of texts and photographs have been arranged geographically: (1) "Rebozo and Resolano: Old Hispanic Lifeways"; (2) "Miners, Merchants, Homesteaders, and

Indians: Western New Mexicans"; (3) "Commerce and Cowboys: The Northeast"; (4) "The Literary Tularosa"; and (5) "Southeastern Scouts, Ranchers and Homesteaders." They are anchored by the two strengths in extant documents—the Hispanic North and the Anglo settlers of southeastern New Mexico. Unfortunately, very few surviving materials deal with Native Americans.

The Writers' Project/Program texts were selected first. They were chosen for geographic, occupational, and racial representation. Although some of the reminiscences are not of the twentieth century, the imaginative interest kindled by their subject matter (old Hispano folklife, outlaws, cowboys, for example) certainly is. Most important, perhaps, is that the accounts stand out as vivid, intriguing, and often amusing glimpses of "ordinary" people living in a period of New Mexico history which has received comparatively little attention.

The photographs do not always correspond exactly to the people and places mentioned in the texts, but exemplify the spirit of the subjects involved. Both texts and photographs have been minimally annotated, with notes to suggest a few additional readings, to clarify historical facts and discrepancies, and to gloss unfamiliar terms.

Biographical sketches of all the artists, photographers, and writers whose work is represented here are given in the appendix. A glossary highlights the organization and activities of all the projects mentioned, both nationally and in New Mexico, and is followed by a selected bibliography.

ACKNOWLEDGMENTS

The major work for this collection was made possible by a 1979–81 grant from the National Endowment for the Humanities to myself and William Wroth, then of the Taylor Museum of the Colorado Springs Fine Arts Center, to study "Governmental Support of the Arts in New Mexico, 1933–1943" (RS-00056-79-0589). Will proved a fine colleague throughout. For my part on the verbal arts (primarily historical records, music, theater, and writing), research assistants Mary Powell and Lois Vermilya-Weslowski helped by ably cataloguing most of the New Mexico holdings in Santa Fe and, in Powell's case, in the Library of Congress. My project consultants, Richard B. Stark of Santa Fe and Joy E. McWilliams of Albuquerque, also provided invaluable assistance.

In 1976 and 1977 I worked with Lorin W. Brown and Charles L. Briggs, the latter then at the University of Chicago, in editing a collection published in 1978 as *Hispano Folklife of New Mexico: The Lorin W. Brown Federal Writers' Project Manuscripts*. Chuck did the field work and helped weave together what we both knew of Lorenzo (Lorin) and his fellows. Sadly, Lorenzo did not live to see the book's publication, but he continues as an inspiration in these matters.

Since 1983 I have been collaborating with Peter White at the University of New Mexico on a book of New Mexico folklore. Peter generously helped me go back through some of the Santa Fe holdings and discussed their significance. Some of the documents and themes in this collection are the result.

Peter Nabokov's enthusiasm for the Historic American Buildings Survey has proved infectious. I am also indebted to Peter Bermingham, director of the University of Arizona Museum of Art, for his photograph of Peter Hurd's Alamogordo mural in chapter five and to Louisa Thorpe for information about her father, Reyes N. Martínez.

The staffs of the New Mexico State Records Center and Archives and the History Library, Museum of New Mexico, Santa Fe, and the Archive of Folk Culture (formerly, of Folk Song) at the Library of Congress in Washington have provided gracious support.

I would like to express particular thanks to Sherry Smith-Gonzales, formerly of the History Library and of the Records Center, and to Gerry Parsons of the Archive of Folk Culture.

In the spring of 1983, Beth Hadas, senior editor at the University of New Mexico Press, sent me a flyer about *Up Before Daylight,* the 1982 University of Alabama Press collection of life histories from the Alabama FWP edited by James Seay Brown, Jr. She asked if a similar New Mexico book could be assembled, and with her expert editorial help through several revisions it has.

As always, Chuck and Nan Perdue lead the way with their Virginia work in all these areas and many, many more.

INTRODUCTION

Government-Issue Grass Roots in New Mexico

In her discussion of the "roots" phenomenon following the Bicentennial and the 1976 publication of Alex Haley's *Roots: The Saga of an American Family,* Tamara Hareven observes that "the search for roots in our time is not entirely new . . . [and] current popular oral history projects are miniscule by comparison to the [1930s] undertakings of the Works Progress Administration's Federal Writers' Project in most American communities."[1] In the 1930s, as in the 1960s and 1970s, there was "a genuine concern for recovering the historical experience as it was viewed and perceived by participants. . . . Alfred Kazin, one of the unemployed writers in the WPA project, described the interview experience as 'A significant experience in national self-discovery—a living record of contemporary American experience.'"[2] Until recently, it has been fashionable to dismiss these 1930s and early 1940s documents as inaccurate, romanticized, and, for the most part, of poor quality. However, both extensively and intensively, they provide a tremendously valuable resource for viewing a significant period of United States—and New Mexican—history.

Although there were documentation projects in cities across the country, the New Deal is commonly thought to reflect rural and especially Southern grass roots. Hareven characterizes this conception as follows:

> Much of the social documentation of rural life resulted from the recognition that that world was fast disappearing, and from the fear that some of its wholesome values would be swept out by a new industrialism. To a large extent, this passion to document rural life was stimulated by the discovery of chronic poverty and deprivation in the rural South and Midwest, which had been ignored while the "pathology" of cities had occupied the limelight during the first three decades of the twentieth century. While they conveyed the suffering and deprivation of their subjects, the photographs and narratives in *Let Us Now Praise Famous Men*

and in other kindred documentaries also conveyed the resilience and wholesomeness of this group. The faces of the "Sharecropper Madonna" and of the Okies also had a sobering effect on those who idealized the myth of self-reliance and frontier life. In addition to the strong humanistic empathy for the subjects and their way of life, these projects also expressed the period's longing for a lost mythical past of innocence and wholesomeness. The very launching of these projects in the midst of a catastrophic depression resulting from the "industrial plant being overbuilt" was a reaction against "progress" and with it, the destructive pace of modern, industrial life.[3]

In New Mexico, this longing and reaction is seen in the abundance of documents describing Hispanic village life in the north and homesteading and cowboy life in the eastern and especially southeastern part of the state. As elsewhere in the country, most of these were gathered as part of the WPA.

On January 3, 1935, President Franklin D. Roosevelt addressed the Congress and declared: "The Federal Government must and shall quit this business of relief. . . . We must preserve not only the bodies of the unemployed from destitution, but also their self-respect, their self-reliance, and courage and determination." He signed Executive Order No. 7034 on May 6, thereby establishing the Works Progress Administration to coordinate "the work relief program as a whole" and to "recommend and carry on small useful projects designed to assure a maximum employment in all localities." White-collar jobs were to be among such "small useful projects," and on August 2 the WPA's Federal Project Number One was announced as follows:

> It is the intention of this Administration to sponsor nation-wide projects intending to employ persons now on relief who are qualified in fields of Art, Music, Drama,

and Writing. The following persons have been appointed by [WPA Federal Administrator] Mr. [Harry] Hopkins to direct each of these nation-wide projects: Art, Holger Cahill; Music, Nikolai Sokoloff; Drama, Hallie Flanagan; and Writers, Henry G. Alsberg.

> Each of these directors will have a staff in Washington and the field to insure the unified planning and execution of the programs.[4]

Thus began what historian William F. McDonald calls the "heart" of a government-supported and -subsidized arts program that "in material size and cultural character was unprecedented in the history of this or any other nation."[5]

In New Mexico, where the WPA soon became known popularly as *El Diablo a pie,* "the Devil on foot," a jocular Hispanicization of its initials' English pronunciation, Roswell's Lea Rowland was appointed state administrator.[6] Arts projects were not set up until the fall, however. Apparently at Commissioner of Indian Affairs John Collier's recommendation, on October 1, 1935, Ina Sizer Cassidy was offered and accepted the position of New Mexico Federal Writers' Project (NMFWP) state director at an annual salary of $2,300. From October 15 through Christmas of 1935, she directed the new program from her home at 924 Canyon Road in Santa Fe, and from 1936 until her demotion in January 1939 she oversaw matters in Room 9 of the Renehan Building on Palace Avenue, Santa Fe.

When Cassidy was demoted to researcher on January 31, 1939, her assistant, Aileen Nusbaum, became acting state director until her resignation for health reasons on August 31, 1939. Nusbaum's administration was enlightened quite literally when the NMFWP offices were moved from the condemned Renehan Building to 418 College Street [now Old Santa Fe Trail] in El Parian Analco, the so-called native market.[7] As she wrote Alsberg on March 15, 1939: "The fact that we have proper light and ventilation alone proves the wisdom of the change."

Nusbaum, a European-educated native New Mexican who had a book to her credit— *Zuñi Indian Tales* (G. P. Putnam's Sons, 1926)[8]—had more facility in working with people than her predecessor. With help from outside FWP writers, notably Jacob Scher from Chicago and Vardis Fisher from Idaho,[9] she managed to finish the bulk of the New Mexico Guide work before her resignation. Her successor, Charles Ethrige Minton, supervised the numerous final details but paid tribute to his onetime supervisor in the preface to the 1940 *New Mexico: A Guide to the Colorful State,* declaring that "most of the credit for the completion of the work belongs to Aileen Nusbaum, former director of the project, who wrote some of the essays and worked mightily under great handicaps to assemble the materials."[10]

The NMFWP was administered from Santa Fe, with some research and editorial help from the University of New Mexico faculty in Albuquerque. The state was divided into quadrants of counties, each directed by a district head who reported to the central editorial staff in Santa Fe.[11] Field writers, who were paid monthly salaries, not, as the popular misconception goes, compensated by the word, submitted field notes and finished manuscripts collected in communities throughout their area and copied historical documents, newspapers, and the like from local libraries and private collections.

Santa Fe poet Alice Corbin (Henderson) served as editor for the American Guide between February 1936, and July 1937. In a four-page letter to Ina Sizer Cassidy dated April 20, 1936, Corbin summarized her work and the serious problems encountered by the Santa Fe editorial staff:

> As you know the personnel of our field workers, and how few, if any of them, are trained writers in any sense of the word— you know that it has not been easy to get this material assembled on first trial in

correct form, or, what is more important, with all the necessary data attached. The State office is naturally supposed to do the re-write for Washington; but one great difficulty encountered is that we have to fill out such great gaps, as regards history, etc.... For instance, the field worker in the little village of Quemado in the Datil mountains [Clay W. Vaden] can send us interesting material on vicinity—but he hasn't the books that give its historic background. Consequently our work here in the State office is more like a case of complete rehabilitation than an editorial condensation or re-write!

She concluded:

> The personnel of the State editorial staff is satisfactory in every respect—all thoroughly cooperative, deeply interested in the work, and more than anxious to produce results, in spite of all handicaps.... Apparently the various state quotas of workers are based on population, rather than area, or wealth of material to be covered. We rank low on population, but large on the other two items. The distances to be covered are great; 75% of our population is rural, and our rural communities and villages exceedingly varied as regards history, archaeology, racial elements, etc. Our field workers in this vast area are few and far between, in addition to being inexperienced writers, and they have no travel expense to make personal investigations. And, in spite of all the books that have been written about New Mexico, mostly the northern part, there are great areas practically untouched. This shows the immense value of the work being done on the American Guide Book, but it also indicates the stupendous magnitude of the job we are tackling—under terrific pressure of time!

The American Guide was initially conceived as a five-volume regional (Northeast,

Southeast, North Central, South Central, and Pacific Coast) encyclopedia written in Washington from information provided by state writers. However, by October 1935, the national office modified this proposal to concentrate on state guides locally written and edited on both state and national levels. National FWP director Henry G. Alsberg, associate FWP director George Cronyn, and Katherine Kellock, who became the national office's tour editor, disagreed about the guidebooks' character.

> Alsberg and Cronyn favored a small encyclopedia for each state, which would contain essays on its history, education, agriculture, industry, and topography. Kellock preferred a volume concentrating on tourist routes with a brief background of the state. Alsberg's view assumed that the staff would write primarily for *readers;* Kellock's, that their audience was *tourists.* The compromise was a guide beginning with a variety of essays followed by comprehensive tour descriptions.[12]

At first, confusing manuals and instructions were issued, and "Alsberg had to admit that, almost a year after the project began, there still existed doubt in a number of states about the nature of a guidebook. Was it a gazeteer? A state encyclopedia? A device for attracting settlers?"[13] This confusion was not resolved administratively in Washington and the states until mid-1936.

Two early letters from Henry G. Alsberg in Washington to Ina Sizer Cassidy in Santa Fe express the initial national concerns. The first is dated January 17, 1936, barely two months after the NMFWP had started:

> We are particularly interested in scenic or human interest subjects—traditions, folklore, oldest settlers, ghost stories— anything that can be visualized as a halo to illuminate some objects which travelers can gaze on with horror or delight or some other form of emotion.

> We are always trying to keep before us the thought and effort to make people "see America first."

The second letter is dated May 13, 1936. Alsberg notes that Europeans have been promoting their countries for the last two hundred years and that everyone goes abroad to spend money.

> The American Guide and the subsidiary local guides are designed by the U.S. government to teach both our travelers and travelling foreigners that we have many things worth seeing on this side of the Atlantic. If the guides keep some of the American millions, normally spent abroad, right here and add to them some of the European millions, which do not normally come here, they will do much to alleviate financial conditions in this country and reduce unemployment—and this in addition to what the Federal Writers' Projects are doing directly [primarily in hiring].

He goes on to remind Cassidy that "no part of the country will benefit more from the influence of the guides than will your part, since you live in one of the most interesting sections of the United States and increased travel will do much to put your unemployed in the way of finding permanent work."

By 1938, the official handbook for NMFWP workers announced that:

> The chief undertaking before the Writers' Project, is the preparation of an encyclopedic publication entitled, "The American Guide." This Guide will be vastly more elaborate and detailed than any guide hitherto published by a firm or City. No section of the State is to be neglected by the Guide. Through the help of educational and commercial leaders in the State, the articles included will be carefully checked for accuracy and inclusiveness of scenic, historic, commercial, cultural and other resources.

> The general aim of these guides is to

turn the attention of Americans to their own land, and to promote their knowledge of America as a whole, and to arouse the interest of the public in the history, the natural resources, recreational facilities, economic and cultural developments of the State, its folk-lore, art and literature, and to disseminate this information for the use of the public, in the form of State and local guide books, and supplemental books on special topics of value such as collections of native folk-lore; contributions to language with glossaries; Place Names and their meaning; Tall stories originating in the State, and supplemental reading books for school use.

The plan of the Federal Writers' Project is arranged as a collaboration of special workers in the field of research, writing and compilation of literary, historical, economic and racial elements, in the hope that much valuable material may be preserved for future generations, which otherwise would be lost.[14]

In June 1938, Louise Lazell visited New Mexico from the Washington office and reported that the Santa Fe editors "do not know the New Mexico scene very well, and did not at all grasp the kind of writing that must go into a Guide that is to be the only reference book on the subject for years to come, and to be read by citizens of New Mexico, of the USA and by foreigners for their information. *Facts* not opinions or 'fine writing' are what we have such a hard time extracting from these writers."[15]

Lazell's criticisms reflect the FWP's continuing dilemma over the project's guidebooks: how to present accurate, objective, nonboosterish material in a natural, vivid style to appeal to both readers and travelers. At first, Washington stressed the guides' essays on history, peoples, livelihood, education, literature, arts, folklore, and the like.

However, in its desire to provide thorough essays, the Washington staff tended at times to overlook the basic objects of the American Guide Series—to guide tourists. Alsberg and some [state] directors like [Idaho's Vardis] Fisher and [Arizona's Ross] Santee preferred to focus on lengthy essays, without realizing the importance of the tours, which could offer an opportunity for creative writing as well. . . .

Only the determination of the tour editor, Katherine Kellock, led to an organizational framework covering the *entire* country in a uniform and entertaining style. "K.K." almost single-handedly undertook a presumably dull task which no one else wanted or could manage and derived from it imaginative and comprehensive final copy. She insisted that the guides satisfy all travelers, whether drivers on interstate highways or hardy trail explorers, and that they cover every mile of the country.[16]

The NMFWP tours were considered unsatisfactory by Washington officials. Kellock's and particularly Henry G. Alsberg's concern for a compelling style was expressed in the following letter from Alsberg to acting director Aileen Nusbaum on June 13, 1939:

Try to make the readers see the white mid-summer haze, the dust that rises in unpaved New Mexican streets, the slithery red earth roads of winter, the purple shadows of later afternoon, the brilliant yellow of autumn foliage against brilliant blue skies, the pseudo-cowboys in the tourist centers, the blank-faced Indians who are secretly amused by white antics, the patched and irregular walls of the older adobes; make him understand the social cleavages and jealousies, the strangely rotarianized "Indian dances," the life of the transplanted Oklahomans, Texans, Mexicans, Greenwich Villagers, and so on.

A letter of July 20 reiterates this request, pleading that "we want the type of visual description that Steinbeck would give—that is, descriptions of the types of buildings common to smaller New Mexican towns, mention of color, smells, sounds, signs, and above all, of the types of people seen along the streets." By this time, Idaho novelist and FWP state director Vardis Fisher had been in Santa Fe for two weeks, helping Nusbaum finish the tours for the state guide, and he answered Alsberg on July 24, 1939: "Nobody knows any better than I how thin some of these are; but it is impossible at this late stage to give them the Steinbeck color and details asked for . . . [because] the person or persons who logged under Mrs. Cassidy did a rotten job of it—a job so bad that it is almost beyond belief."

New Mexico was not alone in suffering the vagaries of local writers' incompetence and state editors' ineptitudes. The production process was a slow and sometimes acrimonious one of instruction, submission, criticism and compromise between the states and the central Washington office. Nevertheless, according to Monty Noam Penkower:

> In the last analysis, the superior guidebooks produced justified the close review given thousands of pages of manuscript. The central staff sought "an appreciation of the value of facts, an unbiased point of view, a sense of organization of material, and a gift of style." It knew that future judgments of the guidebooks would take into account not only the circumstances under which they were produced, but also their quality. As Cronyn put it, these volumes represented "not temporary displays of talents on relief, but permanent printed records of work done." The guides would be exposed, then, to critical scrutiny for all time.[17]

New Mexico's contribution to the American Guide Series was late.[18] Selling for $2.50 and published by the New York firm of Hastings House in August 1940, it never reached New Mexico until September of that year, too late for most of the summertime Coronado Cuarto Centennial activities. The volume's sponsors—the University of New

Mexico and the Coronado Cuarto Centennial Commission—and the state project workers were dismayed by the late publication date, the ugly blue-on-orange cover, and the subtitle *A Guide to the Colorful State*—Sunshine State and Cactus State having been rejected. The 496-page book contains three major divisions of text—(1) essays on state history, land, peoples, arts, and other aspects; (2) descriptive essays and information about Albuquerque, Santa Fe, and Taos; and (3) twenty-five tours covering the entire state, plus a calendar of annual events, a chronology, a bibliography, eight photograph sections, and an official 1940 state road map.[19] Few contributors and informants are named, and it is an essentially anonymous record of hundreds of submissions and interviews (like the ones in the present collection).

NMFWP workers were late in completing the guide in large part because they were attracted to the state's rich folklore and oral history. In fact, one of the first proposals for the study of folklore on the national FWP was submitted by New Mexicans Nina Otero-Warren and President J. F. Zimmerman of the University of New Mexico on December 10, 1935.[20] They suggested that the Southwest (New Mexico, Arizona and southern California) be singled out for an organized collecting project that would include folktales, pioneer stories, cowboy songs, Spanish ballads, folk drama, and place names. Their rationale follows:

> There was a time when standardization was rampant and all efforts, social and economic, converged on the idea of making the country uniform to the point where Southwestern villages would be identical with Middletown. Our art, our literature, and our music became one. Since then, however, we have become more appreciative of the differences in the various localities of the United States. In fact, we welcome a genuine distinction as something that should be preserved. In some cases, we go too far trying to be different. The more genuine

manifestation of true regional culture is embodied in the folklore production throughout the United States. The Southwest with its triple culture: Indian, Spanish, and English, offers a field to the sociologist, ethnologist, and the writer that no other part of America has to offer.

The philosophy of life of regional folk is only arrived at by a study of their culture, a culture that is manifested through such things as song and poetry. There is a group of society that is fairly uniform throughout America. This group wears the same brand of shoes, eats the same foods, sings the same songs, and dances to the same music, throughout the nation. For this reason, this group is of less interest to the ethnologist. It is a person who is a product of the soil; who lives closely to it, that is able to give us the regional and varied aspect of America. Sophisticates at times try to imitate the Southwestern cowboy or the Indian, but because of the lack of sincerity the result is usually ridiculous. We are not trying to maintain a ridiculous civilization; this lacks those elements which give a flavor to a region without imitation or sophistication. This is the true America that lies hidden in the Southwest, and this is the place where a collection of material which will lead us to understand these people lies ready for the folklorist, ethnologist, and anthropologist. A study such as this would be more than a hobby, and while there are those in the field who have already rendered valuable services, much more remains to be done.

Otero-Warren and Zimmerman's proposal was not directly acted upon. In time, however, such concerns were translated into a series of national questionnaires sent to states as supplemental bulletins to the folklore instruction manuals. John A. Lomax helped prepare the following questions, which were distributed on October 24, 1936:

1. Are there any Indian legends which tell stories of your community? What are they? Give the exact location of the scene of the story.

2. Are there any geographic features, canyons, mountains, peaks, headlands, etc., named for Indian legends? What are they?

3. Are there recognized such things as wishing seats, wishing wells, swamps or quicksands with sinister properties, localities with beneficent qualities, proposal rocks or lanes, etc?

4. Are there any stories concerned with animals or animal life, or the relation between human beings and animals, which are native to your community?

5. Are there any special festivals celebrated at special times of the year designed to insure good luck, good crops, good weather, etc? Describe them.

6. Can you discover any local songs or ballads, sung or commonly used by any group of people or passed down in any particular family? Copy them or get them by word of mouth.

7. Are there special fairs or market days, particularly if they are significant as related to local products or local life or industry? Describe them.

8. Is there a particular kind of costume common to a sect or group worn in your district? Describe it. How did it originate?

9. Are there special customs relating to particular days in the year, such as Fourth of July, Hallowe'en, Christmas, etc.? Describe them.

10. Are there special customs observed at the birth of a child, upon the death of a person, at marriages?

11. Are there community gatherings such as quilting, singing schools, etc? Describe them.

12. Are there any peculiarities of table service or dining routine, such as serving the husband first, serving of bread by the father, etc?

13. Are there religious customs, such as public denunciation of wrong-doing, Easter services, blessing of crops or of rivers, camp meetings? Describe them.

14. Are there rodeos, joustings, log-rolling contests? Are there localized ghost stories, witch stories, etc?

Addenda:

1. Are there any words, phrases, or expressions peculiar to your section, such as dialect, slang, unusual "graces" at table, drinking toasts, short rhymes, dance calls, "play party" songs, etc.?

2. Are there any of the so-called "Tall Tales," where the story teller gets the effect either through exaggeration or understatement, stories that are not in print but that are passed around by "word of mouth"?

3. Are there any jokes, anecdotes, about some local character or unusual person of the present or past that are passed around by the campfire or where two or three good fellows meet together?

4. Are there any unusual epitaphs in old graveyards, or signs about abandoned mines or starved-out towns, or painted on wayside stones?

5. Are there any persons in your community who are believed to possess power to see into the future? Tell some of the current stories about such persons.

Such questionnaires, which were distributed to field writers in New Mexico, influenced their submissions and the interviews they conducted.

Even when involved in the work on the guide, New Mexico fieldworkers were constantly advised to pay attention to people with interesting "folklore." In a letter of August 3, 1938, Cassidy assigned field writer Ernest P. Morey of Silver City the task of gathering place name origins for all locations within Catron, Grant, Hidalgo, Luna, Doña Ana and Sierra counties as given on the 1938 road map of New Mexico. She claims: "This is work that can easily be carried on while you are gathering the other material. In interviewing old timers and others for stories have your list with you and ask them if they know anything about the origin of the names of these places." This is consistent with the acknowledgments for the 1941 place-names pamphlet, in which Charles E. Minton thanks the Museum of New Mexico staff, Kenneth Allen of the New Mexico State Tourist Bureau, and "individuals too numerous to mention—oldest inhabitants, school teachers, postmasters, obscure citizens, prominent citizens, newspaper editors, librarians, officials in various departments of County, State, and National government, the United States Land Office, the State Land Office, archives in the Museum of New Mexico, and so on."[21] Thus, although the emphasis is on the official and historical, old-timers and "obscure citizens" are given a voice.

New Mexico had no systematic life history project like the one set up by W. T. Couch for the southern states,[22] nor did the state's fieldworkers develop anything resembling the southern collection of ex-slave interviews.[23] Nevertheless, although constantly admonished to complete the factual, historical, tourist-oriented state guide, they managed to interview an admirable range of their neighbors and fellow citizens. This book combines their documents with the efforts of their fellow art project workers (who were usually given more creative latitude and subject to more "artistic" criticism) and the photographs of the Farm Security Administration photographers (encouraged to exercise considerable creative independence in the field by their Washington chief, Roy Emerson Stryker). The result is a remarkable record of the lore, life, and oral history of New Mexico, most of it previously unpublished.

READER'S GUIDE
With Maps

The 1939 collection *These Are Our Lives as Told by the People and Written by Members of the Federal Writers' Project of the Works Progress Administration in North Carolina, Tennessee, and Georgia* bears a disclaimer on the series title page: "The stories in this volume are of real people. All names of persons have been changed, and where there is any danger of identification, places also." Names and places have not been changed in this volume on New Mexicans' lives. None of the accounts included are libelous, and their value as sociohistorical and artistic documents would be severely diminished by disguising any particulars of time, place or person.

The following manuscripts and all photograph captions have been transcribed directly by the editor from original typescripts and attached captions on materials in the various repositories. However, since most of the NMFWP manuscripts were retyped in the district or Santa Fe offices—and thereby subject to casual error—minor orthographic and grammatical changes have been made.

Accents do not as a rule appear in the originals, but they have been added here. Other editorial corrections and additions are bracketed. The very few cases of editorial omission are indicated by an ellipsis, and any rearrangement of paragraphs or subsections of the original has been noted.

FSA numbers refer to negatives in the Library of Congress, Prints and Photographs Division, Washington, D.C. 20540, which publishes a four-page descriptive leaflet on the Farm Security Administration Collection. Other photographs are from the Still Picture Branch, Audiovisual Archives Division, National Archives, Washington, D.C. 20408; the New Mexico State Records Center and Archives, 404 Montezuma, Santa Fe 87503, referred to here as NMSRC; or the Photo Collections, Museum of New Mexico, Box 2087, Santa Fe 87504-2087.

Each NMFWP selection is identified as fully as possible by giving title, collector, informant, word and page count, date of writing, date of receipt in Santa Fe, and the location(s) of the documents. The following abbreviations are used:

A#: As of July 18, 1983, the Works Progress Administration (WPA) Files at the NMSRC have been indexed by folder number in a list of 268 folders (30 expandable files) prepared by archivist Louellen N. Martínez.

BC: Number assigned in a preliminary compilation by Gilberto Benito Córdova, *Bibliography of Unpublished Materials Pertaining to Hispanic Culture in the New Mexico WPA Writers' Files* (Santa Fe: New Mexico State Department of Education, December 1972). Some of the NMSRC documents are filed by BC numbers.

HC: The alphabetical city files at the History Library, Museum of New Mexico, Santa Fe.

H#: Materials at the History Library, Museum of New Mexico, Santa Fe, were originally filed by file cabinet, drawer and folder numbers, and many remain so. A card file of most of these documents was assembled in the 1970s, but it has not been updated to accommodate new discoveries

from other vertical files or the extensive city files.

LC: In 1980, the Federal Writers' Project files were under the care of the Folksong Archive at the Library of Congress. Ann Banks of the American Studies Center, Boston College, compiled a "Survey of Federal Writers' Project Manuscript Holdings in the Archive of Folk Song, Library of Congress," dated December 28, 1979. Manuscripts are numbered by file and drawer, from 36.2 to 48.4, as they are herein. These holdings are now in the Manuscript Division of the Library of Congress, where another group of FWP documents was released from the Library's Landover warehouse. Those holdings were examined in June 1981 and are listed here as LCms#, indicating file boxes but not individual folder names.

Records from the National Archives are in Record Group 69, for which there is National Archives Publication No. 54-2, Katherine H. Davidson, *Preliminary Inventory of the Records of the Federal Writers' Project, Work Projects Administration, 1935–44* (Washington, D.C., 1953).

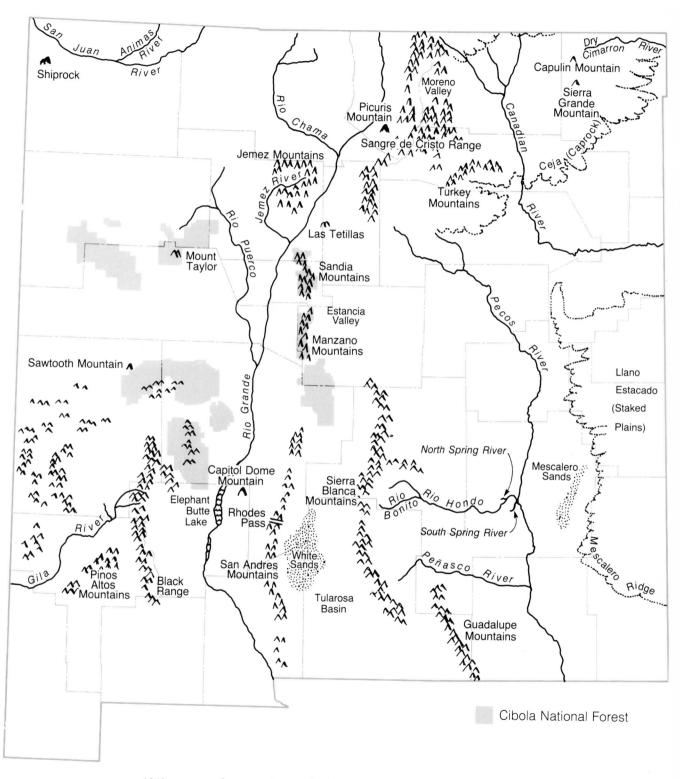

1940 county outline map showing landforms and rivers
mentioned in the text.

TABLE 1—INCORPORATED PLACES OF 1,000 OR MORE

Map Key	Place	Population	Map Key	Place	Population
1	Albuquerque	35,449	18	Clayton	3,188
2	Santa Fe	20,325	19	Lordsburg	3,101
3	Roswell	13,482	20	Belen	3,038
4	Las Vegas*	12,362	21	Hot Springs (Truth or Consequences)	2,940
5	Hobbs	10,619	22	Santa Rosa	2,310
6	Clovis	10,065	23	Farmington	2,161
7	Las Cruces	8,385	24	Lovington	1,916
8	Raton	7,607	25	Fort Sumner	1,669
9	Carlsbad	7,116	26	Mountainair	1,477
10	Gallup	7,041	27	Carrizozo	1,457
11	Tucumcari	6,194	28	Tularosa	1,446
12	Portales	5,104	29	Vaughn	1,331
13	Silver City	5,044	30	Magdalena	1,323
			31	Springer	1,314
14	Artesia	4,071	32	Eunice	1,227
15	Alamogordo	3,950	33	Jal	1,157
16	Socorro	3,712	34	Roy	1,138
17	Deming	3,608			

*Las Vegas City and Las Vegas Town combined.

TABLE 2—THE ECONOMY IN 1940

Activity	Number Units	Employees	Wages & Salaries (millions)	Value Products (millions)
Agriculture	32,830 Farms	178,349*	NA	47.8
Retail Trade	6,617 Stores	12,846	11.6	125.8
Mineral Industries	273 Companies	9,271	7.0	59.4
Manufacturing	272 Companies	3,772	3.8	25.1

*Total farm population.   NA not available.

New Mexico 1940. *Source:* Jerry L. Williams and Paul E. McAllister, eds., *New Mexico in Maps* (Albuquerque: University of New Mexico Press, 1981), pp. 46, 47. Used with permission.

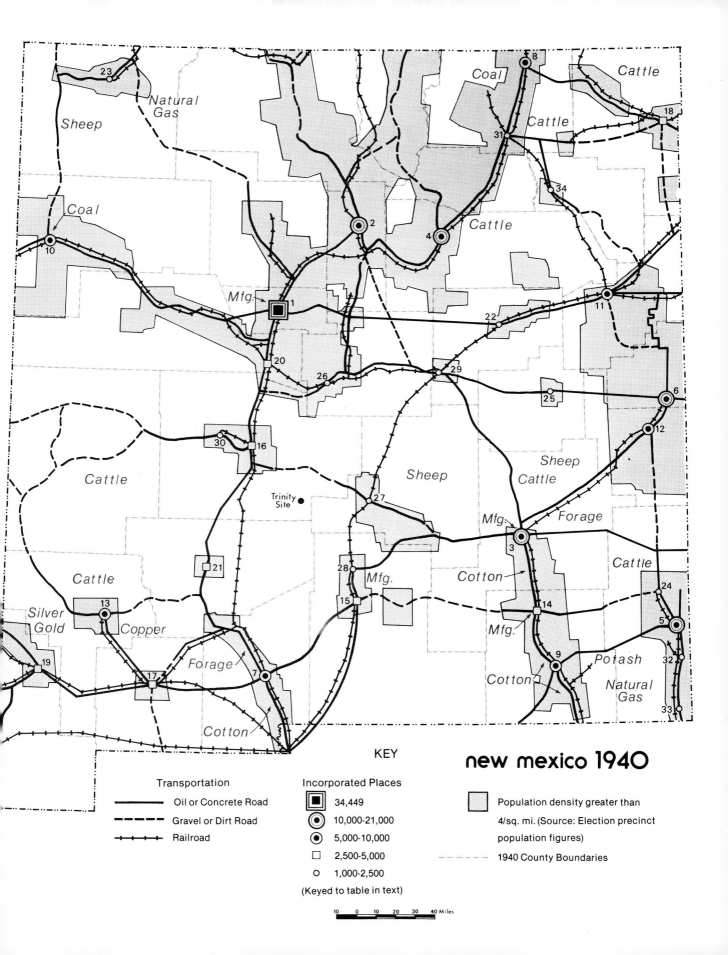

new mexico 1940

KEY

Transportation
——— Oil or Concrete Road
– – – Gravel or Dirt Road
+++++ Railroad

Incorporated Places
■ 34,449
◉ 10,000-21,000
◉ 5,000-10,000
□ 2,500-5,000
○ 1,000-2,500
(Keyed to table in text)

Population density greater than
4/sq. mi. (Source: Election precinct
population figures)
——— 1940 County Boundaries

10   0   10   20   30   40 Miles

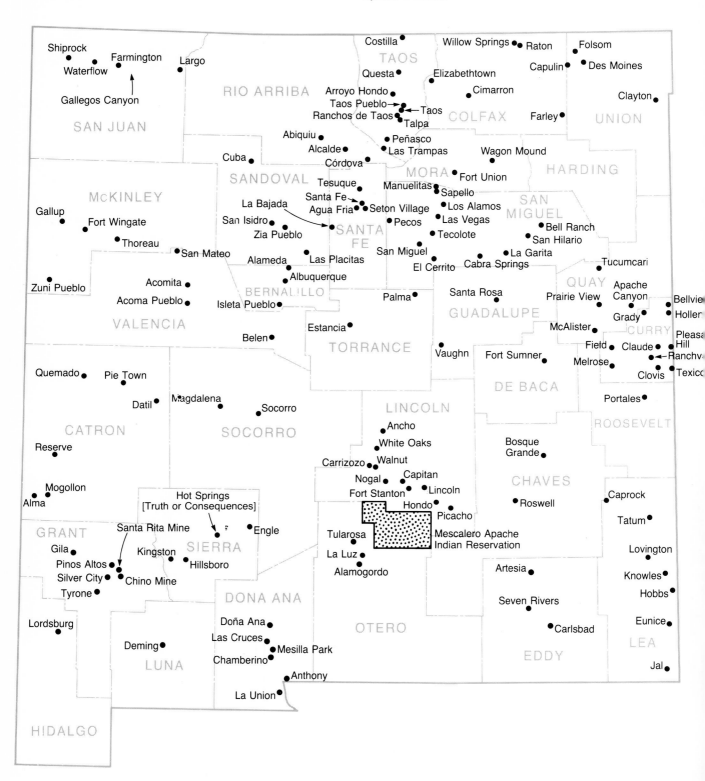

1940 county outline map showing identifiable places mentioned in the text.

REBOZO AND RESOLANO

Old Hispanic Lifeways

William Penhallow Henderson, "The Old Santa Fe Trail—
Sangre de Cristo Mountains." Oil on canvas, 87$\frac{1}{2}$" × 142".
Federal Courthouse, Santa Fe, PWAP-TRAP, ca. 1934–1936.[1]

By the mid-1930s, Hispanic villagers in northern New Mexico suffered acutely from the effects of drought and depression that had closed opportunities for outside wage-work and severely strained local resources, both natural and human.[2] Lorin W. Brown, field writer for the New Mexico Federal Writers' Project, submitted a poignant account of conditions in Cordova. For Brown, writing in 1937, and for his fellow Cordovans, the death of the village idiot Onésimo, who throughout his brief life had been "fed and clothed and treated as one who could withhold the evil hand of misfortune from both the individual and the community," symbolized the end of a good way of life.

Everything remained peaceful in the little village, with no untoward happening out of the ordinary. But about five years ago Onésimo sickened. He crawled into his bed at home and seemed just to give in to his strange sickness. No ministrations helped him. . . .

Dios se acordó de Onésimo, God remembered Onésimo. He was carried to the graveyard with an accompaniment of music, for was he not an *inocente* destined to go straight to heaven?

Shortly after Onésimo's death there was a killing in the place. True, neither the man killed nor the killer were of the village, but it gave the place a bad name, linking it with its neighboring villages in Rio Arriba County which were notorious for the killings committed in them with appalling frequency. Also the crops failed for two years, and work outside in the sheep and railroad camps became very scarce. People would say, "Since Onésimo died we are having bad luck; money is scarce, work is not to be found, and now this killing in our town."

The lame fiddler [of Cordova] brooded more than anyone else over the death of his mascot. We might say his lucky talisman was dead. He took to drinking more than usual, and in this state his inflamed mind

became more alive and suspicious of the indiscretions of his pretty and flirtatious wife. In a moment of insane fury he caught the object of his suspicions and, dragging him to the floor where he could discard his crutches and use his powerful arms, he cut his victim's throat. Onésimo's death had removed a kindly protection from the village and loosed a malignant spirit that bred discontent and hatred with fatal results.[3]

What they perceived as the disintegration of an old Hispanic order in New Mexico stirred Anglo and Hispano field-workers alike. Photographers John Collier and Irving Rusinow foresaw the end of Spanish folk communities like Las Trampas and El Cerrito. Collier, like writers Annette Hesch Thorp, Bright Lynn, Janet Smith, Georgia B. Redfield, and B. A. Reuter, turned to the *ancianos*—old women in black *rebozos* ("shawls") and old men allowed at last to sit on the *resolano* ("sunny side")—for descriptions of their vanishing way of life and its lessons; as Reuter observed, "we Americans have much to learn from men like Octaviano Segura."

To native New Mexicans like Reyes N. Martínez of Arroyo Hondo, the changing Hispanic way of life was symbolized by the *rebozo* or *tapalo*. Martínez mourned its "passing," especially in churches where "the assembly of black-hooded women (shawls were worn covering the head, as well as the upper part of the body) kneeling or sitting on the bare floor (there were no seats in the churches in those years) lent an added air of sanctity to the service, and on funeral service occasion, a gloomy aspect of mourning."[4] In her 1941 folklife book, *Shadows of the Past,* Cleofas M. Jaramillo, Martínez's sister, further described what happened when younger generations discarded such old traditions and began to adopt "the strangers' customs":

The colorful *rebosos* [sic] and *tapolos* [sic] vanished. Modern music, songs and dances, have replaced the soft, musical melodies and graceful folk dances. The quiet reserve and respect has gone, which was so great that even after the sons and daughters were grown up and married, they knelt before their parents to receive their blessing and kiss their hand, and would sooner burn their hand, than to be seen by any of their elders with a cigarette in their hand. I heard my mother's aunt once tell her: "That's one thing my sons have never done to me, is to smoke my gray hairs." The old Spanish courtesy and hospitality has also changed, to the regret of the elders, who have found it hard to get accustomed to the new ways.[5]

In *My Penitente Land*, Fray Angelico Chavez of Wagon Mound reflects on pervasive pastoral and spiritual themes in traditional Spanish life, suggesting that "Palestine, Castile, and Hispanic New Mexico—grazing lands all and most alike in their physical aspects—likewise share a distinctive underlying human mystique born of that very type of arid landscape."[6] San Miguel County natives Fabiola Cabeza de Baca and Alfonso Griego recalled the end of the pastoral as a devastation of family and community. According to Cabeza de Baca, "There was no rain from the fall of 1932 until the third of May, 1935, and the drought was not broken until that winter, when a foot of snow covered the Ceja and the Llano." Finally:

The government started buying the cattle and killing off those which were too poor to move. Papa's cattle were in good condition, but he did not know how long they could survive, so along with other cattlemen he had to sell. . . .

Papa was past sixty and he knew it would be many years before the land would come back; he knew he could not start again.[7]

Alfonso Griego's grandfather Bernardo and his family settled the Valley of La Garita fifty-five miles northeast of Las Vegas in 1878. Don Bernardo Griego (1843–1936) had been a buffalo hunter on the Staked Plains and later became a sheepherder and *ranchero*. He recalled the influenza epidemic of 1918, the blizzard of 1919, and the drought of the early twenties that finally brought herding to an end and scattered the family to find wagework elsewhere. Don Griego advised his grandson "against being fooled by the easy life. 'As I have said many times,' he said, 'as long as people bunch and live together in big cities and live an easy life, they can expect to have times of depression.'" In *Good-bye My Land of Enchantment*, Alfonso Griego writes that when his grandfather and grandmother were buried at La Garita cemetery in 1936 and 1939, "the history of my forefathers . . . ends here. It ends with the great snows, the drought, the Great Depression, the influenza, and the terrible high winds with dust, which forced the sheep-raisers to leave the area."[8]

"Trampas, Taos county, New Mexico. Jan 1943. A Spanish-American village in the foothills of the Sangre de Cristo mountains dating back to 1700 which was once a sheep raising center. Due to over-grazing and loss of range title, its inhabitants now work as migratory labor and at subsistence farming." Photo by John Collier. LC-USW 3-14644-C.

The community land grant of *Santo Tomás Apóstol del Río de las Trampas* (St. Thomas the Apostle of the River of the Traps) was given to a dozen families in 1751 by New Mexico governor Tomás Vélez Cachupín, who wanted the pioneers to provide a bulwark against Comanche raiders.[9] Almost two hundred years later, when John Collier photographed the mountain village in January 1943,[10] the first settlers' descendants could no longer live on the village's land and resources. Collier documented the life of Trampas mayordomo Juan López and his family, including ninety-nine-year-old Grandfather Romero, who "has seen the old world change to the new."

"Trampas, N.M. Jan 1943. The congregation leaving the church after a Mass." Photo by John Collier. LC-USW 3-14628-C.

"Trampas, New Mexico. Jan 1943. Father [Philip] Cassidy, resident priest of the parish of Peñasco, visiting at the home of Juan López, majordomo [sic] of Trampas." [Grandfather Romero sits by the bed at right.] Photo by John Collier. LC-USW 3-17854-C.

In 1940 and 1941, Annette Hesch Thorp, widow of Jack Thorp, began gathering the life stories of old Hispanic village women for a project called "Some New Mexico Grandmothers."[11] Srta. Catalina Viareal of Alcalde told her about filial duties and the lessons of faith.*

Catalina was all of eighty years old, very small and thin with white hair and brown eyes that sparkled when she talked, such a contrast to her little brown wrinkled face. She had on a black dress, blue apron, and a gray cloth tied over her head. She lives alone in her two-room adobe house, which was part of the big house her father and mother had owned.

Her father's name was Antonio Viareal and her mother's María Vigil. They had four children, two boys and two girls. All were born in the same little village of Alcalde.

Catalina was the youngest of the children. Her brothers died when small. When her sister became a young lady, maybe fourteen years old, she married and with her husband moved to Taos. So that left Catalina alone with her parents. Yes, she could have married if she had wanted to. Ever so many men had asked for her. But no, she would not leave her mother and father alone.

She stayed single and took care of them, and when they died they left her the house and land. From then on she lived by herself, planting her garden in chili, onions, *calabazas* and melons. The rest of the land she gave out on *partido* (shares), one part for her and three parts for the one who planted it. Of course, the planter furnished everything and did all the work, and when the crop was ripe he gave her her share.

No, she was not afraid to live alone. She knew everyone in the placita and was related to most all of them. A little girl stayed with her at night. Her sister had tried for years before she died to get her to sell her house

and land and to go and live with her. But no, she did not want to give up all her father and mother had left her. Why, her land was the best in the placita.

Her father had bought it from an Indian when he was married, paying the Indian two *sarapes* (Navajo blankets) and a *fanega* of wheat. (A *fanega* is twelve *almudes*. An *almud* is a wooden box twelve inches square and six inches high. The *almud* was used for measuring grain.) Then he built a room and later on added four more rooms. There used to be *dispensas* (store rooms) and corrals, but they fell down years ago, as did three of the rooms. The remaining two were still good and warm. No, she did not like stoves but had a small one in the kitchen to cook on. In her room she used her fireplace. Heat from stoves gave her headaches.

Catalina's house was more or less like all the other houses in the village with whitewashed walls and corner fireplace and the *vigas* (beams or logs) on the roof almost black with age. Her room was small but clean and cool. In the corner stood an old spool bedstead piled high with freshly washed bedding. On the floor was a *jerga* (carpet) woven from natural colored wool in black and white checks. Against the wall were two or three chairs with gay colored cushions on them stuffed with wool, so high they had to be removed before sitting down.

In a tin nicho hanging on the wall was a figure of a child sitting in a chair with a cloak around its shoulders and on its head a wide brimmed hat with a long plume. In its right hand he held a shepherd's crook and under

---

*"Catalina Viareal," coll. Annette H. Thorp; 1074 wds., 5 pp., 17 September 1940 (H5-5-52#68).

"Wagon Mound, New Mexico. Sept 1939. Spanish-American woman." Photo by Russell Lee. LC-USF 33-12428-M1.

its left arm a lamb, very old and quaint. When asked what the name of the santo in the nicho was, Catalina said it was *El Santo Niño de las Buenas Obras* (The Holy Child of the Good Deeds). Her grandmother told her this story about the Holy Child, for it happened right here in this placita when her mother's grandmother was a child:

There appeared one day in the village a little boy whom no one knew and could not find out from where he came. He went around doing good deeds and helping all those who needed help. If a cow or horse strayed off and the owner could not find it, the little niño would come up to him and say, "I will go and help you hunt for them." No sooner had they left when the stock was found. His feet were sore and bleeding always from walking miles to help someone.

There lived a woman in the village who had been married quite a few years before she had any children and was always sad because she had none. At last a little child was born to her and of course she loved it dearly. The child became very sick when it was about a year old, and all the *curanderas* (women who doctor the sick) came from far and near, but the child got no better. After ten days it was thought that there was nothing that could be done for it.

The mother was crying, for she knew her baby was dying. Just then the little boy appeared at the door and asked for a drink of water. She told him there was none in the house but to stay with the baby and she would go to the spring and get some. He went in and stood by the child's bed and the mother went for water.

When she returned, to her surprise and happiness she saw her child sitting up and playing with a little lamb, perfectly well. And the strange thing was, there were no sheep in the village or close in the surrounding country. The woman called her neighbors and

they came to see what was the matter. She told them about the niño taking care of the baby while she went for water, and when she came back she found the baby well and the little niño gone.

The wise men of the placita talked it over and said that he must be the Holy Child. And so he was. The *santero* of the village made a fine big figure of him out of wood, and the women spun and wove little clothes and dressed him. Then he was put in a nicho in the church. And when the padre came he was blessed.

So there he sits today in his chair, and the devout ones go to him and pray for help. They take little shoes as an offering, for he wears out a great many pairs by walking at night to help those in need.

A conversation between Don Nicolás López of Agua Fria and Lorin W. Brown touches on bygone days of Santa Fe's first archbishop, Jean Baptiste Lamy (1814–88), sheepherding, syrup, and musicmaking—and, above all, water.*

I had stopped for a drink of water from a well in the patio of a group of houses in lower Agua Fria. While drinking I reflected how well named the little village had been. For the water from its springs and wells is very cold and refreshing, and I could visualize how grateful man and beast must have been in those days of slow travel. The magnificent grove of large cottonwoods made an ideal camping spot for travelers on the way from Santa Fe to La Bajada and other points in Rio Abajo or the lower Rio Grande.

While still at the well, I was approached by Nicolás López leading a pair of small horses. After greetings, I helped him draw

water for his thirsty team. "*Que calor amiguito,* if it would only rain so that we would be sure of saving our beans and corn. But the good God knows what he is doing, there is no use in worrying. He will not fail us. Let us go into my house where it is cool." Entering the cool earthen-floored room, I was offered a chair.

From Don Nicolás's conversation I gathered a picture of a much different life in Agua Fria, the life of my host's boyhood. Very meager opportunity for education was his lot. "The teacher was very good at punishing and our textbook was the Catechism and our arithmetic problems were worked on

*"Agua Fria," coll. Lorin W. Brown from Nicolás López; 1011 wds., 3 pp., 11 August 1937 (A#229; HC:Agua Fria; LC47.1).

Kenneth Adams, "Juan Duran," n.d. Oil painting. PWAP
(NMSRC WPA-PWAP #5371).

the surface of the school house door with charcoal. I was not allowed to go to school long. My father took some cattle to herd on the shares from Bishop Lamy and the Sisters of Charity. That was the last of my schooling. For a month at a time I would be gone from home taking care of the cattle, sometimes towards Las Tetillas, other times in the Arroyo Hondo, wherever the grass was best. I will tell you the truth that when I left the school I stole a catechism and while alone in camp I studied this book until it fell to pieces. Before it did fall to pieces it was so greasy and dirty you would have laughed to have seen it.

"And you would have laughed to have seen me when I would come home after a month or more in camp. I would have a head of hair like a buffalo and my clothes would be all torn and in a very sorry state. My father would shear me like I was a sheep. After two days at home I would go back with provisions on my burro for another month or two. A very lonely life, I am telling you, for a boy.

"I used to like to come home when the folks were boiling out syrup from the sugar cane. There used to be two mills here. Everybody would bring their cane to the presses, and while the syrup was boiling or while the cane was being crushed there would be dancing in the patio. Our musician was an Indian captive, Antonio Domínguez, who was very good on the violin. We had very good times then, dancing nearly all night and telling tales while the syrup boiled out. The children enjoyed it too because they were the ones who rode the cross beam which operated the pestle. There, high up in the air, they would rock back and forth shouting and laughing and fighting for their turn to ride.

"Those were great times and I was always glad to get back at those times and I would try to stay as long as I would, enjoying myself, eating too much syrup and candy because in camp I tasted no sweets except when I could find wild honey."

"Why don't you raise any more cane now? Why have the times changed so? I don't see that they raise many crops here any more," I asked.

"Oh, then we had all the water we wanted. Now, the water company has all the water which used to belong to us. You would not believe it but this dry river bed used to have willows growing along its banks from Santa Fe to Cienega. We had good ditches to carry water to all these lands. We raised much corn and wheat. Oh, we lived well then from the land, but now that is all past. Only if God is willing to send us rain do we raise anything now. *'Todo pasa en este mundo,'* everything passes in this world.

"Now we have very much work trying to find a little wood to sell in town. Soon we will have to move into town to find work and abandon our lands. My boys are all in town working now; that is why you find me here alone with my daughters-in-law and my grandchildren. I am getting too old to do any work except feed our *animalitos* and see that they get water.

"But I do not have many years left, and, the good God willing, I want to die here in my home where I was born."

In May 1846, President James K. Polk officially declared a state of war between the United States and Mexico. Lieutenant Colonel Stephen Watts Kearny mustered his Army of the West at Fort Leavenworth and moved to invade Mexico's northern frontier of New Mexico and California. On June 30 at Bent's Fort, Kearny announced that resistance to his occupation would prove futile, and after sending ahead a negotiating team, he proceeded toward Santa Fe. Word of his promotion reached him at Las Vegas, where he issued a proclamation on the plaza on the morning of August 15, and he entered Santa Fe on the afternoon of August 18 as a brigadier general. Governor Manuel Armijo, who served three terms (1827–29, 1837–44, and 1845–46), had retreated south, so acting governor Juan Bautista Vigil y Alarid officially surrendered New Mexico. On August

19, 1846, Kearny addressed an assembly in the plaza and proclaimed them citizens of a United States territory.

In the fall of 1938, Las Vegas native Sra. Guadalupe Baca de Gallegos recalled what her mother, María Ignacia Gonzales de Baca, told her about Governor Armijo and about Kearny's invasion. As presented by Bright Lynn, the Gonzales's family lore is sometimes confusingly interspersed with Sra. Gallegos's own recollections of a pampered pre–Civil War life in the confines of her great grandfather, Don Santiago Ulibarri's elegant old home.[12]*

In the face of Guadalupe Lupita Gallegos is written the story of a long and interesting life, a life that has had more than its share of heartaches and happiness. It is a kind, intelligent face, and devout.

She dresses in unrelieved black. On her head is worn a tight-fitting cap with ribbons tied under her chin in a bow. Around her slender shoulders is wrapped a black Spanish shawl. Her blouse and skirt are black, and on her feet she wears tiny patent-leather shoes.

When asked a question about some incident of long ago, there flashes in her eyes the look of a girl. She smiles half wistfully and begins:

"I was born in Las Vegas, New Mexico, on December 12, 1853. I was baptized by Father Pinal [Pinard], a French priest. My parents, Severo Baca and María Ignacia [Gonzales], were wealthy, owning several farms, many cattle and sheep and much money and jewelry.

"My great grandfather, Santiago Ulibarri, had several children, but I was his only great granddaughter and so I was his pet. Mr. Ulibarri was tall, blond and green-eyed, and very wealthy. His home was Spanish with all the windows opening on the placita, a large yard in the middle. This house was very dark and gloomy and was open to no one except a few Spanish friends. When one entered one of those old Spanish houses it seemed as if one were entering a tomb, so cold and uninviting were they. Several families would live in these houses—the owner's children, their husbands and wives, and their children.

"We lived there shut away from the rest of the world. Mr. Ulibarri was the head of his household, and he knew it. He was virtually the dictator of his family. The women were never allowed on the streets without someone trustworthy to escort them. We obeyed Mr. Ulibarri in everything. Only that which he dictated was done.

"Since it was considered such a disgrace for a lady of the upper class to be seen on the street unescorted, we spent most of our time sewing and playing the piano. We never dreamed of soiling our hands in the kitchen cooking or cleaning.

"In front of Mr. Ulibarri we were always very dignified and well-behaved, but when he was not present we were often silly, as most girls are. I was the only one of the girls who was permitted to go with Mr. Ulibarri very often. He would have his chocolate in bed about eleven o'clock, arise later and have his regular breakfast. Then he would say to the servants in a commanding voice, 'Louisiana, my cape, my cane and my hat.'"

*"The Biography of Guadalupe Lupita Gallegos," coll. Bright Lynn from Mrs. Guadalupe Gallegos; 1650 wds., 5 pp., 27 October 1938, rec. 29 October (BC135; H5-5-51#7; LC47.1).

[Here Lynn switches the narrative from first person to third person.]

The servants would rush to do his bidding. Then he would say, "Lupita, come with me."

"Oh, no! No!" protested the servants. "She is all dirty. Let us wash her."

"You wash yourself. Leave her alone," Mr. Ulibarri would say in a very patient voice. Then he would go to different stores, with little Lupita holding his hand. Immediately upon entering a store, Lupita would go to the candy counter and help herself.

One day, when Mr. Ulibarri was away, all the women got together. They had heard of a strange new toy that had just come to Andrés's doll store. They were very anxious to see it, so much so, indeed, that they sneaked out of the house and went to town to see it. The new toy was a jack-in-the-box. The women had a good time at the store, and when they returned home they made Lupita promise not to tell on them.

Later in the afternoon Mr. Ulibarri returned home, looking very pleased. He called all of his children, servants, and relatives together and told them he had a surprise for them. He laid a large box on the table and told one of the girls to open it. When she opened the box, out jumped the jack-in-the-box. Of course, everyone was surprised.

Only Lupita was unimpressed. "Oh! I have seen it already!" she blurted out. "What, my child?" asked her great grandfather. Before she had a chance to answer, Lupita was carried away to another room and scolded.

Lupita had a Negro nurse who was called Lorenza. She had been brought to Las Vegas by Mr. Ulibarri, who had bought her from the Comanche Indians when she was only seven years old. It is believed that she was the first Negress brought into Las Vegas. People from far and near came to see her. Lupita says it was very pleasant to kiss Lorenza because of her soft, thick lips.

Governor Manuel Armijo was María Ignacia's father's first cousin. He sent word one day from Tecolote that he was coming to Las Vegas to visit his cousin and that he wanted the family to have some delicious hot tamales ready when he arrived.

The governor was in Tecolote already! The house was in an uproar. Servants set to work cleaning the house and cooking chili.

María Ignacia was in the kitchen when Governor Armijo arrived. She had never seen a governor before and was anxious to see what one looked like. She took a bag of tobacco and ran into the room. "Mother, here's your tobacco!"

Her mother was embarrassed. "Go and wash yourself," she said.

"Oh no!" said Governor Armijo. "Don't send her away. Come to me, my child."

María Ignacia ran to him and jumped upon his lap, spilling the cup of chocolate which he held in his hand all over his trousers. María Ignacia's mother was very embarrassed, but the governor only laughed.

When Lupita was eight years old, Santiago Ulibarri died and left her an inheritance. When the Civil War broke out, Lupita was sick with fever and her father wanted to take her south, but her mother refused because the sympathies of the New Mexicans were with the North.

In her home Lupita was a regular princess. She was the only child and had everything she desired. At noon the servants would come to dress her. Then she would come downstairs, roam through the yard, or play with her toys, or go visiting with her parents.

She had an old tutor who taught her to read, write, and to work out problems in arithmetic. When she was ten years old she attended the Loretto Academy in Santa Fe. She had been there only seven months when a fever epidemic broke out, and her parents sent for her at once. She was taught to embroider, to play the piano, and only such things that would make a lady of her.

Lupita's mother, María Ignacia, was just a little girl when General [Stephen W.] Kearny came to Las Vegas [on August 15, 1846] to take possession of the territory. María Ignacia's father got up unusually early and went for a walk. Where the [New Mexico] Nor-

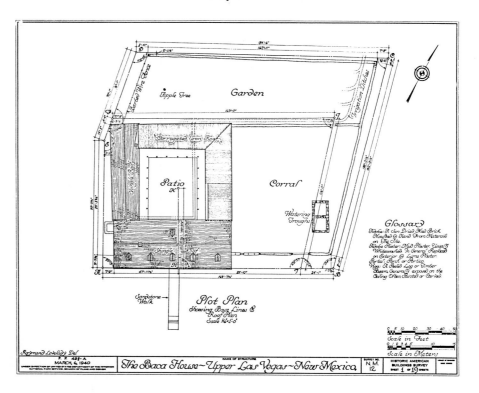

The three-story mansion built in Upper Las Vegas by Don
José Albino Baca between 1850 and 1855 exemplifies the sort of
enclosed, extended family dwelling headed by Sra. Guadalupe
Gallegos's great grandfather, Don Santiago Ulibarri. Raymond
Lovelady delineated the plot plan and four directional elevations
for the Historic American Buildings Survey. There are a total of
nineteen sheets dated March 6, 1940.[13]

mal [now Highlands] University now stands
he saw many cannons all pointing toward the
town. Immediately he rushed to town to spread
the news. The town was in an uproar. Everyone, it seemed, was screaming and crying.
None wanted to become Americans; all wanted
to remain under the Mexican flag.

María Ignacia's father refused at first to
become an American. He left everything he
owned and went to Mexico. All his land was
confiscated and his stock killed to feed the
troops. Only his house remained to him.

The family which Mr. Ulibarri had been
the head of for so many years moved to San
Miguel [del Bado]. After a year Ilario [Hi-
lario] Gonzales, head of the family, came
back to Las Vegas. He made friends with
Kearny, regained some of his possessions,
and moved into his house where some of the
troops had been lodged. Gonzales sent to
San Miguel for his family, and when they
arrived General Kearny, his wife, and their
six-year-old daughter moved in with them.
The little girl was pretty, having fair hair and
blue eyes. General Kearny's men were fed
on the cows, sheep, and other stock belonging to Ilario Gonzales.

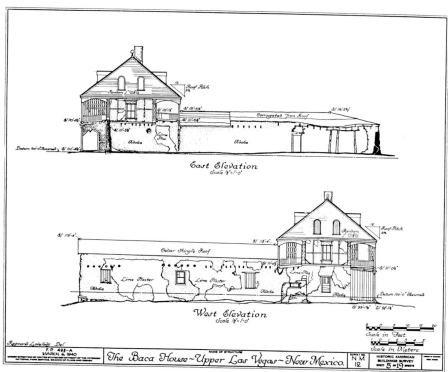

"Patio (North Elevation)," Baca House. Donald W. Dickensheets, photographer, HABS, Library of Congress. 3220/8 MNM.

"South Elevation," Baca House. Donald W. Dickensheets, photographer, HABS, Library of Congress. 3220/2 MNM.

"East Elevation," Baca House. Donald W. Dickensheets,
photographer, HABS, Library of Congress. 3220/3 MNM.

"Patio (South Elevation)," Baca House. Photographer unknown,
HABS, Library of Congress. 3220/12 MNM.

Guadalupe Lupita Gallegos seems first to have come to Bright Lynn's attention because of her abilities as a narrator, particularly in telling old Spanish magic tales.[14] Her stories of her own marriage at age twelve to the much older J. M. Gallegos of Los Alamos, and her subsequent encounters with outlaws Billy the Kid and Vicente Silva, have a fairy-tale quality.*

The family of Guadalupe Lupita's parents had many Indian servants and this is the way they got them, as related [to Lupita] by María Antonia, an Indian servant of the family. The Navajo men would all leave their camps on hunting expeditions in the fall and early winter, taking with them the strongest women and leaving behind them the old women and men with the children. Often, while they were away, the Chimayos, a tribe of Indians living in the area, would come and steal the women and children and sell them to the rich Spaniards. The Spaniards were very kind to the Indians, Lupita says, and the Indians loved their masters. Even after the Civil War ended slavery the Indians refused to leave, preferring slavery with the Spanish masters to freedom.

Before she had grown to a marriageable age, several men had asked for the lovely Lupita's hand. But Lupita was not allowed to know the identity of these aspiring young gentlemen. Her parents were very strict with her. Once in a great while, she was taken to a dance and there she must keep her eyes downcast until she was asked to dance a number.

The boys were always awaiting an opportunity to "make eyes" at the girls, but the latter were not even allowed to look around the room. Mrs. Gallegos says that the only chance a boy had of seeing a girl was at a dance or at Mass.

If a young man wished to marry a certain girl he informed his parents who in turn would have a talk with the parents of the girl, and thus the marriage would be arranged. More often, however, among the upper class, wealthy parents would visit other wealthy parents who lived far off and arranged marriages for financial reasons. In many instances, the bride and groom to be did not even know one another and were not even informed of the impending marriage until all arrangements had been made by their parents.

Often a boy would fall in love with a girl he had seen at Mass or at a dance, and his parents would have a talk with her parents. The girl's parents would take a few days to think it over and then send a refusal to the parents of the boys. *"Les daban calabazas"* (they gave them pumpkins). This expression meant that the girl's parents did not consent to the marriage.

A young Spaniard by the name of J. M. Gallegos lived in Los Alamos and often came to Las Vegas to the dances. It was at one of these dances that he happened to meet Lupita, who was then only twelve years old, and he fell madly in love with her.

Mrs. Gallegos smiles when she says that she doesn't know yet whether he fell in love with her or her money. He was an excellent dancer and they danced much together. One day her father told her that two men had asked her hand in marriage, a Jew named Rosenwall [probably Rosenwald] and a J. M.

---

*"This is a corrected copy of the BIOGRAPHY OF GUADALUPE LUPITA GALLEGOS which was sent in Nov. 8, 1938," coll. Bright Lynn from Mrs. Guadalupe Gallegos; 1450 wds., 6 pp., 30 December 1938, rec. 5 January 1939 (BC137; H5-5-51#7; LC47.1).

Gallegos. Lupita did not wish to marry a Jew so she chose Gallegos.

Lupita, only a girl of twelve, was married in Our Lady of Sorrows church at eight o'clock in the evening. In the church was a beautiful statue of Our Lady of Sorrows. It was customary to dress the statue for every church occasion, and for Lupita's wedding it wore a halo of gold and a necklace of gold which had been given to Lupita by her grandmother's [?] aunt Louisianita.

Lupita was dressed in a white dress of heavy silk called *espuma* (foamy) and wore a short white veil. When the groom's parents came to receive her, she went to the boy's father, as was the custom, and said, "Recognize me as your daughter."

The father replied, "I shall always be at your service." Then Lupita went to the boy's mother and to each of his relatives. After all the customary preliminaries were done with, the ceremony was performed by Father Cuder [Coudert], a French priest.[15]

After the wedding feast, everyone went to the wedding ball, which was held just in back of where the Charles Ilfeld Company is located today. Doubtless, little Lupita was flushed with a new kind of happiness as she glided across the dance floor in the arms of her handsome husband. She was surprised when he suddenly stopped dancing and asked her to go outside with him, for he had a little story to tell her. This is the story he told to Lupita as he held her in his arms, their faces turned upward to the stars:

When Lupita's mother, María Ignacia, and her father, Severo Baca, were about to be married, J. M. Gallegos was a dirty little urchin playing about in the streets. He and several other little street boys saw a wedding procession going by, and they knew that Severo Baca and María Ignacia were going to be married. The boys ran after the coach shouting, "Long live Severo Baca! Long live Severo Baca!" When all the guests were having dinner after the wedding, J. M. Gallegos and his friends crept up to a window to stare at the bride. Little did the young Gallegos

dream that he was staring at the mother of his future bride.

For many years Mr. and Mrs. Gallegos ran a small store at San Ilario. Their store stood close to the main road, and almost every traveler who passed stopped in to buy something and to pass the time of day. One day Mrs. Gallegos returned to the store from a visit with one of her neighbors. Her husband was in front of the store, talking to an American cowboy in Spanish. When her husband saw her come in, he called to her and said, "Lupita, I want you to meet a friend of mine. This is Billy the Kid."

Mrs. Gallegos says that she has always been a brave woman, but when she found herself actually face to face with Billy the Kid she almost fainted. The Kid seemed to be in a talkative mood, for he started telling Mrs. Gallegos about his adventures, and for emphasis he drew his gun and shot a couple of holes in the ceiling. The neighbors all came running to find out what all the shooting was about, but upon finding it was Billy the Kid they all started running the other way.

The next time Mrs. Gallegos saw Billy the Kid she was in the store by herself. He came in, bought some things, and left. Mrs. Gallegos says that he was always very courteous and that he was, in her opinion, a real gentleman.

Mrs. Gallegos knew Sostenes, a member of Billy's gang, very well.[16] His parents were good people and lived in Los Alamos. As far as she knew, Sostenes was always a good boy and it was hard for her to believe that he would turn outlaw. When he did turn, however, he turned with a vengeance. Mrs. Gallegos was acquainted with an old man who was half blind and he told her the following incident:

One day, while he was traveling on his burro, Billy the Kid and Sostenes rode up. Sostenes said, "Billy, let's kill this old blind man just to see how old blind men die."

"Let him alone," commanded Billy. "He's doing us no harm." The old man thought his day had come, and when Billy prevented Sostenes from killing him the Kid became the old man's hero.

Mrs. Gallegos knew Silva, the notorious bandit, very well indeed, for he worked for her husband one year carrying trading stuff from Las Vegas to Santa Fe. She says that he was considered a respectable citizen then. She describes him as tall and handsome, rather fair of complexion and light of hair. Years later, when Mrs. Gallegos was living at Los Alamos she and the neighbors used to see a mysterious person dressed in a black cap and cape with a black cloth over his face walking by the side of the river. Everyone suspected it was Silva, and afterwards they discovered it was he.

Silva had his headquarters at the home of a woman named Cruz, a respectable lady on the surface, who used to come often to Mrs. Gallegos's house to visit. Of course no one knew at the time that her home was being used as the headquarters of such a notorious band of outlaws as the Silva gang.

On November 28, 1938, Bright Lynn wrote that "Mrs. Gallegos has been too ill lately to talk very long at a time. Consequently, I have asked her granddaughter, Mary Elba C. De Baca, to get the remainder of her life a little bit at a time and, in turn, tell it to me." Lynn probably met Sra. Gallegos through her twenty-two-year-old granddaughter because the latter was a fellow student at New Mexico Normal (now, Highlands) University. According to his brief biography of her: "She has been an attentive listener to the tales of superstition, witchcraft, cuentos and legends of the Spanish-American people which her cousins, aunts, parents and grandparents have told her and is an interesting relator of those tales herself once she is persuaded to start telling them."[17]*

After living in Manuelitas, where they had the store, Grandmother and her husband moved to Los Alamos, where they lived on a farm owned by her mother. After living there for about three months, Grandfather came home one day looking very pleased with himself.

"Guess what," he said, "I've bought a saw mill at Manuelitas about five miles from where we lived before." And so Grandmother packed up and they moved back to Manuelitas.

Grandfather became restless before long and went away. Grandmother was left alone with two Indian companions, María and Sabina. She says that they were forced to work very hard. They arose at four-thirty every morning and prepared breakfast for the peons who worked at the saw mill, and spent the rest of the day doing housework and other duties. She remembers an old man, Juan Antonio, who was an idiot. He would sit on her doorstep from early morning until late at

*"The Biography of Guadalupe Lupita Gallegos," coll. Bright Lynn from Mrs. Gallegos and Mary Elba C. De Baca; 2000 wds., 7 pp., 28 November 1938, rec. 5 December (A#227; H5-5-58#14; LC47.1).

night. This old man had a brother who was a very popular person and a smart politician, and Juan Antonio would follow him everywhere on the days that he was not sitting on her doorstep.

Grandmother remembers also that the Penitentes would pass by her house on their way to the morada, singing, singing all the way. There was no other road, and she used to see them punish themselves as they passed by her house. At night she got a horrible creepy feeling as they sang their sad melancholy songs.

At the end of three years Grandfather returned home from his roaming, and they moved to San Ilario where they bought a large store. Grandfather went to Kansas and bought two thousand dollars worth of fine stock, fine stuff that the poor laboring people of the community couldn't afford to buy. As a result, the store was not very successful.

They lived at San Ilario for four years. Four years was a long time for Grandfather to live in any one place, and his restless nature got the better of him. He wrote to Grandmother from Carrizito to tell her that he had found a beautiful place he wanted to buy. He told her to pack everything and come. She did, and they lived in a little shack until their home was built. Carrizito was a beautiful place, but the nearest neighbors lived six miles away. During the day Grandmother was left alone with a little girl, the daughter of a neighbor. At night the owls would hoot and the little girl would say, "Those are witches."

Before long, her husband tired of the new home and decided to move to El Pajarito. Here, they built a lovely two-story home. For three years she lived there while her husband continued to travel. She disliked El Pajarito very much. It was a hot desert land with not a single tree. María and Sabina joined her there, and two days before Christmas she received a letter from her husband telling her to come to Las Vegas. He had bought a home there. On Christmas day they arrived at Las Vegas. Grandfather had bought a house on Grand Avenue, and there they

lived for three years. Again he was struck with the wanderlust, and so they moved to Los Alamos to her father's place. They lived there for a while, and then they moved to San Ilario.

They had been in San Ilario only a short time when Grandfather received word that his mother had died. Immediately he left for Los Alamos and sold Grandmother's mother's rich farm at thirty-five dollars an acre. With this money he paid for his mother's funeral expenses. This is how he did it: He told Grandmother to sign two papers and thus, without her knowledge, gained the right to sell the farm. Perhaps you wonder how Grandmother could have been so dumb. Well, she was only twelve years old when she married, and as her husband was so much older than she was, she was supposed to obey him as one would obey a god.

The second paper was a note for ten thousand dollars to be paid to him. He then advised Grandmother to tell her parents that she had signed the papers. She told them, but they loved her so much because she was their only child that they would not go against her wishes and did nothing about it. Grandfather was supporting all of his brothers and sisters and all of their children on Grandmother's money. Grandmother couldn't possibly protest, for in those days a wife must obey her husband in all things without question.

Now Grandfather had a wicked brother, Isidore [Isador V.?] Gallegos, who was as clever and sly as a fox. This man swindled his brother, his relatives, and everyone he could swindle. Now my Grandmother's aunt Juanita and her uncle Rumaldo [Rumauldo Baca?] were very wealthy.[18] They had no children of their own, and so they brought up mother and a nephew, Felipe, whose mother had died when he was a baby. They treated the boy like a prince. They were giving him an excellent education and loved him as if he had been their own son.

Uncle Isidore probably thought to himself, "If I can only make trouble and cause

Felipe's father to take him back, Aunt Juanita will take one of my children and bring him up." The wicked fellow then went down to Felipe's father, who was an extremely dumb man, and said, "Why don't you ask Aunt Juanita to give you back your son. He'll now be able to help you a lot for he's growing big." Thus he convinced the dumb man, and both went to Aunt Juanita.

Aunt Juanita, a spunky woman, said, "You shall not take Felipe away from me. Take it to court if you wish but nothing can persuade me to give up Felipe."

"Let him go, Aunt," said the tactful Isidore. "Now you may have whichever of my sons you want."

Aunt Juanita, who knew his character well enough, saw through his little scheme and said, "Although yours may be blonde, not one of them will compare with Felipe's little finger."

Now, great grandmother owned ten thousand head of sheep. Grandfather sold them at six dollars a head, making Grandmother, of course, sign a bill of sale. Her parents were very angry, but they swallowed everything for their daughter's sake. They would do anything to prevent a scandal in the family, and besides, they hated to hurt their only daughter.

At San Ilario my great or great, great grandfather owned the Bell Ranch. His name was Ilario Gonzales. Grandfather, finding himself in need of money, sold the ranch without Great Grandfather's knowledge. Great Grandfather was very old, and when the officers went to foreclose on the ranch the old man was griefstricken and died shortly after.

Grandmother's money and all her property were gradually being wasted by Grandfather. Several years after he sold the Bell Ranch, my father's father, Manuel C. de Baca, a lawyer, came to my Grandmother's mother to ask if she wanted him to sell her beautiful farms for her at a considerable sum.[19] She consented, and when my grandfather Baca went to sell them he found that they had been sold already.

When Grandfather finished with most of his wife's money, he started in on her wealthy relatives. Grandmother's favorite aunt, Nanita Louisianita, lived with Grandmother's parents and she owned one thousand sheep. Grandfather sold them. He sold her ranches and everything he could get hold of.

Now, my grandparents had a farm and a thousand head of cattle at Cabra Springs. Grandfather made Grandmother sign a paper giving him the right to sell them. He gave the paper to his brother but died before he could sell it. When my Grandmother's people went to see about the farm and cattle, Grandfather's brother had already taken possession of them.

Now, when Uncle Rumaldo, who had brought up Felipe and my mother, died it was discovered that Isidore had tricked him into making out the insurance in his name. When Aunt Juanita went for the insurance she was informed that Uncle Isidore had already collected it.

As usual, Grandfather was wandering over the country somewhere. Grandmother came to Las Vegas to visit and happened to stop at the mailman's home. There, her last baby, who is now Sister M. Dolores at St. Anthony's Mercy Hospital at Pocatello, Idaho, was born.

When her baby was two months old her husband finally came home. She says that the day before he arrived she felt a terrible sadness creep over her as if something awful were going to happen. Grandfather came home and before long had a heart attack and died [in 1893]. When he died he owed a thousand dollars at the bank and Grandmother's father paid it.

The wicked troublemaker Isidore went to the bank and told them that his brother owed a thousand dollars and advised them to go collect from his widow, for she was very wealthy. The officers went to Grandmother's home with Isidore as witness. Great Grandfather knew that he had paid the debt, and finally, after looking all over, he found the receipt and the bank sent its apology. Aunt

Juanita saw red and she gave Isidore a piece of her mind.

Grandfather left nothing for Lupita but her children to support. Waldo Spiess, Grandmother's lawyer, told her to file suit on the bank, that she could get plenty out of them, but she wouldn't.

You may wonder why Grandmother's people stood for everything, for they were good and noble and honest and they thought everyone was like themselves. Grandmother had lots of spunk in after years, but then she never dared raise her voice against her husband. Her parents would do nothing to him for fear of hurting their adored daughter.

Mary Elba C. De Baca concluded the account of her grandmother's life with a touching tribute to the woman whom she viewed as a "princess now dying like a pauper."*

After Grandfather's death [in 1893], Grandmother went to live with her parents. Exactly one year after his death, Rosenda, her eighteen-year-old daughter, died of a heart attack.

For six years Grandmother and her parents lived at Los Alamos. Then her father was elected probate judge, so they moved to Las Vegas. That year Grandmother's daughter Lele, twelve years old, died of heart trouble. Her oldest son Magin married and then her oldest daughter Cleotilde, and both left her. In 1917 Great Grandmother mortgaged the last of her land and all their money ended. They had little to live on except the pension which Great Grandmother received because her husband had fought in the Civil War.

In 1918 Great Grandmother loaned the Sisters of Mercy one thousand dollars to help build the St. Anthony's Mercy Hospital at Pocatello, Idaho. Great Grandmother, Mrs. Severo Baca, started going blind. Two years later she went completely blind and died.

Grandmother stayed with Mother part of the time. The other part of the time she was in Denver with her grandchildren. In 1928 Grandmother's oldest daughter, Cleotilde, died. Grandmother took the death calmly.

That spring she left for Pocatello, Idaho, to visit with her daughter Sister M. Dolores. She stayed only a short time, for she got homesick for her grandchildren in Las Vegas and returned. That year she started receiving ten dollars a month from the Sisters of Mercy, who were paying back what her mother had loaned the Hospital in 1918.

Grandmother has always been a deeply religious woman. She has always been resigned to God's will and no matter what happens she is never unhappy. In 1934 her son Magin died and she took the news of his death calmly while the rest of us were having fits.

In 1935 her only remaining son, Ilario, died. Mother, Grandmother, and I were present when he died. I saw her kneeling there, praying to God, offering Him the soul of her son. Not a tear did she shed. She comforted Mother and me and then left for church.

After Ilario's death Grandmother attended Mass every single day, and when she wasn't at home she would be in church praying. Her greatest affliction came when she fell sick a year ago and was no longer able to go to her God. She bears her cross with patience and resignation. I have never met a

*"The Biography of Guadalupe Lupita Gallegos," coll. Bright Lynn from Mary Elba C. De Baca; 750 wds., 3 pp., 12 December 1938, rec. 13 December (BC136; A#227; H5-5-51#7; LC47.1).

stronger, braver woman. She has lost everything now, but her great faith in God.

Today is her birthday. She is eighty-six years old and still as happy as she was when I first remember. About a year ago she became totally blind. She wouldn't admit it for the world, but we could see that she couldn't even find her spoon or anything. I have seen her at the point of death, smiling and even telling us that she was feeling better.

In October she received the last Sacraments. She believed, as we did, that she was dying. But now she seems to be getting better and better. It saddens me to see her reduced to such a state—she who had been brought up like a princess, now dying like a pauper without a penny to her name, while those relatives of her husband's are really wealthy.

She can bear anything herself, but as soon as she sees her daughter or her grandchildren unhappy she's unhappy too and does her utmost to cheer them. She has more life in her than all the rest of us put together. She really gives us strength when we are discouraged and feel like quitting.

She is the happiest woman I have ever known.

Don Alejo Herrera, who twice befriended Billy the Kid, spent his formative years in captivity among the Apaches. His passing in 1936 at the age of 117 marked the end of an important link to the Mexican past for Hispanos in Roswell's Chihuahua district, some twenty-two city blocks with, as NMFWP writer Georgia B. Redfield romantically claims, "a population of one thousand Spanish-speaking people [and] the colorful atmosphere of a Spanish village. The people living here, in a world all their own, cling to old customs and live in quaint adobe, mud-roofed houses, the exteriors made gay in the autumn with garlands of bright red chili. Chairs in the cleanly swept patios—yards—are usually occupied, afternoons, by the old men and women of the different households who enjoy mid-day siestas in the sun."[20]*

Alejo Herrera is dead. There is grief in the Spanish American settlement called "Chihuahua" in the southeast part of Roswell, and there is a stillness of respect and love in the district for the fine old Mexican patriarch who lived a hundred and seventeen years. He died on Sunday, December 27th, at the home of Mr. and Mrs. Gus García, 700 East Tilden Street, Chihuahua, Roswell. There was no sickness, not an ache or a pain. It is said he never experienced an illness of any kind during the many years of his life. The cause of his death was only extreme old age.

Alejo Herrera was called "The Methu-

*"Alejo Herrera—Patriarch, Chihuahua District Roswell," coll. Georgia B. Redfield from "notes of Alejo Herrera's own dictation to Ricardo (Dick) Gomez, Carlsbad; J. P. White (deceased) for whom Alejo Herrera once worked as a sheep herder; personal knowledge of writer"; 600 wds., 4 pp., 30 December 1936 (A#186; LC47.1).

"Cordova, Rio Arriba county, New Mexico. Feb 1943. Sheep which belong to Blas Sanchez, a Spanish-American rancher." Photo by John Collier. LC-USW 3-19210-C.

selah" of the Chihuahua settlement. He was a friend for many years to the Mexican people of that district. Thrilling adventure, perils, and helpfulness are written through the pages of his life's history as told by himself, his friends, and various records in reckoning the milestone of his long, interesting life.

Apache Indians captured Alejo when he was eleven years old. They took him from his home at Saltillo, Mexico, to the Guadalupe Mountains and later to the White Mountains. He was guarded and watched constantly by his captors. Not once in the nineteen years of his captivity did he find an opportunity for escape. He learned the language of the Apaches, their habits and customs of living, which clung to him all the days of his life, and he could ride like an Indian.

When Alejo reached thirty years of age, while camping with the Apaches in a deep canyon in the White Mountains, a stranger brought "firewater" and gave it freely to the Indians in the camp. This gave him his longed for chance of escape. During the drunken brawl there was fighting among the tribe, and the guards and their chief were knocked out. Alejo, realizing this was his chance for escape, caught and saddled a horse, crept back within a few feet of the unconscious guards, and took a white girl who had been in captivity with him for three years. Together they rode the one horse and safely made the perilous journey to Santa Fe, with the Apache Indians in hot pursuit and others camped on every trail.

Arriving at Santa Fe, Alejo turned the rescued girl over to a man by the name of Johnson who lived on a ranch in Santa Fe country. He secured work for himself on another ranch as a "bronco buster," wild horse rider. He rode and broke the horses on many of the first ranches settled in New Mexico.

The Lincoln County War was an interesting experience in Herrera's life. He was a brave fighter in that war and in several Indian uprisings. His body and hands showed many bullet marks and arrowhead scars, some of which he received protecting women and helpless children. These he bore proudly to his grave.

After the Lincoln County War and the

Indians had been subdued and were safely guarded in reservations, too old then for bronco riding, Herrera was a sheepherder for many years. He worked for José Analla, the first sheepman of Lincoln County. Afterwards he was herder for J. P. White (Senior), a well-known sheepman and one of the first stockmen of the Pecos Valley. Herrera also worked for Juan Chaves, who had a ranch and the only residence on the land which is now Roswell. At that time provisions for the Chaves Ranch were brought over from Santa Fe by Herrera in a two-wheel "carreta" drawn by two oxen.

Billy the Kid had no better friend than Herrera, who concealed him from the sheriff on two different occasions. He rolled the Kid up securely in his bed roll one time, leaving only a small opening at one end for air.

The old patriarch had no family. He was cared for by his friends, and his word was law in their home. The Garcías cared for him tenderly until the end.

Another former shepherd, Sr. José García y Trujillo, was living in Albuquerque when Janet Smith interviewed him about Billy the Kid (1859–81). Sr. García had once served on a posse which, in trying to capture the Kid, unsuccessfully staked out Pete Maxwell's Fort Sumner house. He related many familiar aspects of the Kid's legend, notably his Robin Hood qualities and his immortality.[21]*

José García y Trujillo doesn't believe that Billy the Kid was ever shot. He feels sure he got away to South America. He wouldn't be surprised if he is alive somewhere today, an old man with many memories and a quick mind, like himself. When I showed him a book by the man who killed Billy the Kid

[Pat Garrett, *The Authentic Life of Billy, the Kid, Noted Desperado of the Southwest* (1882)], he was unconvinced.

"No, *señora,*" and he shook his forefinger back and forth before his face. "You think Billy the Keed let himself be shot in the dark like that? No, *señora*—Billy the Keed—never.

*"Interview with José García y Trujillo," coll. Janet Smith as "Pioneer Stories"; 1800 wds, 7 pp., 26 August 1936 (A#212; LC47.1; LC47.2).

I see Billy the Keed with these eyes. Many times, with these eyes. That Billy, *tenia un agilesa in su mente—in su mente aquí.*" He pointed to his forehead.

Mr. García could speak but little English, and I knew almost no Spanish, but I understood that he meant that Billy the Kid had an extraordinary quickness of mind. Again he pointed to his forehead and then with a quick motion to the sky. *"Un función eléctrica,"* he said. Something that worked like lightning.

When I stopped to see Mr. García he was sitting on the ground under the cottonwood tree that shades the cracked adobe walls of his long narrow house. His hat was pulled down over his eyes and he seemed to be sleeping. As I stopped the motor of my car, however, he raised his head and pushed back his hat with one motion. He squinted at me a minute, then pulled himself to his feet.

"Cómo se va, Señora?" Mr. García placed the one chair in the shade for me. He found a box behind a heap of wagon wheels and car fenders and sat down beside me. He squinted his long blue eyes and asked in Spanish, "What's new?"

I patted the black kitten stretched on a bench at my elbow. Beside it perched a cock and two hens. Two little brown dogs nosed at my shoes, and a big shaggy fellow laid his head against my arm. The flies buzzed.

A thin, dark old woman stepped over the little goat sleeping just inside the doorway of the house, its head resting on the doorstep. She gathered up some green chili from a table in the yard, giving me an intent look as she stood there, and went back into the house without saying a word.

Mr. García asked me again, "What's new? You bring me those history books of Billy the Keed?"

I showed him the picture of Pat Garrett, who shot Billy the Kid. "I don't want to dispute against you, Señora, but in my mind, which is the picture of my soul, I know it is not true. Maybe Pat Garrett, he give Billy the Keed money to go to South America and

write that story for the looks. Maybe he kill somebody else in Billy's place. Everybody like Billy the Keed—*su vista penetrava al corazón de toda la gente*—his face went to everybody's heart."

Mrs. García came out again and sat on a bench beside her husband. Her skin looked dark and deeply wrinkled under the white towel she had wrapped about her head. She rolled a brown paper cigarette from some loose tobacco in a tin box. As her husband talked she listened intently, puffing on her cigarette. From time to time she would nod her head at me, her eyes dark and somber.

"What did Billy the Kid look like?" I asked.

"Chopito—a short man, but wide in shoulders and strong. His forehead was big. His eyes were blue. He wore Indian shoes with beads on his feet. His clothes—*muy desarollado*—"

"Desarollado?" I asked.

"Like yours," he said, pointing to my blue denim skirt and shirt. "Any old way.

"Muy generoso hombre, Billy the Keed—a very generous man. All the Mexican people, they like him. He give money, horses, drinks—what he have. To whom was good to Billy the Keed he was good to them. *Siempre muy caballero, muy señor*—always very polite, very much of a gentleman. Once lots of mens, they go together after Billy the Keed to shoot him. They pay us—we go—sure. But we don't want to shoot Billy. We always be glad he too smart for us."

In broken English mixed with Spanish phrases, Mr. García told me how he went in a posse of thirty-five or more men to capture Billy the Kid. He didn't know the sheriff's name, but the description sounded like Pat Garrett himself—*"muy, muy alto,"* very, very tall, and Pat Garrett was six feet four and a half. José García was working at the time as sheepherder on the ranch of Jacobo Yrissari about ninety miles southeast of Albuquerque. The tall sheriff came by one day with a band of men and offered him five dollars a day and food for himself and his horse to join

"Cimarron, New Mexico. Aug 1939. Statue [of Lucien B. Maxwell] by a local artist [D. P. O.]." Photo by Russell Lee. LC-USF 34-3409-D.

the posse in search of Billy the Kid. He said he didn't think there was any danger of their getting Billy, and five dollars was a lot of money. The plan was to surround the Maxwell Ranch on the Pecos River where Billy the Kid was known to spend much time.

This ranch belonged to Lucien Maxwell. *"Un muy grande hombre, un millonario,"* said José García.

Lucien Maxwell was indeed one of the most striking figures of the early mountain frontier.[22] Every trader and plainsman in the Rocky Mountain region knew him. He came to New Mexico from Illinois, when the country was still a part of Old Mexico. There he married Luz Beaubien, daughter of a French Canadian, Charles Hipolite Trotier, Sieur de Beaubien, and a Spanish woman. With Guadalupe Miranda, Beaubien had received from the Mexican government during the administration of Governor Manuel Armijo [1841]

a huge grant of land as a reward for pioneer services. Beaubien bought Miranda's share, and at Beaubien's death Lucien Maxwell, his son-in-law, purchased all the land from the heirs and became sole owner of more than a million acres. He made huge sums of money selling sheep, cattle, and grain to the government and built a great house at Cimarron [ca. 1857].

There he lived in as much magnificence as the times and the country could afford. His guests included cattle kings, governors, army officers, and later, when he moved to the ranch near Fort Sumner [1870], Billy the Kid. Nearly every day his table was set for more than two dozen, and it is reputed that they ate on plates of silver and drank from goblets of gold. José García said he didn't know anything about that for he had never been inside of the house, but he thought it quite likely. He had been by the place at

Cimarron several times, when he was working for some people by the name of Martínez who had a ranch north of Las Vegas.

The Maxwell house was *"una grande mansión,"* but it was to the Maxwell house on the Pecos near Fort Sumner that he went in search of Billy the Kid. Maxwell retired to his place at Fort Sumner after losing much of his wealth. His son Pete later became the richest sheep man in that part of the country. It was Pete who was a friend of Billy. José García said he and the other men surrounded the house for two weeks, but they never got so much as a glimpse of Billy the Kid.

Mr. García said he knew a good friend of Billy the Kid, José Chávez y Chávez. When he was herding sheep on the Yrissari Ranch, which was not far from Santa Rosa on the Pecos River, José Chávez y Chávez was sheep herder on a nearby ranch. One day the two of them were sitting under a tree smoking when a pack train on the way to Arizona came along on the other side of the Pecos. Just opposite the tree where the two sheepherders were sitting, they tried to ford the stream, but the water was swift and the horses floundered. José García and José Chávez pulled off their clothes, jumped in, and guided the horses to the bank. After the pack train went on, José Chávez showed Mr. García the twenty-one bullet scars on his body. "He had an innocent face—didn't look as though he could break a dish, but he was bad with a gun. *Qué hombre!*"

"Did they try to get José Chávéz to go with the posse after Billy?" I asked.

"José Chávez y Chávez," he corrected me. "No, *señora,* he had left the country at that time."

According to Walter Noble Burns, who wrote *The Saga of Billy the Kid* [Garden City, N.Y.: Doubleday, Page and Company, 1926], it was this José Chávez y Chávez who was responsible for the friendship between Billy the Kid and the wealthy Maxwells. Billy the Kid had ridden over to Fort Sumner from Lincoln with several of his men, among whom was José Chávez y Chávez. The fiancé of one of the Maxwell girls was drunk and met José Chávez y Chávez on the street back of the Maxwell house. The two men quarreled and José Chávez pulled his gun. Mrs. Maxwell ran out of the house and tried to pull her future son-in-law away, begging Chávez not to shoot him as he was drunk and didn't know what he was doing. Chávez replied that drunk or sober he was going to kill him, and he was going to do it immediately. Just then a young man walked rapidly across the road, touched his sombrero to Mrs. Maxwell, said something in Spanish to Chávez, and led him away. It was the Kid. From that time until his death he made Fort Sumner his head-quarters and was a frequent visitor at the Maxwell home. It was in Pete Maxwell's room that Pat Garrett shot him.

Mr. García asked me if there were any books in Spanish about Billy the Kid. "My wife," he said, "she taught me to read. I didn't know the letters when I married her. She didn't know the words but she knew the letters and she taught me. I taught myself how the words went, but I never could teach her how to read, *ni con cariños ni estím[ul]os*—neither by coaxing nor praising—she never could learn anything more than the letters."

Mrs. García shook her head. *"Nunca, nunca, nunca,"* she said. Never had she been able to learn more than the letters.

I promised to look for a Spanish book about Billy the Kid. I sat for a minute longer watching some pigeons perched on a water barrel. They pecked at the water. The ripples reflected on their green and lavender breasts. The little goat came out of the house and sniffed the dirt around my chair.

As I rose to go Mr. García stood up and took off his hat. *"Muchas felicidades y buena salud, Señora,"* he said with a little bow. Much happiness and good health to you.

Mrs. García put out her hand. Her dark eyes were always somber. *"Adiós,"* she said, *"no se mas que decir Dios se irá con usted."* Goodbye, I can only say God be with you.

"Vuelva," they called after me as I drove away. "Come back."

Like shepherds, traditional craftspeople were threatened by changing economic conditions. Reyes N. Martínez believed that the old weaver whom he interviewed in Talpa in 1936 followed a doomed and unjustly miserable way of life.*

At Talpa, a village five miles south of the town of Taos, on a side road a few hundred feet to the east of State Highway 3 stands a three-room adobe house. A visit to this house ushers you into an atmosphere reminiscent of a past era.

In answer to your knock, the door is swung open by a stocky-built old man, grizzled and crippled by the years. Stooping as you enter the low doorway, you are invited to sit down on one of the homemade benches in the room as he also sits down at another similar bench and asks the purpose of your visit. There, before you, you see the Old Weaver of Talpa, suave and quiet of manner and uniquely interesting in his narrative of the events of his long life, for he is eighty-four years old. Two old women keep him company. One of them, he informs you, is his wife, seventy-eight years of age; the other is the widowed mother of his son's wife and about eighty-five years old. The bench on which you sit is hard, but you feel comfortable in the coolness of the dirt-floored room.

Curious to know, you ask how he makes his living. The question strikes his favorite topic, and he at once assumes an intensely interesting attitude. He relates to you the story of his life:

Becoming an orphan at twelve years of age, he was left with an old weaver with whom he lived for many years and learned the trade which later became his chief occupation and means of livelihood. In his younger years, the stream at Talpa was very rich in trout, and he used to make frequent trips to Taos to sell his catch and bring back in trade some provisions from La Plaza de Don Fernando, as Taos was known at the time.

Later he confined his activities to the weaving of blankets and rugs. He became very proficient at it, and his trade drew business from the whole valley of Taos, including the Indians, who became his regular customers. Getting up at four o'clock every morning, he plied his trade sometimes till dusk. He was making a very comfortable living till the depression swept his business along the downgrade with the rest of the business world, forcing him to seek aid from the government relief agencies. Notwithstanding his miserable circumstances, he tells you, no relief has been tendered him, and he still plods along at his old trade, doing a little weaving now and then for the neighbors or selling a blanket occasionally to effect a scanty means of sustenance for himself and the two old ladies who comprise his household.

He invites you to see his loom. Across an open space, in another house, stands his loom, a relic of the olden days but still useful, already smooth and shiny from long years of use. A spinning wheel stands at one side of the loom. This is an apparatus of his own invention, combining the old with the new and consisting of a discarded bicycle wheel with a handle attached to the axle for turning by hand and a driving-band extending back toward the old-fashioned spindle. Taking a quantity of carded wool, he demonstrates to you his method of spinning the yarn and the winding of it on a quill inserted at the end of the spindle. He then takes the quill and places it into the shuttle, a hollow boat-shaped piece of wood, pointed at each end and about ten inches in length. Throwing the shuttle first to the left through the opening made in the warp-threads by the heddles, then back

*"The Weaver of Talpa," coll. Reyes N. Martínez for S-240 Folk-Ways; 715 wds., 3 pp., 13 May 1936 (BC495; A#234; H5-5-4#3; LC38.1; LC47.1; LC47.2).

"Costilla, New Mexico. Sept 1939. Spanish-American woman carding wool at a Works progress administration weaving project." Photo by Russell Lee. LC-USF 34-34208-D.

"Costilla, New Mexico. Sept 1939. Spanish-American woman spinning woolen thread at the WPA weaving project." Photo by Russell Lee. LC-USF 34-34266-D.

to the right, he carries on the process of weaving till a considerable part of a rug is made for demonstration to you.

The years have not yet dimmed his eyes or incapacitated him in a way to prevent him from plying the trade that he has loved and carried on for a span of more than seventy years. The pity of it is that such a humble trio have to plod along in the evening of life under such miserable circumstances. Fate, sometimes, is an unkindly weaver of circumstances. Here an opportunity presents itself for charity to serve a noble purpose.

"Costilla, New Mexico. Sept 1939. Spanish-American woman
weaving rag rug at a Works progress administration project."
Photo by Russell Lee. LC-USF 34-34289-D.[23]

"Peñasco, New Mexico. Jan 1943. Blacksmith shop." Photo by
John Collier. LC-USW 3-17335-C.

Octaviano Segura of Pecos was known for his skills
in ironwork and rhetoric.[24] B. A. Reuter, who was interviewing the Pecos descendants of Donaciano Vigil,
governor of New Mexico between 1847 and 1848, also
learned a valuable lesson from the blacksmith.*

Julio Segura was a man of some education,
intelligence, and otherwise gifted beyond his
ability of hammering steel. He was a blacksmith by trade and erected a shop to take
care of the needs of the settlement of Pecos
at that time. He taught his trade to his oldest
son Octaviano, who after his father's death
carried on the work. Octaviano married Mar-
iana, the daughter of Hermenejildo Vigil, a
descendant of Governor Donaciano Vigil, and
became the father of Antonio, Juan, and
Cleotilda.

Octaviano was a man of some education
and did considerable reading, but just how

*From "Governor Donaciano Vigil's Ancestors," coll. B. A.
Reuter of Pecos from Teodosio Ortiz Refugio Vigil, José A. Vigil,
Lora Vigil Sena, Antonio Segura, "a great grandson of the Governor and other living descendants and old people of Pecos"; 3300
wds., 11 pp., 11 August 1939, rec. 14 August (A#228; H5-5-
9#9).

he got his education I have not taken thought to find out. However, I intend to make a survey of the subject of the development of education facilities in Pecos. I feel sure that Governor Vigil and the Segura family must have played a principal role.

Octaviano Segura was one of the most gifted orators in handing out well-arranged and appropriate bouquets of rhetoric whom I have ever listened to. He was not only gifted in flowery figures of speech but was informed and used his information in a logical and convincing manner. He was a champion for better schools in Pecos and the most of his speeches were directed to that end. I have never met a man of more natural refinement and yet he lived a humble life in Pecos, little known beyond a few precincts surrounding the district.

I once had Octaviano do some blacksmithing for me, for which I had to owe him for a few weeks. One day, when I was enroute to his shop to pay him, I met him unexpectedly walking on the road. I brought my car to a quick stop and hastily put my hand in my pocket for the money and started to hand it out to him. Instead of taking the money, he looked at me as if I had done him wrong and told me to lay the money down and first give me your hand, for I would rather have your heart and your hand than that money. I have never quite recovered from that rebuke. He did it nicely but resolutely, and the lesson has served me well in dealing with his type of man. We Americans have much to learn from men like Octaviano Segura.

Irving Rusinow also learned from Hispano villagers. When he photographed the tiny San Miguel County village of El Cerrito between April 10 and 16, 1941, for the Bureau of Agricultural Economics, Rusinow saw a community threatened by change, persisting "not because of economic conditions, but in spite of them." Villagers were "devoted to their village and they resist change. . . . When they leave . . . they go out among strangers. Their thoughts are always of home and when they will return there."

Rusinow's introduction to his camera report concludes: "Here, then, is a village until recently pretty much apart from the rest of the world. But resources have so dwindled and opportunities so shrunk that the people are convinced that radical changes must be made in their way of life. And many think that these changes will mean the end of some of the customs and traditions and values that have always been of the first importance—the things, in fact, that have made life worth living."[25]

"The families who have always lived in the village welcome to their homes those who show good will. They are by nature friendly, courteous people.

"A few who have lived for a while in some Anglo town are suspicious." [Neg. no. 83-G-37828.]

"Most of the pictures in the rooms are religious. The rest are usually family portraits." [Neg. no. 83-G-37826.]

"Here, the family, including even distant relatives, is almost a sacred institution." [Neg. no. 83-G-37825.]

"Men get together for a half hour of talk after the service. This is almost as much a part of going to church as the service itself." [Neg. no. 83-G-37865.]

"Recreation here is simple and limited. Older people go to town once in a while, but they have no money to spend on such luxuries as movies.

"Often there is a dance in the village. When there is, everyone goes to it and has a fine time. Then, there is fishing in the river, ... " [Neg. no. 83-G-37880.]

" . . . and music. . . ." [Neg. no. 83-G-37824.]

"The people understand that, despite its isolation, their village is coming to depend on the outside world." [Neg. no. 83-G-37877.]

"It has taken generations of living to build up the patterns that hold the people of these villages together, but they were built, many of them, on a foundation of natural resources that no longer exist.

"Unless the old ways can somehow be made to support the people, they will have to go out into the towns and cities of the Anglos and make for themselves a new life based on, instead of isolated from, the new and changing conditions of the world of today." [Neg. no. 83-G-37831.]

MINERS, MERCHANTS,
HOMESTEADERS, AND INDIANS

Western New Mexicans

North wall of lobby in the new post office, Gallup, showing
oil paintings by Warren E. Rollins, "Indian crafts and
ceremony," 3′ × 3′ and 4′ × 6′, n.d. PWAP.[1]

The Gila country boasted many colorful loners who readily attracted comment from Writers' Project field-workers. Mrs. Frances E. Totty of Silver City wrote about a gamut of such independent souls, from the reclusive Bear Moore to the solitary artist Bill Warner, who

> when he first came to Grant County lived in Tyrone but at present is living at Gila. He has had paintings hung at all important hangings in the Southwest. Among the places that he has had pictures hung are El Paso, San Diego, Los Angeles and Santa Barbara. He paints pictures of the Southwest of ranch life and the deserts of Arizona. He especially likes to paint pictures of the country surrounding Tyrone and spends many hours in this locality. He does not spend all of his time in Grant County but spends hours in the desert as he loves nature and tries to put the glories of the scenes that he sees in painting. Mr. Warner has paintings at Schiffs Clothing Store and Himans Hardware, but they do not remain long at a time for they sell rapidly.[2]

However, most loners were mountain men and prospectors, like amateur naturalist "Wild East Joe" Griggs, who lived alone in a cabin north of Silver City.

> Joe has led a hermit life in the wild spot where his cabin has stood for years. In the early days a town was laid there by some one, known as "North Virginia." A few houses were built and some mining work erected in and about the place, which had hardly been laid out by its enthusiastic [founders] as a town before a mining slump came and laid it out as a corpse. Only Joe Griggs was left. He has continued there as sort of a watchman over the remains, and ever since has had the whole town to himself.
>
> Mr. Griggs doesn't very often come to town, but yesterday he did. Having thawed out, he says he had a regular arctic time of it this winter. All the hills and valleys were buried in snow-pure white, dazzling his eyes wherever he might turn. His place has during the winter been a regular stamping ground for all manner of wild animals. He has experienced everything but white bears. The beasts of prey focusing about his cabin having carried off and devoured every living thing but himself and dog, Mr. Griggs is a regular authority on the ways and means of all the wild animals of the hills.[3]

James A. ("Uncle Jimmie") McKenna (1851–1941) chose as epigraph for his 1936 memoirs, *Black Range Tales*, Stewart E. White's comment on "The Old-time Prospector":

> As you come to know him better, you must love him for the kindliness, the simple honesty, the modesty, and the charity that he seems to draw from his mountain environment. There are hundreds of him buried in the great canyons of the West.[4]

By the late 1930s, Bear Moore, Sophie Hansen, and Eugene Davis, prospectors noted by project writers and photographers, still had not been dislodged by the large company mining operations that flourished at Santa Rita, Chino, and Mogollon.

Mining required transportation, and railroads gradually replaced the old stage and freight wagon lines. New Mexico's major railroad, the Atchison, Topeka and Santa Fe, divided the state when it pushed southwest from Raton to Albuquerque and then to Deming and El Paso by June 1881. Many communities and commercial enterprises were fostered by these connections, among them the businesspeople and homesteaders of Anthony, whom Mrs. Marie Carter interviewed in 1937.

Northwest of Anthony, it was the development of roadways, not railroads, which spurred the economy and gave an impetus to successful businesspeople like Mrs. Loraine Morley Warren Reynolds of Datil and

H. L. Craig of Pie Town. Mrs. Reynolds's brother, William Raymond Morley, Jr. (1876–1932), was influential in establishing the New Mexico routing for Highway 60 from Socorro through Magdalena, Datil, Pie Town, Quemado and into Arizona.[5] The road brought homesteaders and travelers in need of roadside services.

The Morleys had been Datil ranchers since 1886. Mrs. Reynolds's sister, Agnes Morley Cleaveland, claimed that "it was the homesteaders who, more crushing than the drought or the failure of the wartime market, dealt the final blow to the open range and the Morley enterprises."[6]

'On to Pie Town,' Ray would say as the slow caravans passed through Datil. No, Pie Town is not our symbolic Promised Land; Pie Town is a very literal place. The man who first set up a roadside eating-place, when there was promise that Highway 60 would be a popular transcontinental route, had named his shack 'Pie Town' and had given authenticity to the name by serving pies of his own manufacture. It had struck a chord of popular fancy, and Pie Town it remained as it grew into a trading center for the homesteaders who settled to the north, east, south, and west of it. It lies fourteen miles beyond the Continental Divide and twenty-four miles from Datil Post-Office. Another twenty separate it from Quemado, still further west, and all these miles are dotted with homesteads. Their clearings may be seen with the stumps of the piñons still showing, or the dust of their plowed fields blowing across the face of the sky. A windmill is a rare exception, but 'dirt tanks' for restraining flood water during the rainy season are adjuncts of many of them.[7]

In June 1940, FSA photographer Russell Lee documented this "community settled by about two hundred migrant Texas and Oklahoma farmers who filed homestead claims." Mr. Craig was still the major Pie Town merchant. He and other local businessmen annually bought piñons and sold them to a network of buyers, processors, and sellers of the nuts stretching from Pie Town and Magdalena to Albuquerque and New York City.

In the northwest, pioneers Nettie and William Locke settled in Farmington, where Mrs. Locke maintained a business selling honey and eggs. Helen Gage Simpson, who interviewed Mrs. Locke at Waterflow in 1936, was the fourth wife of Navajo Indian trader R. T. F. Simpson. When the Navajo Indian scout and pensioner Hola arrived at the Albuquerque Veterans Administration Hospital from Gallup in 1941, it was an Indian trader like Simpson who acted as interpreter and guide during the unfamiliar medical proceedings.

B. A. Reuter first visited Acoma Pueblo with architect John Gaw Meem in 1926. During Reuter's three years as construction foreman on the restoration of the Pueblo's Spanish mission church, he talked with many Acoma Indians, later submitting long descriptions of the Pueblo and its traditions to the NMFWP. Among these lengthy manuscripts, many of which were first written in pencil, is an account of the oldest Acoma residents, remarkable men over a hundred years old in the 1920s and 1930s.

Catron County was home to at least two noted hunters—Ben V. Lilly (1856–1936), who lived in the Alma area and between 1913 and 1915 killed 110 mountain lions, and Englishman Montague Stevens (1859–1953), who owned the SU Ranch and professionally hunted grizzlies.[8] Stevens had lost his left arm in a California goose-hunting accident, but he did not suffer injury from his professional encounters with grizzlies.

Gila country recluse Bear Moore was not as lucky as Stevens. He suffered the ravages of a grizzly mother's attack in 1892.[9] John Casey of Deming told Betty Reich about the old hunter and prospector in 1937.*

Bear Moore lived in what is known as the Upper Gila country. He was a prospector and did quite a bit of hunting and fishing.

He received the sobriquet of Bear from a battle with a bear that came near costing him his life.

One day while hunting he shot at a grizzly bear and wounded him. The bear charged and knocked the gun out of his hand. He then continued the fight with his hunting knife. The bear tore the flesh from his chest and his cheeks and crushed his chest. Finally he killed the bear.

He was sent East to be treated of his wounds. When he recovered he was a horrible sight. His eyes were pulled down and his face was badly scarred. He grew a beard to hide some of the scars. From that time on he was known as Bear Moore. He did not like to meet people and lived the life of a recluse in the mountains until he died.

*"Bear Moore," coll. Betty Reich from John Casey of Deming; 1 p., 15 July 1937, rec. 17 July (A#213; LC47.1).

John Oglesby of Pinos Altos told Mrs. W. C. Totty a slightly different version in November of 1937. According to him, Bear Moore's first name was John, and he killed a troublesome grizzly named Old Club-Foot, who "must have lost his foot while a cub." Moore came to Oglesby's house after killing the bear.*

Bear Moore stayed at my house several days and rested up, but poor fellow never went around people after his fight with the bear; he was so self-conscious of the condition of his face. I must admit it was the most horrible thing I ever saw. His face was half gone, and, having healed without any medical treatment, it was badly drawn, and the scars looked horrible.

Mr. Moore was called Bear Moore until his death. Children would run from him if they saw him. He cut himself off from the human race, but he sure did this part of the country a favor when he killed Club-Foot.

Mr. Moore was a very independent person; he always paid for everything he received. In the early days even a stranger, outlaw, or respected citizen was never asked to pay for anything, but Bear Moore would never accept this Western hospitality.

*"Bear Moore," coll. Mrs. W. C. Totty from John Oglesby of Pinos Altos; 2 pp., 17 November 1937, rec. 20 November (A#153).

"A gold prospector putting tin can containing his claim deed into his monument on his claim." LC-USF 33-12703-M1.

In May 1940, Russell Lee photographed Eugene Davis, a gold prospector who lived with his milch goat in Pinos Altos. Davis told Lee: "The 'Lost Adams' diggings? Say, I've read all them books about the Lost Adam's [*sic*] diggings and I tell you this is it. Now if I just had a little grubstake so I could work it right. Say, we'd all be rich."[10]

"Gold prospector pouring water into a rocker." LC-USF 33-12692-M4.

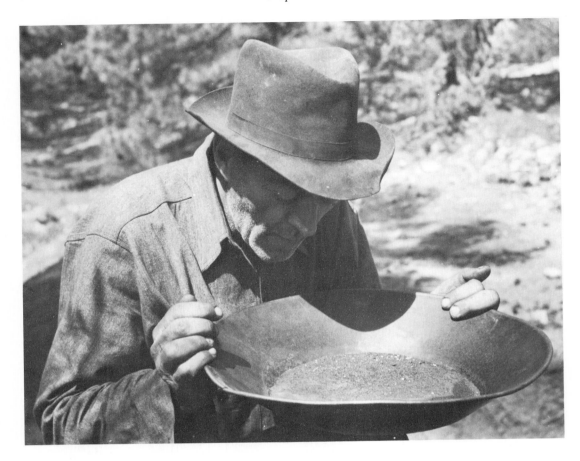

"A prospector blowing on pan of fine dirt containing particles of gold, in order to blow the dirt away and leave the heavy gold. In dry panning the pan is rotated until the dirt is on one side and then, with a decisive toss it is thrown into the air. The light dirt being blown away by the wind while the heavy gold is caught in the pan." LC USF 33-12700-M2.

"Eugene Davis, gold prospector, making a pot of coffee in his
shack on his 'diggings.'" LC-USF 34-36459-D.

Women too were prospectors. In 1936 Clay W. Vaden interviewed Sophie Hansen, an eighty-year-old as optimistic about Kingston as Eugene Davis about his Lost Adams Diggings.*

When Kingston, New Mexico, was a booming mining town in the Black Range, one of the most interesting residents there was Miss Sophie Hansen, Swedish owner of the Occidental Hotel. A short time ago, at the age of 81, she was living alone with her chickens, with which she shared her humble shack, when a terrible winter blizzard struck Kingston.

At one time in the good old days, Miss Hansen owned a large herd of cattle for which she was offered $12,000.00 during the World War, but she refused the offer and later lost them all during a terrible drouth. She remained very active in her old age,

energetic and optimistic, doing her own assessment work on her mining claim, a few miles west of Kingston, and joining in with other oldtimers who always believed that Kingston would stage a comeback. At the age of 81 she walked eight miles to Hillsboro, the county seat, to make proof of labor on her claim, and returned the same day on foot.

Sophie Hansen is a true example of a real pioneer New Mexican who had many hardships to endure and difficulties to overcome but who met them courageously and would not admit defeat. Such as these Madonnas of the West are the salt of the earth.

*"One of the Last Women Prospectors at Kingston," coll. Clay W. Vaden for S-240-Folk-Ways; 216 wds., 1 p., 1 September 1936 (H5-5-53#19; LC47.2).

Kingston had been known as the "Gem of the Black Range" in the nineteenth century. Silver City began to boom by the turn of the century when, according to Erna Fergusson (1888–1964), it "contained all the elements of New Mexico's frontier in highest concentration: miners from Wales, southeastern Europe, Mexico, and the States; squatters on the big cattle ranches still held by cattlemen who did not hesitate to shoot, a 'Chink' washee-washee conducting a brisk smuggling in opium and compatriots; merchants trying to do business and stay out of trouble; and a lurid and luxurious red-light district across the arroyo . . . and to top the pile was a group of sophisticated Main Liners from Philadelphia, brought by mining interests or by tuberculosis to Dr. Bullock's fine Cottage Sanatorium."[11] Mogollon was a contemporary Kingston and Silver City when Russell Lee photographed its miners above and below ground in June 1940.

"Gold miner looking at his watch before going down in the mine for work." LC-USF 33-12793-M2.

"Gold miner inserting a fuse into a stick of dynamite." LC-USF 34-36934-D.

"Workers in a gold mine coming out of a cage which brings
them to the surface at the end of a day's work." LC-USF 33-
12757-M3.

"Crowd of men on the boardwalk in front of a bar in a gold mining town." LC-USF 33-12791-M2.

"Bar room on payday in a gold mining town." LC-USF 34-36797-D.

The Atchison, Topeka and Santa Fe Railway, which traversed New Mexico from Clovis to Gallup and divided it from Raton to Deming and El Paso, was crucial to mining, commerce, and settlement in communities like Anthony, which straddled the Texas–New Mexico border some twenty miles north of El Paso. The Santa Fe railroad station was on the Texas side and called La Tuna, while the New Mexico location was known as Half Way House. That the post office was called Anthony in 1884 may have been due to a Spanish chapel dedicated to San Antonio or an outline of "St. Anthony's Nose" on the mountain.[12]

Until the completion of Elephant Butte Dam in 1916, farming (and bridge building) in this rich part of the Mesilla Valley was constantly jeopardized by the vagaries of the Rio Grande.[13] Doña Ana County pioneer Charles C. Geck recalled these perils in a 1937 interview with Marie Carter. Many of the early businesses he remembered were connected with travelers along the railroads.*

Charles C. Geck was born in Doña Ana, New Mexico, January 27, 1880. He married Ramona Benavides of Las Cruces, New Mexico, 1912. . . . Mr. and Mrs. Charles C. Geck have five children: Margaret, Charley, Mary Estella, Tela, and Harry. Margaret is now Mrs. Mike Apodaca of San Miguel, and Charley is in the United States Navy. Mary Estella, Tela, and Harry are pupils in the Anthony grade school.

Charles C. Geck's parents, Mr. and Mrs. W. C. P. Geck, had seven children: Charles, Beatrice, William, Josephine, Epifanio, Louis, and Alvina. Charles is a farmer of Anthony, New Mexico; Beatrice lives in Las Cruces; William is a businessman of El Paso, Texas; Epifanio is a farmer in San Diego, California; Louis is a resident of Los Angeles, California; Alvina is the wife of Louis Provincio, a valley farmer.

Charles C. Geck's father, W. C. P. Geck, moved his family to Anthony in 1902, where he built a home which is still standing in the town proper, a short distance east of U.S. Highway 80. W. C. P. Geck served Anthony as Justice of the Peace for fifteen years, and his son, Charles C. Geck, held the same office for two years—1932 and 1934. . . .

In recalling the early days of Doña Ana County, Charles C. Geck of Anthony, New Mexico, said: "I was born in the family home where my father, W. C. P. Geck, was born before me, and where my grandfather Geck lived a life time. I say a life time because he came to this country so very long ago. He came to America from Germany almost ninety years ago. Our house is one of the oldest houses in the town of Doña Ana; it is in good condition and occupied by my aunt, Mrs. W. C. Weir."

In mentioning his grandfather, Mr. Geck said: "Grandfather Geck was a trader and a merchant. In the early days, when a shipment of merchandise was ordered, the merchants

---

*"Old Timers Stories—Charles C. Geck (Wife: Ramona Geck)," coll. Marie Carter on May 17, 1937; 1300 wds, 5 pp., 24 May 1937 (A#197; HC:Anthony; LC38.1; LC47.1). The last three paragraphs of Carter's account have been placed first to give a better biographical orientation.

never knew when they were going to receive it, if at all, for the Indians would ambush the pack trains and wagons, murder the drivers, rob the caravan and burn the wagons. My grandfather told me many an exciting tale of the early days. I sometimes thought that he knew everything; that he was the wisest man in the whole world. No matter what I wished to know he could tell me something about it."

Mr. Geck's parents craved new scenes. "So they piled their household goods in the old covered wagon and headed for Las Cruces," he said. "That was in 1888. Las Cruces was a mere village. Then my parents left Las Cruces and went to La Unión. The reason people moved up and down the valley in the old days was because the Rio Grande wouldn't let them remain in one place; it was like a mad dog at their heels. They would no sooner get settled than it would rise and flood them out. During the flood of 1905 the valley was covered with water from San Miguel to White Spur, where the El Paso Electric Light power house stands."

Mr. Geck paused, then resumed: "My parents, who had moved from La Unión to Vinton, not far from White Spur, were forced to move to Chamberino. There in Chamberino it was not so good either, for as soon as they would plant their crops the Rio Grande would rise and wash their seed away. It was a common sight to see some poor rancher's adobe dwelling floating down the river; they couldn't bother about their homes when it was all they could do to save their lives. I think the Rio Grande should have been called mad river. During the flood of 1905 the Provincio family and other ranchers had to come to town to shop in skiffs. *Por Dios*, it was an ocean! The Provincios are some of the very early pioneers. Louis Provincio, Nemecio's son, married my sister Alvina. In 1902 my parents moved to Anthony."

In speaking of employment, Mr. Geck said: "Work was scarce in the old days. I would work for fifty cents a day and sometimes had to take my wages out in trade. Farmers ploughed with a small hand plough and cut wheat with a scythe. The principal crops were wheat, corn, frijoles (beans), and alfalfa. The old Santa Fe office was a small adobe house west of the Santa Fe tracks. This whole valley was bosque or woodland with trees, nothing but trees everywhere; we were kept pretty busy clearing the land. But in the old days neighbor helped neighbor, and to say how much do I owe you would have been an insult, for when your time came they would all flock to your ranch and lend a helping hand."

In comparing old main street with new main street, Mr. Geck observed: "The old business street is very quiet and the new business street is noisy with traffic—in the old days it was a wagon road. Charley Miller built and ran the first store on the old business street west of the Santa Fe tracks. And this same man gave me my first job in Anthony. His store was next to Mrs. O. C. Story's place of business."

Resuming the subject of the old business street, Mr. Geck said: "We were proud of the old street. Mr. and Mrs. Pat Coleman ran a boarding house until Mrs. O. C. Story bought the house they lived in. Then the Colemans moved to Chamberino and started a sheep ranch. Mrs. Story, who had a sick husband, also ran a boarding house. But at a later date she quit keeping boarders and started a notions store, which was the foundation for the dry goods store she runs today on U.S. Highway 80, or the Broadway of America."

In speaking of the boarding house business, Mr. Geck explained: "Anthony was a stopping place for travelers; that's the reason so many of the townsfolk kept boarders. Mr. and Mrs. Alvarez ran a boarding house after they lost heavily in the flood of 1905. The Alvarez family lived in the house at the north end of the street, where Judge and Mrs. Smith live at the present time."

In the course of his conversation, Mr. Geck mentioned the Valdez family of La Unión, saying: "Mrs. Valdez was born in La Unión. Her people were among the first to colonize

"Thoreau, N.M. Mar 1943. Conductor C. W. Tevis, with the Atchison, Topeka and Santa Fe railroad for 32 years." Photo by Jack Delano.[14] LC-USW 3-21190-E.

"Acomita, N.M. Mar 1943. Brakeman R. E. Capsey, standing on the platform of the caboose, waiting to hop off, as the train on the Atchison, Topeka and Santa Fe railroad between Belen and Gallup, New Mexico pulls into a siding." Photo by Jack Delano. LC-USW 3-21154-E.

this valley. They are connected with my family by marriage. Before her marriage, Mrs. Valdez was an Enríquez. Her brother, Emeilia [sic] Enríquez, married one of my sisters. *Por Dios!*" he chuckled, "we are like a chain letter."

When asked about the style of houses built by the early settlers, Mr. Geck replied: "Since we had plenty of trees we used them to build pole houses. The poles were placed straight up and down and then plastered in between with adobe mud. We used poles for our ceilings too. Then we whitewashed the house inside and out. The floors of our houses were just plain dirt. Americans and Mexicans, we all fared alike in the old days. Gradually people began to build houses out of adobe, which were warmer in winter and cooler in summer."

They had good times in the old days. "Innocent fun," Mr. Geck called it. "We had picnics, barbecues, dances, chuck wagon suppers and rodeos. The last rodeo was staged about eight years ago by a group of old timers, and the last chuck wagon supper ten or eleven. The good old days when we took our guitars and sang love songs to the girl of our dreams will never return. Pretty soon the mothers will be like the girls and buy all of our native dishes in tin cans."

"Albuquerque, New Mexico. Mar 1943. Joseph Pina, boilermaker in the Atchison, Topeka and Santa Fe railroad locomotive shops for 34 years." Photo by Jack Delano. LC-USW 3-20526-D.

On April 17, 1937, Marie Carter wrote New Mexico's state WPA administrator Lea Rowland to apologize for omitting crucial information in her submissions. She continued with a description of business in Anthony:*

Now I shall proceed to tell you more about the "Old Main Street" of our community. It isn't a very long street, in fact, if measured, I doubt if it would be as long as the shortest city block. Although refurbished, most of the houses have that aged allure so obviously lacking on the new main street. Perhaps if it could speak it would say: I am the street, old but superior, the pioneer rock upon which the new street built its success. I was a busy street when the new street was a mere wagon road. What does the new street know about the hardships, stamina, struggles and achievements of the early pioneers—etc.

Mrs. O. C. Story, who had a sick husband and two small children, brought them west in a covered wagon. . . . At that time houses were scarce in the little village of Anthony. She had to have a place to live, so bought the house in which Mrs. Coleman lived and kept boarders. After buying the house, which is still a store building, she also kept boarders. At a later date, however, she started a notion [*sic*] store. That same notion store was the nucleus for the dry-goods store which she conducts on the new main street today. It seems that the boarding house business flourished in the old days because Anthony was a stopping place for travelers. Mrs. Alvarez kept boarders too. Charley Miller, who seems to factor in all of the old-timers' stories, ran the old Valley Mercantile store adjoining Mrs. Story's place of business.

*Copy of letter, which actually went to Ina Sizer Cassidy, not Rowland, attached to manuscript in HC:Anthony.

Earlier, Carter had written up her interview with "Mrs. O. C. Story, born 1872, Metropolis, Ill. [who] came to Anthony, New Mexico, in a covered wagon in . . . 1901 [and] . . . is a successful business woman."†

The other day I dropped into our local drygoods store to chat with a friend and old-timer who has lived in our community since the year of 1901.

"What," I inquired, "did Anthony look like when you located here?"

"Lordy me," she exclaimed, "I wish you could have seen it. All this business section on the highway was jest a wagon road. We drove horses 'n' buggies in them days, 'n' wagons, of course. It took us a whole day to get anywhere—south to El Paso or north to Las Cruces. S-cuse me." She opened the stove door to expectorate, then explained: "It's snuff. Bin chewin' it for twenty years 'n' ain't got used to it yet."

I waited until my friend had reclosed the stove door, then resumed my quizzing: "Where was the principal business street when you located here?"

"West of th' Santa Fe tracks. Guess how many houses was on that street? I see you

†From "Old Timers Dictionary in Detail," coll. Marie Carter; 1000 wds., 5 pp., 8 March 1937; HC: Anthony; LC38.1; LC47.1).

can't guess," she added quickly, "so I'll have to tell you. There was five. I run a little notion store 'n' Charley Miller run a store next door. He sold whiskey but had to quit 'cause the Mexicans would get drunk in his place 'n' start fights. One day he got so mad that he took all his whiskey barrels 'n' dumped 'em in th' street."

"I suppose land was cheap," I said.

"I'll say it was. Good valley land ranged from eight to ten dollars an acre," she said. "Twenty-five dollars was a fancy price."

The street referred to by this old-timer was in 1901 a mere country lane with narrow trails branching off in different directions. One trail turned north to the town of Mesquite. A second trail turned west to the Rio Grande and Bosque or low land.

Today the ranch land known as the "Dairy Farm" commands a top price, but in 1901 it was bought by a Mr. Howser for six dollars an acre. Mr. Howser leveled the land and sold it to C. F. Carpenter for twelve dollars an acre. Mr. Carpenter made some improvements and sold it to the El Paso Dairy Farm Company. This company bought the ranch to raise alfalfa and grain to feed their cattle. At the present time the principal crops are cotton and sugar-beet seed. The seed is shipped to Colorado to grow sugar beets.

In the early days of this town the chief amusements were picnics and barbecues. The men usually barbecued the beef. Sometimes they remained up all night preparing, cooking, basting and turning it on the spit. As one old-timer commented, "ye can't hurry barbecue."

In 1870, William Raymond Morley, Sr. (1846–83) was a railroad engineer when he was hired by the owners of the Maxwell Land Grant to handle surveying and development. He married Iowan Ada McPherson (1852–1917) in 1873, and they lived at Cimarron. Morley resigned from the Grant in 1875, but the family was deeply embroiled in the Colfax County turmoil for years.[15] Morley then did railroad engineering in New Mexico, Colorado, and Mexico, where he was accidentally shot on January 3, 1883, leaving daughters Agnes (age nine) and Loraine (age five) and son Ray (age seven). In 1886, the family moved to the Datil ranch and a challenge described by Agnes Morley Cleaveland as *No Life for a Lady* (Boston: Houghton Mifflin, 1941).

According to her nephew, Norman Cleaveland: "In 1918, my Aunt Loraine, a divorcee, was running the Datil post office, general store, cafe, gas station and the early-day motor court of five rooms."[16] At that time she married Morley ranch foreman Tom Reynolds.

Sometime after that Mrs. Reynolds's brother Ray moved their mother's great log house from White House Canyon nine miles into Datil, rebuilt it, and renamed it the Navajo Lodge. There, Morley entertained guests with yarns of the Old West and "to add color . . . arranged for several Navajo families to reside on the premises, where the women could weave blankets and sell them to the passersby. From the Indians, he had learned the art of handling live rattlesnakes and whenever there was a favorable opportunity he would demonstrate this art to fascinated or terrified onlookers."[17]*

Mrs. Loraine Morley Warren came to New Mexico in the fall of 1916, after resigning as supervisor of public recreation in Redbank, New Jersey, and bought Fred Baldwin's stock of general merchandise and leased the ranch for two years. At her own expense, she built the first schoolhouse at Datil out of her own funds, then immediately after having the keys of the schoolhouse turned over to her, she discovered that a man by the name of Richardson from Tucumcari, who was camping nearby, determined to file on the public land where the school was erected. This forced Mrs. Warren to file on the 160 acres, the only public domain open in the vicinity where Cibola, formerly known as Datil, is now located.

The squatter who laid his plans to jump the schoolhouse property or land and thereby force Mrs. Warren either to sell the building or move it within thirty days to another site made his brags that he was goin' to outwit that clever widder and take the land, move into the school building and set up housekeeping. Mrs. Warren, always a staunch prohibitionist, can truthfully say that liquor was in that instance a great boon for the innocent, for Richardson became intoxicated to the braggart stage and exposed his nefarious plan to the crowd in the post office.

Mrs. Warren overheard his remarks and decided to take a hand and checkmate his proposed plan. She engaged him in conversation and offered him an exorbitant price for a load of freight to be hauled by him from Magdalena for her store. She gave him a cup of coffee and detained him until nearly dark. Then she arranged for the mail carrier to come very early in the morning and stepped into her car and beat him to Magdalena by about forty minutes, where she filed on the 160 acres before A. A. Sedillos, land commissioner. (Sedillos afterwards became a prominent attorney in Albuquerque.)

Immediately after filing, she started to build her residence. She moved into it in 1918 and eventually moved the post office and opened a store in the large room which is now used as the dining room and kitchen of the present residence.

About this time she married Tom Reynolds, who had been the general manager and foreman for the Morley ranches. They moved to the new residence and commenced building a village. (So Seton Village at Santa Fe wasn't the first village built by a white resident of New Mexico.) Mrs. Reynolds is probably the only woman in New Mexico to have established a village. Frequently it is true that the originator of any town is never known, but in this case a pioneer lady, a native of the state, really founded the town and deserves credit for this worthy effort to aid posterity.

She also persuaded her brother, William Raymond Morley, to move the old family home, then called The White House, as his land joined her property on the east, to the present location of the Navajo Lodge. About twenty months later, Mr. Morley had completed the Navajo Lodge and it was opened to the public. Mr. Morley's dynamic personality made the lodge one of the outstanding places of interest to tourists and guests in the Southwest. In this way their home was restored to its beautiful appearance and use-

*"A Woman Builds a Town," coll. Clay W. Vaden; 1165 wds., 5 pp., 11 March 1936 (A#182).

"Navajo Lodge formerly an old ranch house in the mountains.
About thirty years ago the rancher [Ray Morley] who owned it
had it dismantled and moved it piece by piece and rebuilt it at
its present location. He is now dead and the house is used as a
hotel principally for summer visitors." Photo by Russell Lee,
Datil, April 1940. LC-USF 34-35886-D.

fulness and added greatly to the community
and to the convenience of travelers along
Highway 60.

In 1928 Mrs. Reynolds built the tourist
camp, having the store and post office at the
forks of the two roads, U.S. 60 and No. 12
state road, and called the village Datil, that
being the original name of the Cibola National Forest there. In 1932 she sold the
camp, sixty acres, and the store to Harry H.
Watson of Oklahoma City, who, in 1933,
sold to Mrs. Julia Mae Parrott and Mrs. Lois
Parrott of Oklahoma City. At that time Mrs.
Julia Mae Parrott and her husband, Russell
Parrott, moved here and have since built two
additional modern cottages and several out-
buildings and are at the present time con-

structing a residence which is being joined
into the store building.

The FERA [Federal Emergency Relief
Administration], after carefully considering
the proper location in Catron County for its
main offices, decided to locate in Cibola because of the fact that long distance telephone
facilities were already established and the location was more favorable for reaching Santa
Fe. Quemado, which might have had the
headquarters, was too isolated without a telephone service and with only a tri-weekly mail.
The erection of the FERA building of native
pine logs has added much to the attractive
appearance of the buildings of the village,
which are mainly of logs. Until this FERA
building was erected the original Datil school,

"Proprietor of the Navajo lodge before the fireplace." Photo by
Russell Lee, Datil, April 1940. LC-USF 34-35889-D.

which Mrs. Reynolds built in 1917, was used
for the FERA offices. Since that time three
filling stations, two garages, the very attractive and unique Navajo Lodge and stores
comprise the main business establishments,
and all the cottages are occupied by FERA
officials.

The village is built on the historic site of
Camp Datil, established in 1887 or 1888 by
General Miles for the purpose of protecting
the citizens from the murderous, roving bands
of Apaches under Chief Geronimo. The location has always been considered most ad-

vantageous because of its being on the Old
Trails road, and now the two federal aid roads
make it very accessible to all points from
Cibola.

The picturesque Sawteeth range of mountains in the Cibola National Forest have some
of the most gorgeous scenery in Catron
County. The Capitol Dome Mountain, four
or five miles east of Pie Town, is very distinctive and worthy of an artistic highway
sign to attract the attention of numerous
tourists. Other natural attractions in this range
of red sandstone of gorgeous changing colors,

"Living room of the Navajo lodge." Photo by Russell Lee, Datil, April 1940. LC-USF 34-35893-D.

which surpass the scenic beauty of the Palisades along the Hudson River in New York, are: the mountain pass through Sawteeth Mountains by way of Cathedral Rock on Cibola forest reserve (part of this is on Goesling's lease, now owned by Badger-Bruner of Amarillo, Texas), the Veiled Nun and the Monk, rock images or natural monuments, very lifelike in appearance, etc.

After having sold the store and camp, conditions during the depression forced Mrs. Reynolds to open up her house and home, which she humorously calls "The Dump,"

for appreciative guests, and is at this time entertaining some very interesting and prominent guests. Mrs. Reynolds, like her illustrious brother Ray Morley, has a wide reputation for her intellect and spontaneous wit. She recently said to her interviewer, "One who builds a village leaves a living monument and needs none of stone to keep his or her memory green," and quoted from that remarkable educator and philanthropist, Horace Mann: "Be ashamed to die until you have achieved some victory for humanity."

Photos by Russell Lee, all taken in June 1940:
"Business section." LC-USF 34-36796-D.

Loraine Morley Reynolds also had a hand in establishing Pie Town, the homestead community which symbolized the end of the Morleys' ranching fortunes. Pie Town was described by Clay W. Vaden for the American Guide project in 1936, and it was extensively photographed by Russell Lee in June 1940.[18]*

The rustic little friendly village of Pie Town, on U.S. Highway 60 twenty-two miles east of Quemado has quite an interesting bit of history concerning how it got its distinctive, original, and outstanding name.

Clyde Norman, an ex-service man, came to Catron County at the close of the World War looking for a homestead claim, but failing to find just what he wanted in that line he took up a mining claim of forty acres at the present location of Pie Town, originally called "Norman's Place" and so designated on old state highway maps. He went into the oil, gas, and grocery business first and later opened a small eating place where he served coffee and doughnuts in a small one-room picket house. He bought his doughnuts from the bakery at Datil, run by Miss Helen McLaughlin.

His trade grew until the little bakery could

*"Origin of Pie Town," coll. Clay W. Vaden; 300 wds., 1 p., 17 October 1936 (HC: Pie Town).

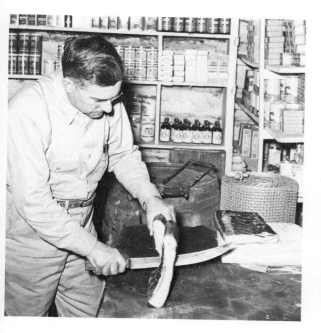

"Mr. Keele slicing bacon in the general store." LC-USF 34-36832-D.

"Josie Caudill getting resin from pinon tree for chewing gum." LC-USF 33-12766-M3.

not supply his demand for doughnuts. Mrs. Tom Reynolds, who had financed the Datil bakery, suggested that he "build pies" at his place and name the village PIE TOWN, and she assisted Mr. Norman in stenciling the letters for his first Pie Town sign.

About two years later, H. L. Craig, a veteran of the Spanish American War who had lost all his possessions in cattle during the early depression and bank failure at Mag-

dalena, bought a working interest in Pie Town. Mr. Craig started adding other baked products. Eventually he bought out Mr. Norman's half interest and the latter returned to Texas. Later Mr. Craig, now the sole owner of the entire town, married a widow, Mrs. Ora Baum. She and her daughters assisted Mr. Craig in building up Pie Town of today, and they have continued to specialize in pies "like mother used to make."

"Mrs. Fero Caudill looking at canned goods in her storage
cellar. Notice the slab roofing." LC-USF 34-36551-D.

"Fero Caudill pouring water from his well into a watering
trough made of hollowed-out log." LC-USF 34-36541-D.

"Mrs. Bill Stagg, homesteader's wife, putting the coffee on the table for dinner which consisted of homecured ham and gravy, pinto beans, corn, homemade pickles, homegrown tomatoes, homemade bread and hot biscuits, fruit salad, cake, two kinds of pie, milk and coffee." LC-USF 34-36660-D.

"Mrs. George Hutton irrigating her garden. The Huttons have ample water at their farm. This was the only irrigated garden seen in the section." LC-USF 34-36755-D.

"Young Hutton feeding clabbered milk to the chickens." LC-USF 33-12729-M3.

"Mrs. George Hutton putting the food on the table for dinner."
LC-USF 34-36679-D.

"Mr. and Mrs. Besson eating cake and coffee at a forty-two
party at their home. They farmed in Oklahoma near Frederick
before homesteading here." LC-USF 34-36578-D.

Pie Town was also a center for piñon sales. A bumper crop of eight million pounds was recorded in 1936 in New Mexico. Pickers realized about $700,000 cash on nuts eventually sold on the New York City market—a not insignificant sum during hard times.[19]*

Few people realize that the piñon industry in the Pie Town district in Catron County this season compares favorably with the income from stock raising, but the following facts speak for themselves: Good crops of piñons usually occur from every three to five years, and this year's crop is a bumper one.

There are from five hundred to a thousand Indians, mostly Navajos from near Gallup and Zunis from Zuni, that are working under orders of thirty local white men who have set up several commissaries for the Indians' convenience near their camps where each member of the Indian families works picking piñons on land the white men have leased from the owners within a radius of twenty-five miles of Pie Town, New Mexico. H. L. Craig, Pie Town merchant and biggest local buyer of piñons, said in a recent interview: "I have bought $16,000.00 worth of pinons from September 20th to the present time, November 25th, and with continued good weather the season of piñon gathering should last much longer."

Other buyers in Pie Town district are J. McPhaul, Jesse Padon, Ellis McPhaul, Messrs. Kennedy and Baldwin, Teat Lehew, and W. R. Thomas. These men sell their piñons to four buyers in Magdalena: Becker-McTavish Co., Chas. Ilfeld & Co., George Goze, and Mr. Jones of Thoreau, New Mexico. Prices at Magdalena vary from eight to nine and a half cents delivered in Magdalena. The pickers themselves often get from six to eight cents a pound. While this does not sound so big, the fact remains that this year's God given crop of piñons in this small area itself has helped fifty poor families in Catron County to be dropped from the direct relief rolls according to the ERA authorities.

Ninety percent of the piñons are first shipped from Magdalena to Ilfeld's roasting plant in Albuquerque. From there they are shipped to New York City where Jewish dealers practically control the piñon industry.

The Indians engaged in piñon gathering have an efficient method all their own, gathering the little nuts which are considered such a delicacy. They thresh the piñons from the trees, letting them fall on wagon sheets or tarpaulins spread under the trees, or else they use light bamboo rakes to collect the nuts in piles, then screen the nuts with handmade heavy screen netting tacked on wooden frames similar to those used in screening gravel for mixing with cement. The squaws later winnow the chaff and fine debris from the piñons by using finer meshed screens and tossing the nuts and trash in the air during a bit of windy weather.[20]

If the profit from piñon picking continues to improve, the U.S. Government's valuation of thirty-five cents placed on each piñon tree will be raised.

*"Profitable Pinon Picking Near Pie Town," coll. Clay W. Vaden; 458 wds., 2 pp., 1 December 1936 (A#182).

Karl Pitschner (b. Iowa, 1899) was a metallurgist and chemist who in 1945 was described as: "owner of the Albuquerque Food Products Company, located at 3407 East Central Avenue, manufacturers of candy in which the famous piñon nut is utilized, and also producers of potato chips, pop corn and chile, [who] made a remarkable contribution to the agricultural economy of New Mexico when he perfected a process for adapting these famous nuts to candy and other confections. While on a trip through the west some years ago Mr. Pitschner was requested to undertake the designing of equipment for shelling piñons. While engaged in this effort he became interested in the piñon industry and in March, 1932, founded the Albuquerque Food Products Company. He started the business on a very small scale, but it was a decided success from the very beginning and early in 1941 the company completed a new building with four thousand square feet of floor space."[21] However, when Janet Smith interviewed him in 1936, he was at 1116 East Central.*

One of the unique industries of Albuquerque is the Piñon Nut Company at 1116 E. Central, owned and managed by Karl Pitschner, who is an accepted authority on the piñon (pronounced *pin-yon*) industry and the inventor of a piñon nut shelling machine.

Piñons are one of the most important economic products of New Mexico. The piñons used in Mr. Pitschner's factory come from an area of over 500,000 square miles, of which about one fifth is piñon country. They come from Gallup, Magdalena, Cuba, Santa Fe, and Las Vegas, and from parts of Arizona, Utah, and Colorado.

The piñon trees grow on dry foothills, mesas, mountain slopes and the sides of canyons at an elevation of from 5,000 to 9,000 feet. The trees, although evergreens, somewhat resemble old apple trees in appearance from a distance. They have short trunks, and low hanging branches, usually crooked, and ranging in height from 10 to 35 feet. The trees are slow growing and often reach an age of 300 years. An individual tree may produce as much as 40 pounds of nuts. There are usually 2 or 3 cones to a tip, and 12 to 14 nuts to a cone. Mr. Pitschner says that piñons are capable of semi-cultivation. If a tree is pruned, and a furrow plowed so that the moisture will go to the roots, the nuts will be large and the crop can be thus increased. He also mentioned that Professor English, near Zuni, has made experiments of this kind.

There are 4 species of piñon trees of which the *Pinus edulis* Englemann and the *Pinus Monophylla* are the most common. The former has the thinnest shell and is superior in flavor and color.

Mr. Pitschner says that the piñon tree will bear a crop only every two years. If, for instance, the tree bears pollen this June, by next fall the nut will be only partly matured. Not until a year from next fall will it be ready to pick. The cones ripen in September, and during the latter part of September and Oc-

*"Unusual Albuquerque Industries," coll. Janet Smith; 1200 wds., 5 pp., 4 May 1936 (A#128; LCms#1).

tober shed the seeds. Each scale of the cone covers two wingless brown seeds which are the piñon nuts.

The nuts are gathered chiefly by Indians and native New Mexicans. The favorite method is to rob the pack rats' nests. A nest will often hold from $1/2$ to $1 1/2$ bushels and all the nuts will have kernels—the rats never gather empty shells. The nest can be robbed from 2 to 3 times during the fall. The nuts are also picked from the ground. A Navajo squaw can often pick as much as 20 pounds a day. Sometimes a tarpaulin is spread on the ground and the trees shaken. The ground is occasionally swept with a broom, but this results in sticks and dirt which have to be separated from the nuts. After cleaning the nuts, Indians and Spanish-American natives then take them to the stores and trading posts where they sell or trade them.

Mr. Pitschner described to me the method by which the nuts are prepared after reaching his factory. They are cleaned and then polished in the shell by tumbling with sand in a steel drum through which an air blast is blown to remove dust, dirt, and abraded shell. The nuts can then be roasted in the shells, and if so desired are placed in large cylinders which have a 500 pound capacity. In Mr. Pitschner's plant, electricity is used for heating, as he has found it more satisfactory than moist, gas heat.

Special machines are necessary for the shelling of piñons because of their tiny size. Mr. Pitschner invented such a machine and set up his present business March 1932, at the suggestion of an Indian friend.

If the piñons are to be shelled after cleaning and polishing, they are sized. This calls for a series of screen with graduated opening so that after being shelled the kernels may be separated from the uncracked nuts. Before shelling the nuts are exposed to a hot steam for a sufficient length of time to kill germs and insect life. The shelling machine proceeds at the rate of about 100 pounds an hour, and not more than 2 percent of the kernels are broken. The sterilized nuts are

fed into the machine through a hopper. The shells and brown inner skins are blown through a pipe in the rear of the machine, while a mixture of kernels and uncracked nuts drop through the bottom. The mixture is then passed through screens which separate the uncracked nuts from the kernels. The uncracked nuts are then returned to the machine. The kernels, which may contain a small amount of shell, are run through another device which completes the separation of kernel from shell. The kernels are then sent to sorting tables where girls remove any rancid or discolored kernels, or remaining bits of shell. The machine does its work so well that the girls can sort as many as 40 pounds in an hour, and there are approximately 2,900 kernels to the pound.

After the kernels are taken from the sorting tables they are spread thinly on screens, and thoroughly dried. In the summer time they are exposed to 7 hours of direct sunlight. When the drying process takes place in the winter, they are first dried in an oven, and then given direct sunlight. It is said that the sunlight increases the vitamin content.

The piñon nuts may be kept for months, sometimes as long as 3 years if they are dried properly and kept at a temperature not more than 40 degrees F.

The piñons are sold as roasted and salted nuts, and are made into piñon taffy, creams, and piñon brittle. Mr. Pitschner says the demand for them is growing. In lean years, after a drouth, the demand exceeds the supply. There is a market for them from coast to coast, and exporters have recently made inquiries with the idea of sending them to Hawaii and China.

Mr. Pitschner said that Dr. John Kellogg of Battle Creek is interested in piñons from the dietetic point of view, as they are rich in proteins, carbohydrates, and fats.

A clear yellow oil is made from the nuts by a process of suction filtering after slightly roasting and grinding the nuts. It is thought that this oil could be profitably used for dietetics and also for cosmetics.

The shells make good fuel. Chemists of the Bureau of Standards are of the opinion that the shell has other valuable uses. Experiments show that it could be used as a raw material for destructive distillation, decolorizing, and deodorizing. When heated in retorts an excellent charcoal is produced and a mixture of organic materials is driven off which with proper treatment should produce chemicals such as wood alcohol, furfural, tar, etc. The charcoal obtained is of a type useful in gas masks.

During certain seasons Mr. Pitschner employs about 8 people and says that he sees great possibility for future development of the industry.

In 1876, Animas City, Colorado, residents William Hendrickson, Charley and Milton Virden, Albert Puett and Henry Wood stopped at To-Tah, the confluence of the Animas and San Juan Rivers, and eventually named their settlement Farming-town, christened in a shorter version as Farmington. They were soon followed by other pioneers, among them Mr. and Mrs. William Locke, also from Colorado. Remembering late nineteenth-century Farmington life, oldtimer John Arrington said: "William Locke, who had thirteen children to support, found time to organize and conduct what was known as the 'Saturday Night Literary.' Readings were interpreted in the elocutionary manner and with guitar or fiddle accompaniment. Folk songs were rendered by members and guests."[22] Mr. Locke (1836–1919) served with Ricardo López as members of the House from the eighth district (Rio Arriba, San Juan and Taos Counties) during the Territory's 31st Legislative Assembly, convened in Santa Fe the last Monday of December, 1894.

Mrs. Nettie C. Locke (1854–1937) supplemented the family's agricultural income with proceeds from beekeeping and egg sales. She lived at Waterflow near Farmington when Helen Gage Simpson interviewed her in 1936.*

Mr. William Locke and his wife "Nettie," now some eighty years of age, with their children on March 19, 1879, started from the Cockle Burr Ranch near Florence, Colorado, to locate in the San Juan Basin near the junction of the San Juan and Animas rivers, San Juan County, New Mexico. They traveled in a four-horse wagon and a hack drawn by two horses and were just thirteen days on the road.

They crossed Red Mountain and camped that night with a brother of Mr. Locke, who

*"Personal Interview with Mrs. Nettie Locke—S-240-Folk-Ways," coll. Mrs. R. T. F. Simpson from Mrs. Locke at Waterflow; 750 wds., 4 pp., 11 September 1936 (A#225; LC47.1).

lived in that valley, and worked slowly over toward Alamosa. The night they made camp near that town they were so near a sheep camp that they took turns to keep guard all night to ward off Mexican sheepherders who were said to have made away with some campers not long before. They were known to be an ugly lot, hence their caution.

Traveling on to their new location, they finally came into Largo Canyon, quite near their goal. They made their last camp in this Spanish-American settlement and found these people most friendly. In seeking fresh eggs and milk from them, the fact that Mr. Locke spoke Spanish freely seemed to give them an open sesame to their homes. Mrs. Locke well remembers the friendliness extended to them in giving them shelter for the night, saying it was too cold for the baby to sleep outside. They also gave good care to their tired horses and started them off on the last leg of their journey well supplied with some of the beef they had just been butchering. This was in sharp contrast to the type of Spanish-Mexicans encountered near Alamosa.

It was but a short distance from Largo to the junction of the San Juan and Las Animas Rivers, and in a few days Mr. and Mrs. Locke were established in a three-room house of "pole" construction where the Farmington Fair Grounds are now located. This was an improvement on camping, to be sure, but Mrs. Locke was sorely disappointed "that the rooms had no floors. I couldn't put the baby down in the dirt." Mr. Locke found her in tears about it, so to console her he hastily covered one floor with hay and put a Navajo rug on the hay where the baby sat and played in cleanliness.

This room had a fireplace in it for heating; the kitchen was heated by a cookstove which they had brought with them and of which they were justly proud. The third room had no heat. Before long they were able to floor one room where the fireplace was for the baby to play in. Soon after, the kitchen was partially floor, that is, the part that held the cookstove.

This was not a very desirable location as it was too low and damp, especially in rainy weather when it was almost a swamp. For this reason and because of an Indian scare they moved nearer to the town, which was higher ground. Mrs. Locke exhibited a 12 × 12 photograph of what the town was in the very early days which was quite interesting. In the foreground to the right was the much talked of 18 × 24 schoolhouse, then a one-room structure, today a two-story, nine-roomed house bearing no resemblance to the earlier schoolhouse. To the left was a big open space, then a tent next to a small adobe building now gone altogether but which was then the location of the Bowman Drug Store where there was a hold-up sometime later. On the north side of "Main Street" could plainly be seen the long narrow roof of the first business block, The Markley Building beyond the two small stores just east of it, all still standing.

In the center background was the home of Mr. Oliver McGordon, the man who named Farmington. This was the adobe house now owned and occupied by Mrs. Lorena Mahany and the home of the Farmington Library. Mr. McGordon was a man of uncertain temper, and one day in a rage he shot and killed his wife and was hung for it.

In the farthest northwest corner of the photograph could be seen the tall trees on the Markley Estate nearly a mile away, now the home of R. T. F. Simpson. In the center or near foreground were a few people afoot and on horseback and an open ditch with ice on it. There was nothing else in the picture except the wide open spaces of very rough ground, some water or mud in the street edged with ice, and considerable space given to a clear sky.

Mr. Locke set out his first fruit trees on June 2d, 1880. This was the nucleus of what later became the largest orchard in San Juan County. Mr. Locke's first alfalfa seed was a gift from the friendly Spanish-Americans in Largo Canyon. It was a tobacco sack full of the seed, and from this small quantity he in later years raised large quantities of alfalfa.

From four beehives from Canon City, Colorado, was started the bee culture in the county, which soon became the property of Mrs. Locke. She learned to handle them and was never stung, and from these four hives she supplied many people of the valley with bees. This she told with considerable pride. The orchards, alfalfa fields, and the cleome or wild bee weed furnished plenty of pasture for the bees.

Mrs. Locke's chickens were such good layers there was considerable income from the eggs, especially in the winter when they

were somewhat scarce. One winter they brought her in a dollar a dozen, her one regret being they went to the White House Saloon. However, saloon or no saloon, she could not resist the price.

Mrs. Locke is the mother of fourteen children. She is a little woman with pure white hair, soft voice, pleasing manner, and clear memory, but so frail with the burden of her eighty or more years that her strength gave out in less than an hour. Therefore, here ends the history she gave me of her first years in Farmington.

Navajo scout and pensioner Hola traveled from Gallup to Albuquerque by bus in 1941. Unfortunately, there is no indication which New Mexico Writers' Program worker submitted the following perceptive account of Hola's encounter with the medical profession.*

Early in the evening of October 14, 1941, Hola, seventy-four-year-old Navaho Indian scout and pensioner, arrived unescorted at the Veterans' Hospital in Albuquerque, New Mexico. He had an admission card to the hospital and a return bus ticket to Gallup, New Mexico. A telephone call from the bus station brought a car from the hospital to pick up the old man.

Hola could speak neither English nor Spanish. Half a dozen people were certain he could understand Spanish, and all were talking to him at the same time. When the old man realized that no one could understand him, he remained silent, retaining his serenity and dignity. An ex-Indian trader, who was a patient at the hospital and who had a

fair knowledge of "store Navaho," was enlisted as an interpreter. Hola was delighted to find someone who could understand him.

Hola, who was making an application for an increase in his pension, had come to the hospital for a routine examination. Other scouts whom he had served with had received an increase, and he was applying for one.

With the exception of his eyes, Hola was in good condition. Like many old Navahos, he was almost blind, probably due to many sweat baths and smoke from the open fire inside the hogan. Poor eyesight is not inherent with Navahos, for when young they have unusually good vision.

If there is such a thing, Hola is a typical Navaho, in looks, dress, and demeanor. His

*"A Navaho Scout at the Veterans' Hospital in Albuquerque," no coll. given; 1773 wds., 6 pp. (A#65).

features are strong and regular; he is five feet nine inches tall and weighs 170 pounds. He has lost only two teeth, but those he has have been worn down almost to his gums. His hair is long and almost white. It is kept in place by a black silk kerchief, for he wears no hat. A small pair of turquoise eardrops dangle below the kerchief. He wears a single blue cotton shirt, which has a tendency to stay on the outside of his waist overalls. If it is chilly, he wraps his Pendleton robe around his shoulders. When it gets colder, he will probably put two or three more shirts on over the one he is wearing. His drawers are made of colored calico and he wears a G-string which is tied with a buckskin thong. He wears cheap work shoes and long cotton stockings. In Navaho style, he cuts the toes out of his stockings.

His robe cost about ten dollars. The rest of his clothes did not exceed six dollars. Three or four dollars would be an outside price for his eardrops.

With the fifty-five dollars a month pension Hola receives, he could live in luxury on the Navaho Reservation, but three of his sons and their families live with him. It is doubtful if there is much left for the old man after his children's wants are supplied. He owns three horses, but no sheep, goats, or cattle. The horses are a necessity. The old man must have some way to get to town when his pension check comes each month.

Young people "sponging" off of their elders happens as often among the Navahos as it does among the whites. Superintendent McCray, who was at the Shiprock Agency in the early 1930s, became so indignant over the treatment that some of these old pensioners were receiving from their relatives that he had several moved in close to the Agency where they would be better cared for.

Hola's was a plain case of where his children were keeping him in abject poverty. A Navaho of Hola's standing and receiving his income should have been better dressed. He should have been wearing a good shell and

turquoise necklace, a large silver belt, and at least one good bracelet. Also, he should have owned a blue serge coat with silver buttons on it. If he receives the seventeen dollars increase in his pension it will mean just that much more for his children to spend. It is doubtful if he benefits from it.

Hola could not get his examination until the following day, so he spent the night at the hospital—as a guest and not a patient. He said that he had been in a hospital only on one other occasion, to have his eyes examined. It was obvious that he had never used a clinical thermometer. When the nurse wanted to take his temperature, she had no trouble in getting him to open his mouth so she could insert the thermometer, but she couldn't make him understand that she wanted him to close his mouth. When he did close his mouth, he insisted on keeping the thermometer on top of his tongue.

The old scout was put in a private ward. When shown which bed he was to sleep in, he immediately started to disrobe. The nurse made a hasty departure. Some of the patients predicted that he would sleep on the floor, but he didn't; with only a word from the interpreter, the old man put on the pajamas furnished by the hospital and climbed into bed. This was probably the first pair of pajamas he ever wore, and it is doubtful if he had slept in many beds.

True to Navaho custom, Hola was up at break of day. After he had given his face and hands a thorough scrubbing, he was ready for a stroll around the grounds with his guide, the Indian trader. At 7:15, breakfast was served in the mess hall. From the way some of the patients stared, they had probably never seen a real Indian. The old scout's manners at the table were above reproach. He was just a little awkward with knife and fork, which were more than just a little strange to him. No doubt he would have preferred using his fingers and a spoon as he was accustomed to using at home. He surprised his trader friend by eating two fried eggs. Fish, fowl, and eggs are taboo to most old Navahos.

Nils Hogner, "Navajo Indians," oil painting, 36 × 44, n.d.
PWAP (NMSRC WPA-PWAP #5417).

When taking bread, he always broke a slice in two pieces and left half of it on the bread plate, but at that he made away with fifteen or sixteen slices, besides drinking three cups of coffee. It is not good manners among Navahos to take a whole slice of bread. When eating fried bread or tortillas, they never take a whole cake; only small portions are broken off from the whole. Judging from the amount he ate, the old man was hungry, preparing for a fast, or just being polite and showing good manners by eating a lot. The waitress in the mess hall was especially considerate and saw that he was well supplied.

At eight o'clock the doctors started with their examinations. First there was a Wasserman blood test. When the doctor stuck the needle in his arm to extract blood, the old warrior never flinched or batted an eye. Navahos, especially the older ones, are like the Plains Indians; they seem to take pride in appearing indifferent to pain.

The next step was to get as complete a history as possible. The attendants, a doctor, a nurse, and a secretary all insisted that he should have a Christian name. Old Navahos as well as other old Indians seldom had but one name. If they do, it is usually given to them in school. The old scout had been receiving his pension check under the single name of Hola. To add any more to his name would be inviting trouble and confusing his records. The interpreter compromised by tacking on "Hosteen." Hosteen is a title of courtesy given to many old Navahos; it means about the same as the English word "mister."

Hola could date his birth fairly accurately. He had heard his parents say that he was almost old enough to walk when they left Bosque Redondo near the present town of Fort Sumner in the summer of 1868. It is unusual for an old Indian to have any idea of the date of his birth unless it is dated by some special event.

Next came Hola's family. He said he had been married only one time and had nine living children, six boys and three girls. His wife had been dead for ten years. If he had any children dead he made no mention of them. It is customary for the Navahos not to mention the dead or speak their names. It seemed strange to Hola's questioners that he could not give the English name of a single child.

After Hola's history had been recorded, doctors on the first, second, and third floors of the hospital gave him examinations. These examinations lasted until noon. The doctors were very considerate of the old man and did everything to make him feel at ease. Hola cooperated one hundred percent. If the old man was embarrassed at having to disrobe before the doctors he did not show it. There was never any loss of dignity. These exam-

inations lasted until noon. Hola and his interpreter and escort, the Indian trader, were all morning making the rounds. True to Indian fashion, Hola insisted on walking single file instead of abreast with his trader friend. This gave the appearance that he was following the trader, but neither Hola nor the trader were bothered about what others thought.

After a big dinner, Hola was x-rayed from head to foot. He seemed greatly interested in some x-ray pictures shown him. When he saw his own, he showed signs of uneasiness. If there is one thing a Navaho is afraid of, it is a dead person. No doubt these pictures looked too much like human skeletons for him to be comfortable.

The doctors enjoyed joking with the old man. Those who think Navahos do not have a sense of humor do not know them. There was much amusement all around.

At two o'clock a hospital car was waiting to take Hola to the bus station, and he got in and was driven away. He will have strange tales to tell his friends on the Reservation about his visit to the hospital, and there will doubtless be many times when he will think of the meals he had, when he ate all he wanted and there was no fear of a shortage.

In 1922, at the instigation of Miss Anne Evans of Denver, a group of Santa Feans—among them the Right Reverend Archbishop Albert Thomas Daeger (d. 1932), Museum of New Mexico director Edgar Lee Hewett (1865–1946), artist Carlos Vierra (1876–1937), and architect John Gaw Meem (1894–1983)—informally organized a Committee, later, the Society (in 1932), for the Preservation and Restoration of the New Mexican Mission Churches. Through the help of William P. McPhee of Denver, restoration of the roof on the church at Zia Pueblo was completed in December 1923, and in 1924 plans were underway to begin work at Acoma Pueblo and Las Trampas.[23] The restoration of the mission church of San Esteban del Rey at Acoma Pueblo, from 1926 to 1929, was the group's most extended project.[24]

Pecos resident Bernhardt A. Reuter was chosen by the committee to serve as construction foreman on August 17, 1926. According to him: "The Society had done some restoration work on the Mission two years before and the agreement between the Society and the Acoma Pueblo was well understood by the Indians. This agreement was, in short, that the Society would pay for certain necessary materials which the Acomas could not well furnish, and also pay the salary of a construction foreman, selected by the Society and whose supervision of the work the Acomas would respect. The Acoma Tribe, on the other hand, was to furnish free labor for the enterprise. This labor was to be furnished in relays of a certain number of men each week."[25]

John Gaw Meem supervised Reuter's work. "My first visit to Acoma was in company with Mr. Meem and it was he who introduced me to the place and its people. On our arrival at Acoma, Mr. Meem and I met the Acoma governor, and fortunately for us the Acoma councilmen were at the old village. Mr. Meem informed the Governor of our mission, and while the Governor was getting his Council together, Mr. Meem and I went about making an inspection of the church and monastery."[26] In the course of his subsequent labors, Reuter worked with and interviewed many Acoma residents, including Old Santiago (132 at the time of his accidental death), with whom he last spoke in 1929.[27]*

A great deal of skepticism exists concerning the great age claimed by some of our American Indians. In the first place, few even claim to know the number of their years, and even they do not know the day or month of the year of birth.

Old Santiago claimed to be in his one hundred and thirtieth year when he was interviewed. The next oldest men of the tribe said that Santiago was far and away the oldest man in the pueblo. Santiago said that his father was a very intelligent man and regretted that he did not know his own age,

so he decided to keep the age of his son and when he was ten teach him how to continue the count of the years.

He said it was quite simple to learn: In the count of ten, the left hand thumb was number ten. When the right hand thumb is reached in the count of ten, a recount of ten is begun with the thumb of the left hand, which also stands as one complete count of all the ten fingers. When the count of the years again comes to the right hand thumb, the count of the second ten was kept by often playing with the index finger on the left hand.

---

*"Approximate Ages of Old Acoma Indians," coll. B. A. Reuter from "information by interviewing old Indians"; 2500 wds., 5 typed pp., 30 December 1938, rec. 3 January 1939 (A#62; H5-4-15#6a; handwritten, pencilled original, 25 pp. LCms#5).

In this manner the old man claimed to have kept count of his years. He said that at the next winter solstice ceremony, which is the beginning of their year, he would for the second time bring down the middle finger of the left hand in the count of how many times ten the fingers on his two hands showed he had lived in years.

Two years after this, he fell backward into an irrigation ditch and received an injury in the spine that resulted in his death soon after. According to his count, he was 132 when he died. The oldest members of his family then living said that the old man had, since their earliest recollection, been most faithful in keeping count of his years after the manner described. This man gave full details of events that other old men had heard about but could tell nothing worthwhile. From all of the checking done backward and forward, it was evident that Santiago was really as old as he claimed.

Another man in Acoma, though he did not know his age, had certain clear memories of personal and historical events by which his age could reasonably be approximated. This man's name was James H. Miller. He was at the other end of the line, the youngest of the older set.

The baptismal records of the Catholic Church would be the surest way of establishing the ages of these men, if as infants they were all baptized and later remembered their given names. They were given Spanish names in baptism, but some of these old men were not christened, and some of them, in the long years that followed, have become confused about their Spanish names, and therefore identification of the individual and the name in the records of close to a hundred years ago is next to impossible. For instance, there was one centenarian who was usually called Pedro; however, he thought his name was San Juan Pedro, but whether it was Pedro San Juan or Juan or San Juan Pedro, he was not sure. He was also not sure whether either of these or some other name was given him in baptism or if he were ever baptized.

James H. Miller still could remember the soldiers rounding up the Navajos when the government took them to Bosque Redondo in 1864 and their release four years later.[28] He said he must have been between nine and fourteen years at the time of the Navajo Captivity. If he were twelve years old in 1864, then he was seventy-five years old in 1927 when he was interviewed about these matters, and that is about what he appeared to be. When asked how much difference there was in his and Pedro's ages, he said that Pedro was already a man of family in his first recollection of him. When Pedro was asked about the difference in their ages, he said: "Oh! I remember the day Miller was born. I was a grown man at the time. I was herding sheep, and we were shearing at the time. Miller's father was working with us, and his mother was there also and while there gave birth to Miller."

Pedro said he had already been married for some years and must have been close to twenty-five years old. In 1926, Pedro's grandchildren said they had estimated his age at ninety-seven, but when they tried to explain their system they became confused and never succeeded. If Pedro were near twenty-five years at the time of Miller's birth then he could hardly have been less than ninety-seven in 1926. Ten years later Pedro died.

Pedro remembered well the visit of Lieutenant [James W.] Abert, the naturalist who visited Acoma shortly after the entry of Kearny's troops into Santa Fe [in 1846]. He said he was a developed young man at the time, and this visit was just eighty years before 1926. This event was about five years before the birth of Miller, and what Pedro said of his age in both events checked with both his own testimony and Miller's.

Sometime in Miller's late teens he was sent to Carlisle [Pennsylvania] Indian School, where he stayed for a couple of years and then hired himself out to a devout Presbyterian by the name of James H. Miller for whom he worked for a long time. This man gave the Indian youth his own name, and he

"Church at Acoma Pueblo before restoration," n.d. (National Archives, *American Guide* Neg. No. 14802-C.)

has carried it since. Miller is perhaps the only Acoma man of the older set who can converse freely in English. His mind was disturbed between the teachings of the three religions: his old Indian faith, Catholicism, and Presbyterianism. He had been three times governor of his pueblo and was slated by the caciques for another term, but because he showed a white friend the pictographs in the hidden places he failed to become governor again.

Old Pedro was one of the most loved men in the pueblo. He had a fine sense of humor and was a born actor. He was of medium height, lithe and sinewy, intelligent, and of a most cheerful disposition. Though he was a mischievous practical joker, nevertheless he was a man of high honor, truthful and utterly dependable.

He once said that on two occasions in his early life, during severe droughts and food shortage, the caciques commandeered the entire food supply of the pueblo and ordered the various kiva groups of women to work in relays and prepare the food so it could be rationed out to all the people alike and made to last until another harvest. Before the food was all put in certain rooms under one management, a sufficient seed supply was taken and put away for the future. Old Santiago

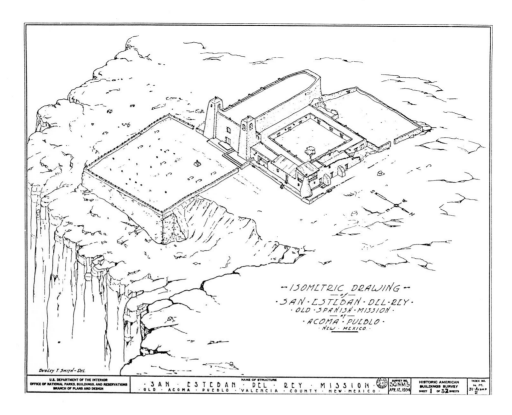

"Isometric Drawing of San Esteban Del Rey Old Spanish
Mission at Acoma Pueblo, New Mexico," delineated by Dudley
T. Smith, 1 of 32 pp., HABS, 12 April 1934.[29]

verified these accounts of Pedro's and the
oldest cacique, who said he was much younger
than Pedro and did not experience the events,
but that in such cases the caciques do have
the authority to take charge of the entire
food supply. According to tradition, this has
happened many times.

It was from Pedro and several other old
men near his age that much was learned about
Old Santiago. There was no doubt in their
minds that Santiago was as old as he claimed,
for as Pedro said, Santiago was already a
mature man in the tribe in Pedro's earliest
memory of him. Santiago looked his age. He
was so bent that his hips and knees were
almost the same distance from the ground,
and when his hands hung straight down they

almost touched the ground. His eyes were
small, beady, and deep set, and he had a
rather cunning look.

The most difficult man from whom to get
information was old Martín. He was tall,
heavy boned, very muscular, and somewhat
unkempt, and he always refused to talk. In
his earlier years Martín was one of the most
enduring runners Acoma ever had, and it was
suggested that flattery about his former running ability would cause him to open up in
his blunt way and tell of his great running
feats.

One day, when a good interpreter was at
hand, the trap was set and Martín broke
loose. He told how, when the priest had forgotten his ceremonial wine he started at day-

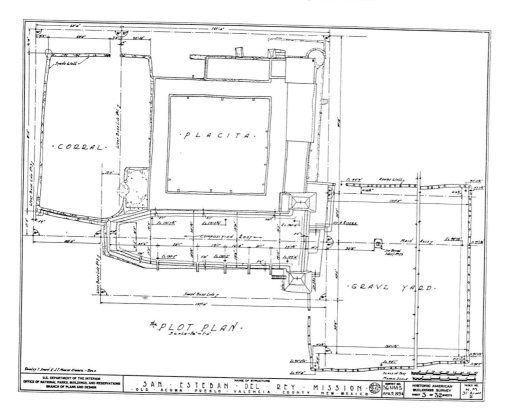

"The Plot Plan," San Esteban Del Rey Mission, delineated by
Dudley T. Smith and J. T. Morse Kidder, 3 of 32 pp., HABS, 5
April 1934.

light Saturday morning, ran to Isleta and back for the wine, reaching Acoma shortly after dark. He covered not less than 110 miles on this run. He said he once ran a twenty-mile race against a man on a mule. The run was in a big circle around Acoma. The mule led in the first half of the course, but after that he led the mule, and when he reached Acoma the man and the mule were nowhere in sight. Martín moved from one story to another so fast that the interpreter could give only a résumé of what he said, but in his prime he had defeated all comers— Hopis, Zunis, Navajos, and Rio Grande Pueblos. From all that could be gathered, he was ninety or over.

All of these old men are now dead excepting Francisco Chino, who is evidently well over the century mark. According to Pedro and Santiago he was five or six years older than Pedro and just a little older than Zemati, an old magician now dead, whose age was between that of Pedro and Francisco Chino.

In 1938 friends and relatives figured Francisco to be 128, but that was probably too high. If Pedro were living he would then be about 110 and Francisco Chino somewhere between 115 and not over 118. His hair had just turned white and he had all his teeth. He was tall and sinewy like most of the men who live to an old age. When last interviewed he was still very animated. Francisco, one of the finest characters one could know, spent most of his life in camp tending his own sheep.

COMMERCE AND COWBOYS

The Northeast

Manville Chapman, "Willow Spring Ranch—1870 A.D." Oil on
canvas, 24″ × 84″ (approx.). Shuler Auditorium, Raton, PWAP,
1934.[1] According to Chapman, Willow Springs was built as a
government forage station in the 1860s and became a stop on
the Barlow and Sanderson stagecoach line. "Later on early
rancher families leased the ranch house . . . [selling] water . . .
out of the well for 25 cents a bucket and provisions . . . to
travelers. . . . The first store owner in the Raton area, George J.

Pace, who lately passed away at his home in Denver, Colorado, made Willow Springs ranch house his place of business for a time. For years the old house stood on the northeast side of the railroad tracks on North Third Street, a modest reminder of pioneer days. Then finally it was replaced by a more modern house. But an addition to the original town of Raton bears the name Willow Springs in memory of this early habitation of northern New Mexico."[2]

The Santa Fe Trail and, later, the Atchison, Topeka and Santa Fe Railway came to symbolize the socioeconomic development of the Anglo Southwest. The Mountain Branch of the Trail and the first track of the AT&SFRR entered New Mexico over Raton Pass from Trinidad, Colorado, while the Trail's Cimarron Cut-off crossed the Oklahoma Panhandle and came into the territory in the Clayton area. Although Clovis became the eastern gateway for the AT&SFRR, smaller lines like the Santa Fe, Raton, and Des Moines; the Colorado and Southern; the St. Louis, Rocky Mountain, and Pacific; the Burlington; and the Elkhart and Santa Fe connected Clayton, Des Moines, Raton, Wagon Mound, Las Vegas, and other northeastern towns.

Taos was peripherally associated with the Santa Fe Trail, as Marc Simmons explains:

> In 1825 Commissioner George C. Sibley and his trail survey party reached Taos. . . . He had intended that this town serve as the official end of the SFT, even though it was locked in by mountains and virtually inaccessible by wagon from either the east or south. But its attractions were several. Taos was becoming a resort for American trappers operating in the Southern Rockies and a center of the fur trade. The Mexican government maintained a port of entry there. And because of its location in the northeast part of the province Taos was the closest settlement to both Raton Pass on the Mountain Branch and the Rock Crossing of the Canadian on the Cimarron Cut-off. Notwithstanding, Taos failed to become a major trail terminus.[3]

However, Taos did become the first art colony in New Mexico, and the artists and writers who portrayed Taos Pueblo and Don Fernando de Taos provided the nucleus for what became a major twentieth-century commerce in arts, crafts, and tourism throughout the state.

In addition to the attractions of Taos Pueblo, New Deal field writers and photographers recorded a full spectrum of commercial ventures—from Mrs. Bertha Gusdorf's banking transactions in Taos, through Mr. J. J. Rogers's real estate development in Des Moines, to Mr. and Mrs. Arch Dunn's work in leather, fur, and taxidermy near Clayton. Clayton businesspeople like retired cafe owner John Spring and eleven-year-old Billie Carroll, who did the major work for the Carroll Goat Dairy, were also interviewed, as were craftspeople like furniture-maker Ancil Swaggerty, jeweler John Beebe, and embroiderer Mrs. Fannie Potter.

The cattle industry held sway throughout much of this area. Businessmen often owned ranches as well, working them along with or after retiring from their occupations in town. Others, like William F. Sumpter, George Turner, Matt Emery, George McJunkin, and George Mutz, were primarily cowboys and cattlemen. Wagon Mound's Bean Day rodeo was popular, and there were successful businesses catering to cattlemen like the harness, saddle, and boot making enterprises in Clayton.

As elsewhere in New Mexico, however, the northeastern cattlemen were suffering from the effects of prolonged drought, which, according to Kenneth Fordyce of Raton, had "cut down the grazing capacity of the range, caused the expense of feeding to mount, caused poor breeding and smaller calf crops. A cow that does not produce a calf does not pay her way and is an expense chargeable against the cow that does." In 1938, he quoted the lament of the late John Clay:

> What a wonderful country Northeastern New Mexico was for grass. There was nothing but grass and more grass; the bluejoint with its ripening heads, good as corn for fattening. Mossy stretches of buffalo grass made unexcelled winter feed. Never before or since have I seen such fat cows, calves, steers, and heifers, all were fat. And then to think that three years from that time this fair land should be as bare as Sahara.[4]

"Taos pueblo, New Mexico. Sept 1939. Jerry, famous Taos Indian, artists' model and fisherman." Apparently, this man is Sharp's "favorite Taos model, Jerry Mirabel."[6] Photo by Russell Lee. LC-USF 33-12409-M1.

In the early twentieth century, Taos Pueblo gained worldwide attention through the efforts of artists and writers in nearby Taos, New Mexico's oldest art colony. Although the colony dates from 1898, when artists Ernest L. Blumenschein (1874–1960) and Bert G. Phillips (1868–1956) ended a Denver-to-Mexico sketching trip there due to a broken wagon wheel, its "father" was Joseph Henry Sharp (1859–1953), who first visited the region in 1883 and told the two younger artists about

W. Herbert Dunton, "Taos Pueblo Indian Man," charcoal
drawing. PWAP (NMSRC WPA-PWAP 5389).

it in Paris in 1895. Sharp himself did not settle permanently in Taos until 1912, and in 1915 he, Blumenschein, Phillips, Oscar E. Berninghaus (1874–1952), E.
Irving Couse (1866–1936), and W. Herbert ("Buck")
Dunton (1878–1936) began the Taos Society of Artists.
Their artistic endeavors were complemented by the work
of Mabel Dodge Luhan (1879–1962) and her more
literary circle.[5]

✳

New Mexico Federal Art Project artist Majel G. Claflin told NMFWP Taos field supervisor Muriel Haskell about her conversation with Juanita Luhan of Taos Pueblo on August 12, 1936.*

Two Taos citizens had made an appointment with one of the prominent members of the Taos Pueblo Indians for an amole shampoo. Sufficient notice had been given so that the soap-weed root could be soaked overnight. During the shampoo, the conversation turned to the beautiful black hair of the Indians and why they did not turn gray—except in rare instances. Those who are gray are usually very old.

Juanita Luhan suggested that perhaps it was because the hair was washed only in cold water—and then spoke glowingly of her grandmother who was very, very old and still had coal black hair. "You know, we Indians believe, that if as a child your head is rubbed with the blood of a black crow that you will never have gray hair—that was why my grandmother never became gray!"

*"Why the Indians' Hair Stays Black," coll. Muriel Haskell from Majel G. Claflin; 1 p., 14 August 1936 (H5–4–12#1; BC321; LC47.2; LCms#6).

Artist and writer Blanche Chloe Grant (1874–1948) first came to Taos in 1919. By the time she joined the NMFWP in 1936, she had already written several pamphlets—*Taos Indians, One Hundred Years Ago in Taos,* and *Taos Today,* all published by the author in Taos in 1925—and a book on the pueblo and town, *When Old Trails Were New: The Story of Taos* (New York: Press of the Pioneers, 1934). She based the following American Guide description of Taos Pueblo on these earlier publications.*

Among the famous personages of the Taos Pueblo . . . was Pablo Zapato, or Pablo Romero, who wore shoes and was the rich man of his day. The late Captain Smith [H.] Simpson [1832–1916] told of going out to Zapato's house to secure a loan for Ceran St. Vrain [1802–70], the well-known Taos trader. Zapato took up the planks which made

his bed and lifted out one thousand dollars in silver! Zapato died about 1870. Following his day, Ventura Romero came to be the head-man at the pueblo, the highest post in the community, over the governor or the priest. He was a remarkable man in his knowledge of the history of his people, especially.

*From "The Taos Pueblo," coll. Blanche Grant from books and "interviews with old-timers and Indians" for S-600; 12 pp., 22 January 1936 (A#50). She also states that "the writer has lived in Taos for 15 years."

"Taos pueblo, New Mexico. Apr 1936. Governor Sandoval."
Photo by Arthur Rothstein.[7] LC-USF 34-2956-E.

A few years ago, Tony [Antonio José] Romero was the outstanding Indian at the pueblo. He was a jovial soul and a real wit. Many a time as the pitcher on the Taos town baseball team he was much more fun than the game itself. He had a good education, enjoyed reading the newspaper, kept himself in touch with affairs in general and, although thoroughly Indian, came as near to understanding the Anglo-Saxon as any man in the pueblo. He was still in his forties when he died under strange circumstances, possibly a victim of Indian jealousy which, since the red men are human, does come to the fore at times. Unfortunately, the manuscript on Taos Pueblo history which Tony Romero was writing was, according to rumor at least, destroyed. The Indians do not yet realize that their story must be written down if it is to be preserved for, in spite of their effort to hand it down by word of mouth from father to son, much that is of interest is being lost.

Alexander Gusdorf brought his eighteen-year-old bride from Germany to New York, then to Santa Fe, and finally to Ranchos de Taos in 1878. Mr. Gusdorf (1848–1923) had immigrated in 1864 and first worked for his uncles at the Staab Mercantile Company in Santa Fe. He then started a mercantile business of his own at Peñasco and later operated a flour mill at Ranchos de Taos. His banking career, carried on by his wife after his death, began in 1894 as president and chairman of the board of the First State Bank of Taos.*

Among the courageous women who accompanied their men to the Southwest in the '50s and later in the '80s were the wives, many of them young brides, of German and Jewish merchants and clerks, to whom the country was especially fearful on account of complete difference in language and customs. Among these pioneer women who came to New Mexico with the coming of the railroads was Mrs. Bertha Gusdorf, who came to Santa Fe and a little later to Taos in 1878. At that time an immigrant girl bride of eighteen years, she made the long arduous journey from New York to Trinidad by train, by stage coach to Santa Fe, and thence to Taos over an almost impassable trail, the latter part of the journey taking four days where now an automobile makes the trip in two hours over a none-too-good road.

Bertha F. Gusdorf (Bertha Ferse) was born of Jewish parents in November, 1860, in the village of Oberlistungen near Cassel in the Duchy of Hesse-Cassel in the central part of Germany. She attended school in her native village, similar to our primary and grammar grades. She was married in the spring of 1878 to Alex Gusdorf, who had returned to Germany after fourteen years in America, most of which time was spent in Santa Fe, Peñasco, and Ranchos de Taos, where he was in business for himself, operating a large flour mill and other mercantile business.

The young couple came to New York May 1, 1878, and traveled by train to El Moro, Colorado, about five miles east of Trinidad, which at that time was the terminal of the Santa Fe Railroad while the contractors were boring the tunnel through the Raton range. They then traveled by stage coach to Santa Fe, where they lived a short time, and then moved on to Ranchos de Taos to make their future home.

At that time Ranchos de Taos, even more so than at present, was almost one hundred percent Spanish-American. About the only Anglos living at Ranchos were the teachers at the Alice Hyson Mission, a Presbyterian institution. The Anderson brothers with their families came to Ranchos in the same year (1878) to enter the employ of Mr. Gusdorf in his flour mill.

The young German woman was under the necessity of learning two languages: Spanish to be able to talk to her neighbors and maids, and also English to talk to the Andersons and the few other Anglos in the village. This she accomplished mainly by the trial-and-error method, aided by Mr. Gusdorf, who had already spent some sixteen years in New Mexico. She now reads and writes English and speaks Spanish fluently.

Mrs. Gusdorf's two daughters were born and spent their childhood years in Ranchos de Taos. They are Elsa, wife of C. D. Weimer

---

*"From Immigrant Bride to Bank President—Mrs. Bertha Gusdorf—S-240-Folk-Ways," coll. James A. Burns; 1030 wds., 5 pp., 19 September 1936 (A#234; LC38.3; LC47.1).

"Questa, New Mexico. Jan 1943. Siegfried Kahn, who was a
storekeeper in Germany, then a store owner in Albuquerque for
thirty years, before business reverses brought bankruptcy and
forced him to start fresh with a general store in this town."
Photo by John Collier. LC-USW 3-18149-E.

of Colorado Springs, born in 1894, and Mrs.
Corinne Wylie, also of Colorado Springs,
born in 1890.

In 1894, after the destruction of Mr. Gusdorf's flour mill at Ranchos by fire, suppos-
edly of incendiary origin, the family moved
to Taos where Mr. Gusdorf went into business with Gerson Gusdorf and J. H. Mc-
Carthy. They lived for some time on the lot
in the rear of the store building now occupied
by MacMarr's and the Taos Variety Store.

In 1909 they erected their new home on
the Santa Fe road, on the brow of the hill
overlooking the lower Taos Valley with the
north slope of Picuris Mountain in the distance. At that time adobe houses and pueblo
architecture were not customary and the
building was sheathed with steel, and the

interior finish of hard wood. In later years she had installed steam heat fired with oil burners. She and Mr. Gusdorf planted trees on the south and west sides of their lot. They also planted apple and cherry trees, shrubs, and flower and vegetable gardens, making a most attractive home-site.

Here Mrs. Gusdorf lived, and here her two daughters were married. Here, too, Mr. Gusdorf died in the fall of 1923, and here she still makes her home, mostly alone, except for a woman coming in to help clean house and a gardener to look after the gardens, the shrubbery, etc.

After the death of Mr. Gusdorf in 1923, Mrs. Gusdorf took charge of the business of his estate, consisting of about twelve thousand acres of land in the Cristóbal de la Serna Land Grant south of Taos and surrounding the villages of Ranchos de Taos and Talpa and extending up the timbered north slope of Picuris Mountain to the summit; also other property in Taos and Taos County.

In 1924 she was elected a director of the First State Bank of Taos, of which Mr. Gusdorf had formerly been president, and continued in that capacity until 1935, when she was elected president of the bank after the death of the late Dr. T. P[aul] Martin. In all these years she has been anything but a dummy director, visiting the bank almost daily, consulting and advising with the cashier and other officials on loans and other business matters. She still maintains the same routine as well as her health and advancing age permit. Mrs. Gusdorf is now one of only two women bank presidents in the state of New Mexico, the other being Mrs. H. B. Sammons of Farmington.

In November 1935, her daughter Mrs. Wylie, assisted by other ladies of Taos, gave a banquet to celebrate her mother's seventy-fifth birthday. This banquet was attended by about fifty of the prominent women of Taos. To the writer, who offered his congratulations and wished her seventy-five more birthdays, she remarked that she did not care to live that long, that "fifteen or twenty-five years would be plenty." So this woman, who came to America in 1878 from Germany, a Jewish girl bride, has lived to see her children's children and to gain the respect, love, and affection of the entire community, which when she came to it was entirely foreign in language, customs, and race prejudices.

Like many who followed the railroads, developer J. J. Rogers was able to harness the growth of Des Moines by providing housing for settlers and locating homesteading claims for them. His nickname of "Shack Builder" seems not to have been derogatory, and he was one of the charter members of the Des Moines Chamber of Commerce in February 1920.[8*]

The earliest settler and one of the outstanding businessmen of the town is J. J. Rogers of Des Moines, New Mexico. A self-educated man, as he terms himself, coming here when Des Moines was only a station on the railroad, he perhaps has done more for the growth and development of the town than any other one man there.

Mr. Rogers, who was born northeast of Fort Worth, Texas, in September 1866, has lived a life enriched by a variety of experiences. At the age of five the family moved to Jack County, Texas, where they lived in a tent until the father could erect a log house. Even at this early age Mr. Rogers, who was the only boy in the family, helped his father look after their cattle.

It was during their stay in Jack County that Mr. Rogers had his most thrilling experience with the Indians, who frequently came into Jack County on raiding parties. On this trip (1873) they had stolen nearly all the horses in the neighborhood. The settlers had joined the soldiers and were in pursuit of the Indians, trying to regain their stolen stock before the Indians could get them onto their reservation. Mr. Rogers—who was just "Jimmy" then—was left at home with his mother and two sisters. Early one morning, as he was returning from taking the milk cows to pasture, he saw his mother run out into the yard and heard her screaming, "Run, Jimmy, run! Run, Jimmy, run!" He was used to his mother becoming excited over little things and never paid much at-

tention when he heard her calling then. He dismounted from his horse and leaned down to put the hobbles on him. As he raised up, a big Indian was reaching over the horse and almost caught him by the shoulder. To use Mr. Rogers' own words, "No one had to tell me to run then; I just flew!" Later, when the men returned with the horses, one of the horses had a very beautiful silver mounted bridle.

When Mr. Rogers was fourteen years old his father died. The year following his death was a fine crop year, following three years' drought. Mr. Rogers then took his mother and three sisters to Mineral Wells to live, and he went back to Weatherford, Texas, and freighted there for three years to make a living for them. He then went back to McKinney, Texas, to live. There, he began working in a store and planned to make this his life work.

Mr. Rogers declares he was eighteen years old before he knew that there was such a thing as a man "beating his debts." His father—as was customary with all ranchmen—paid his bills once a year. It was during his job in the store that he had his first experience of this kind. He had hired out for a month, and if at the end of this time he had given satisfactory service he was to continue working. At the end of the month his employer asked him to take charge of the store, doing all the buying and selling. One day two well dressed men came to the store and wanted to open an account, which Mr.

---

*"Biographies—J. J. Rogers—S-240-Folk-Ways," coll. W. M. Emery from Rogers on August 25, 1936; 1152 wds., 4 pp., 11 September 1936 (A#239; LC47.1).

Rogers refused to do. But Mr. Pierce, the proprietor of the store, did, taking a mortgage on the team and buggy the men were driving and duly recording the same at the Court House. For several days the men bought big bills of goods, each time buying enough to run the ordinary ranch for three months. Then, one Saturday they came in and again bought a large bill of goods. That night they left for the Indian Territory and were never seen or heard from again.

After five years of working in this store Mr. Rogers decided to come further west, moving this time to Dalhart, Texas. Being "broke" when he arrived there, he hunted up an old friend who was working in a supply house and through him got a job on the rip tracks. After working for three months he obtained work in the supply department of a grocery store. As he was an experienced clerk he tried to get on in that line, but the owner of the store was afraid he could not handle the trade. His opportunity came to prove himself one day when the regular clerk was out and two of the store's most important customers came in. Mr. Rogers, through his natural tact and cleverness, sold each lady a large bill of groceries. The manager, who had been watching the sales, made him a regular clerk and the ladies became his regular customers.

In May 1907 Mr. Rogers filed on a claim near Des Moines, New Mexico, which was then only a station on the Colorado and Southern Railroad. In October of the same year he came to New Mexico with the intention of opening a store for himself in the new settlement. His first work was that of hauling wood and water for the settlers; he then began erecting shacks as the people were coming into the new community faster than shelter could be provided for them. Within three months he had built seventy-five shacks and had acquired the sobriquet of "The Shack Builder." He also began locating people from Texas and other parts of the country on homesteads around Des Moines, for which he was paid five dollars per claim. This was the nucleus for the business he is still in, that of realtor.

For the past sixteen years Mr. Rogers has held the position of United States Commissioner, his present and fourth term expiring July 16, 1938. He is also Justice of Peace of Des Moines, the only town in the United States under "Petticoat Government."

In June 1910 Mr. Rogers was married to Marie Record. This wedding took place on the very highest point on Sierra Grande Mountain, with all the principals mounted on horseback. The ceremony was witnessed by everyone in the community who could possibly reach the top of the mountain, some going on horseback, some walking, and others going in buggies or wagons as far as possible, then climbing the remaining distance.

Mr. Rogers and his wife live on their ranch a few miles from Des Moines in the summer and make their home in town in the winter. He has watched the town grow from a little railroad station, whose only inhabitants were the station agent and his family, to one of the most prosperous towns in Union County, and has also watched its decline during the recent years of drought and depression. Through it all he has retained his jovial disposition and his faith in his town and fellowmen. Such characters as Mr. Rogers are the real backbone of the country.

In 1936, Genevieve Chapin described some of the "unusual industries" in Clayton and environs, claiming that "few people in Union County, New Mexico, stop to reflect any more on the fact that we have several industries in our midst that many larger towns do not have, and that few, indeed, of the towns the size of Clayton can boast of."*

The Dunns

Still another interesting industry in leather is that being carried on by Arch Dunn and his wife at their home about six miles south and three miles west of Clayton. These people are taxidermists, furriers, and tanners, and some truly beautiful pieces of work are being sent out from their place of business.

Mr. Dunn has been in this work as a profession only the last three years, but previous to that time it had been a lifetime hobby with him. He is what might be called a self-trained artist. Aside from his own study and experimenting the only training he received was through watching the Jonas brothers, taxidermists in Denver.

Since about four years old Mr. Dunn has studied animal life, either domestic animals or their wild kinsmen caught on the trapline. It is his greatest aim and care now in his chosen work to get his specimens true to life. Just a fraction of an inch's difference in post, just a fleeting change of expression, is all it takes sometimes to spell the difference between success and failure in taxidermy.

Included in their taxidermy work is the mounting of whole specimens of the following animals: the porcupine, coyote, prairie dog, squirrel, white rabbit, and the very rare ring-tailed cat. Still more rare is the head of the double-horned deer which was mounted by the Dunns. They have also mounted many antelope, deer and doe heads, as well as the head of a Chinese leopard. In addition to this they have also made rugs from the skins of bear, lions (one of the latter measuring eight feet two inches from nose to tip of tail), coyote, bobcats, and from one black Abyssinian leopard from Ethiopia.

They also mount all sorts of birds, each year shipping in several dozen pheasants from Michigan and Iowa. Mrs. Dunn does all the bird work.

To a lover of animal life, even though utterly ignorant of the art of taxidermy, it is a fascinating subject. Very briefly reviewed, the process is about as follows for the larger animals. After the measurements are secured, a clay duplicate is made of the subject to be worked on. And here it might be interesting to the uninitiated to add that Mr. Dunn states that if the distance from the end of the nose to the eyes is known, all the other measurements may be secured from that, so uniformly do animals adhere to the laws of symmetry in their physical set-up.

After the clay model is completed true to the original muscular development and joints, a cast is made in plaster of Paris. This is in three sections—one for each side and one for the underbody. Then this plaster cast is removed in sections, and each section filled with strips of wet red building paper and paste laid in layer upon layer. When dry, they are trimmed until they fit exactly; then they are pasted together and the specially prepared and tanned skin is put on the form.

*From "Unusual Industries," coll. Genevieve Chapin from Clayton residents Swaggerty, Dunns, Beebe, Potters, Carroll; 2100 wds., 10 pp., 25 July 1936 (A#238; LC47.1).

"Moreno valley, Colfax county, New Mexico. Feb 1943. George Turner, a gunsmith as well as a cattleman, checking the mounting of a telescopic sight on his rifle." Photo by John Collier. LC-USW 3-18693-C.

The eyes are all artificial, imported from Germany. Oil painting is used to restore the natural colors and to provide background for the mounted specimens, this being also Mrs. Dunn's work.

Besides the mounting and rug work the Dunns also make all sorts of fur pieces, most of their work in this line at present being neck pieces. They buy their furs mostly from Missouri and Iowa.

They also make to order many varieties of leather articles such as purses, belts and billfolds and buckskin shirts, jackets, gloves, and coats. They use as decorations the almost lost art of Mexican handcarving brought over from Spain. In this work the pattern is applied to the leather and then with a sharp instrument the surface is cut following the outline of the pattern. Then the background is hammered down with some sharp pointed tool about like the point of a nail. Sometimes the background is then stained, leaving the raised pattern standing out very clearly and making a beautiful piece of work.

The Dunns have all the work they can do—having customers from some seven states.

Ancil Swaggerty

Ancil Swaggerty is primarily an architect by training, being associated at present with his father in the lumber business at the west end of Court Street in Clayton.[9] In addition to this the younger Swaggerty manufactures Spanish style furniture and makes two very interesting machines. One of them is called by the Spanish people the malacate and is used to make wool into yarn. The other is a sort of loom on which can be woven blankets or rugs in the Navajo style.

John Beebe

Another artist in his line is the proprietor of Beebe's Jewelry Store, which is located on the Main Street of Clayton just two doors east of First Street on the south side. Mr. Beebe served a four years' apprenticeship under different jewelers, beginning his actual jeweler work in 1908 in Little Rock, Arkansas. For twelve years he has conducted his own business, having been in Clayton the past three and a half years.

Besides being an expert and conscientious repairman, Mr. Beebe makes jewelry to order, working in platinum, gold and silver. He makes rings, pins, bracelets and necklaces, even ornamental leg bands. Mr. Beebe is an outstanding artist in his particular line, and his conscientious work and cheery courtesy have won him many friends wherever he is known. Most towns have their jewelry repairmen but comparatively few are fortunate enough to be able to have their jewelry manufactured right before their eyes as the Clayton people do.

Mrs. Fannie Potter

Working in still different fabric we find another artist in the person of Mrs. Fannie Potter who lives two doors east of First on the south side of Walnut Street in Clayton.

Mrs. Potter, who is a native of Old Mexico, specializes in fine Spanish needlework and has worked at her chosen art since early childhood. She received most of her training from her mother, later perfecting her work during five years spent in the Convent School at Aguas Calientes in Old Mexico. Now she, in turn, is passing on her skill to her young daughter Susie, who works with her and acts as her interpreter.

The skillful fingers of these two Spanish women have many beautiful works of art to their credit—mostly in Mexican drawn work, Italian cut work and embroidery. One can scarcely realize the infinite patience and exactitude that has directed these women in the setting of these beautiful, painstaking stitches.

Besides the pieces she has made herself, Mrs. Potter has given private lessons for some fifteen years. During the past three years she has had a W.P.A. teaching project for needlework in Clayton. During this teaching work numerous films for educational purposes have been made of her work. She sells to many out of state points and has donated several valuable pieces to different churches.

The Carroll Goat Dairy

We do not present this goat dairy exactly as a work of art, but it is at least rather an unusual feature. It is located on the south side of Cherry Street about midway of the block east of Third Street in Clayton. Here we find the family of Lawton Carroll, who is the owner of the goats, although the work of the dairy is done by the two children—Billie aged eleven years and Freda aged twelve years.

They have six milch goats and three young ones. During the past two or three years that the dairy has operated they have served from three to seven customers at a time, selling up to six or seven quarts per day. Most of it is sold for the use of invalids or undernourished children. Billie states that the six

107

goats, which are fed ordinary cow feed and not tin cans as generally reported, are kept for just about the same cost as the upkeep of one cow and that the Carroll Dairy has one goat that gives her two and a half quarts per day.

Like Mr. Rogers of Des Moines, Mr. John Spring (1866–1932) found his livelihood in servicing homesteaders and travelers, and later he went into ranching. According to Clara Toombs Harvey, in his early years at Clayton, "Mr. Spring owned a restaurant, sometimes he had a combination of enterprises, the market, grocery, with space for serving food, all in one building." She also claims that "Clayton's only law enforcement officer for many years" was "to our Mexican population . . . lawyer, doctor and Priest. Most of them took his word against another man's oath. He was the only man I ever heard speak Spanish with a Scotch burr."[10]*

John Spring, whose death occurred at Clayton, New Mexico, on December 14, 1932, was one of the sterling pioneer citizens of that place since about 1892. Mr. Spring was born September 8, 1866, in Aberdeenshire, Scotland, where he spent his childhood days. In early manhood he came to the United States, landed in New York, and gradually emigrated westward until he reached Clayton, where he since made his home.

Shortly after his arrival in the United States he was employed in a car factory in Cincinnati, Ohio, where railroad cars were manufactured. It was his duty in this factory to handle the red-hot wheels while in the process of manufacture. After working in this factory for a time, Mr. Spring drifted on westward to the Black Hills, thence to Cripple Creek, Colorado, where he followed his profession of cook, eventually landing in Denver. He had served a four-year apprenticeship of cook in Scotland, which served him to good advantage upon his arrival in America.

Shortly after the arrival of Mr. Spring in Clayton, he secured a position as chef in a cafe and followed this profession for some time, later owning and operating a cafe of his own. He became manager of the hotel known as the Clayton House in 1895, which position he held for a number of years, then became proprietor of a meat market and fresh vegetable stand. He was at one time a member of the town board and later was elected marshall, a position which he filled continuously until his death.

He took an active part in civic affairs, always trying to make his town a better place in which to live. He was an ideal officer of the law and had the personality to win the wrongdoer to the better things of life. All children were his staunch friends. His ever kind and watchful eye was upon them and none feared him, even when aware of a

*"Biography: John Spring," coll. Carrie L. Hodges from Mrs. John Spring on August 19, 1936, Col. Jack Potter on November 30, 1936, and personal knowledge; 578 wds., 4 pp., 4 December 1936, rec. 11 December (A#239; LC38.3).

"Capulin (vicinity), New Mexico. Sept 1939. Sign along the road."[12] Photo by Russell Lee. LC-USF 34-34116-D.

wrongdoing. None mourned his passing more than did these children, though many of them had grown to maturity during his service in the capacity of officer of the law. He was an active member of the Masonic Lodge and Chapter No. 8, Order of the Eastern Star and Past Master and Past Worthy Patron of these Orders.

Early in life Mr. Spring united with the Scottish Presbyterian Church but never moved his membership to the United States.

After a few years of residence in New Mexico, he proved up a claim in Apache Valley, three miles north of Clayton, later on becoming a partner in the Spring-Lackey and Ball Ranch in Apache Canyon. After a time he purchased the partnership holdings of

Lackey and Ball and became sole owner of said ranch.

Mr. Spring was united in marriage to Louise Bushnell, who preceded him in death in 1903. In 1918 he was married to Emma Perkins, who is still living. He is also survived by a foster daughter, Mrs. Goldie Gute.

Colonel Jack Potter states, "John Spring was the friendliest man I ever saw, always ready to serve the needy. He fed more hungry men without pay during the time he operated his cafe than any one man I know of."[11] So an old timer has left our midst, one who was not only interested in the up-building of the community but was interested as well in ministering to the needy. Truly a "Good Samaritan" indeed.

Cattle raising was the important industry in northeastern New Mexico. Pioneer rancher William F. Sumpter (1857–1935) had told his story to W. M. Emery, his half-brother Matt Emery's son, before he died on his ranch near Folsom. When Emery interviewed Sumpter's sister Sarah Jane Gleason in 1936, she had become the oldest resident of Union County.*

When W. F. Sumpter went to his eternal reward, March 21, 1935, Union County lost one of its oldest pioneers and one of its best authorities on the history of Union County.

In recent years Mr. Sumpter had been visited by men from Kansas, Oklahoma, Colorado, and New Mexico who were interested in gathering data on the early history of the cattle industry in these states, as he had a reputation for giving accurate and dependable information.

W. F. Sumpter—more commonly known as Bud—was born at Leavenworth, Kansas, June 6, 1857. He spent his first birthday in the arms of his mother as she walked across the plains toward Denver. The family was traveling by ox train to Denver when they were put on a blind trail by a dishonest storekeeper and all their stock was stolen by a band of renegades and they were left afoot two hundred miles from Denver.

Shortly after reaching Denver his mother married Madison Emery, and Bud was better known as Bud Emery by the men with whom he worked.

The family moved from Denver to Old Fort Bent on the Arkansas, then over to the San Luis Valley, which they were warned to leave by the Indians. Then they moved to the Maxwell Grant where they lived five years.

In 1865 they moved to Madison on the Dry Cimarron River. Here Mr. Sumpter received his schooling at the small country schoolhouse. At the age of ten Mr. Sumpter and his mother assisted the soldiers from Fort Union in capturing the notorious and elusive outlaw Coe.[13]

When Bud was thirteen he killed his first bear. This made him one of the proudest and happiest boys in New Mexico, even though he was one of the sickest from eating the bear meat without salt.

At the age of fourteen Mr. Sumpter began working for the Hall Brothers, original owners of the now well-known Crossell Ranch. He later became foreman of the ranch.

After working for the Hall Brothers for several years Mr. Sumpter went into the cattle business for himself, on the same ranch on which he was living at the time of his death and a few miles west of the Crossell holdings.

When the Hall Brothers sold out to the Prairie Cattle Company in 1881, a Mr. Green, representative of the Prairie Cattle Company, came to Mr. Sumpter with the following offer:

"Sumpter," said Green, "William Hall speaks well of you. He says you are a good cowman and that you have a creditable bunch of cattle. We are forming a new, great cattle company, financed by Scotch capital. We want more stock. I am here to offer you $135,000 for your cattle. If you will sell out to us, we will make you range manager of the new company, at a salary of $2,500.00 per year. Will you take the offer and accept the position?"

Sumpter promised to think the matter over. At the time he owed $40,000.00 on his cattle,

*"William F. Sumpter," coll. W. M. Emery from personal knowledge and interview with S. J. Gleason; 1009 wds., 4 pp., 12 December 1936, rec. 23 December (A#239; LC38.1; LC47.1).

"Moreno valley, Colfax county, New Mexico. Feb 1943. Dinner in the kitchen on the ranch belonging to George Turner, a second generation cattleman." Photo by John Collier. LC-USW 3-18622-C.)

which he had bought on time from his friends. He could have paid all of his indebtedness and had $95,000 clear. But for some unknown reason he turned the offer down, a decision which he was soon to regret. In 1884, the price of cattle declined. Then the hard winter of 1885–86 came on with severe losses, and Sumpter was forced out of the cattle business, with one old black cow all that was left from the $135,000 herd.

Mr. Sumpter worked as foreman for several of the larger cattle companies of northeastern New Mexico. He rode the range from the Arkansas River to the Canadian River and made numerous trips to Denver, Dodge City, and Coolidge with trail herds.

At the age of twenty-seven Mr. Sumpter was married to Miss Minneta Darling. One child, a girl, was born to them but died a few years later.

During the eighties Mr. Sumpter spent one year in South Park, Colorado, the only year of his entire life spent out of the state of New Mexico.

In 1896 he remarried, this time to Miss Daisy McLaughlin of Folsom. They made their first home on a ranch near Capulin, New Mexico, later moving back to the old home ranch on the Dry Cimarron.

To this union seven boys were born. They are Lewis F. of Great Falls, Oregon; Leonard H., who now owns and operates the home ranch near Folsom; Robert F., manager of one of the Doherty ranches near Officer, Colorado; Raymond P., of Kenton, Oklahoma; Benjamin F., Folsom; William Homer, of Fort Gibson, Mississippi; and Howard B., who is foreman of a Doherty ranch near Trinchera, Colorado. He also has a sister, Mrs. Sarah Jane Gleason, of Folsom. His half-brother, Matt Emery, died in 1915.

During his career, Bud Sumpter at one time was owner of one of the largest cattle ranches in this part of New Mexico. He formed partnerships at different times with various persons, among them John Milliken, J. M. Johns, and Dr. Owens, in livestock and ranching interests.

He took an active part in all movements for the betterment of the community and served several terms as a director on the school board.

The Sumpter ranch on U.S. Highway 64 was widely known for its oldtime Western hospitality. Its doors were ever open to friends and strangers alike.

W. M. Emery's father, Matt Emery (d. 1915), "rode the range for years" with the famous black cowboy George McJunkin, who discovered the Folsom site in August 1908. Emery's family knew McJunkin as a cowboy,[14] and he apparently was unaware of the latter's historical importance when he responded to a Santa Fe directive to report on Union County's "racial elements" in 1936.[15]*

The first explorers and settlers in northeastern New Mexico were the Spaniards and the Anglo-Saxons, and the population today is made up principally of these two races. However, there are also a few Jews, Italians, Syrians, Czechoslovakians, and a very few Negroes. There are about six families of Negroes now residing in Union County. Most of these are in or within a few miles of Clayton.

The largest number of Negroes to come to the county at one time came in during the construction of the Santa Fe Railroad from Pelt, Oklahoma, to Farley, New Mexico, in

*From "Negroes," coll. W. M. Emery from Thomas E. Owens, Clayton, son of Dr. T. E. Owens; Emmett Coble, Clayton, husband of Mrs. Coble, teacher of the black school; A. B. Baker, Clayton, who "lived at Mineral, Oklahoma, at the time of the Blizzard of 1889, and was personally acquainted with the men who were saved by 'Nigger George'"; Matt Emery, "father of writer, who rode the range for years with George McJunkin"; 1557 wds., 6 pp., 18 September 1936, rec. 26 September (A#85; A#149; LC38.1; LC47.1).

1931. As soon as the line was finished these people all moved away. Occasionally a few drift in and work around the barber shops or filling stations for a short time then move on to some other town.

In 1926, a separate school for Negroes was established in Clayton. This is held in the home of Mrs. Emmett Coble, who has been in charge of it since its beginning. The classes are held only in the mornings, Mrs. Coble teaching in the Clayton Public Schools in the afternoons. The largest number of pupils enrolled at one time in this school was seven; part of these pupils are Spanish and Negro, as no pupil with Negro blood is allowed to attend the Public Schools.

Within the past year a Negro Church has been erected on the outskirts of Clayton. A Negro pastor from Raton conducts the services.

The first Negroes to come to this country were brought in by cattlemen from Texas, who, upon returning home left the Negroes here. Some drifted in voluntarily, and obtained work as cooks or cowboys with the cattlemen who were settled here. . . .

. . . "Nigger George" [was] one of the most highly respected citizens of the colored race that ever settled in any community. He was known all over northeastern New Mexico and the Panhandles of Oklahoma and Texas for his honesty, bravery, and integrity.

George McJunkin, more commonly known as "'Nigger George,'" was born in southeastern Texas during the days of slavery. As a small boy, he with his mother and brother were sold as slaves for the sum of $600.00. Small George was put in charge of the horses on the plantation. His master was always kind and thoughtful of his slaves and could not endure the mistreatment that he saw given to other slaves.

On one occasion when a new family moved into the neighborhood with a number of half-starved and overworked Negroes, George was sent to tell their master that his "Massa" was butchering the next Saturday and if Mr. McBride would send some one up to their plantation Mr. McJunkin would give them a quarter of beef for the starving Negroes.

As George rode up to Mr. McBride's home, one of the Negroes was receiving a severe whipping. George respectively tipped his hat and said, "Mr. McBride, if you will send up to the McJunkin place next Saturday, Massa will give you a quarter of beef for your starving Negroes."

Mr. McBride flew into a rage.

"You insolent black nigger," he cried, "don't you dare to call me 'Mister,' you call me 'Massa.'"

He tried to jerk George off from his horse and whip him, but George kicked his horse and went home, telling his master of his experience.

It was not long before Mr. McBride arrived at the McJunkin home and demanded that George be whipped for insulting him. Mr. McJunkin, after hearing his story, quietly replied, "Mr. McBride, I teach my slaves to call me 'Master'; everyone else they are taught to call 'Mister.' George will not be whipped."

After George was freed by President Lincoln's Emancipation Proclamation he was given the name of McJunkin.

In 1876, he was brought to New Mexico by Hammett Roberds, a horseman. After working for the Roberds family a short time he went to work for the "Pitchforks," a large cattle company owned by Dr. T. E. Owens, with headquarters ten miles west of the present town of Folsom.

It was while he was working on this ranch that he performed one of his greatest acts of bravery.

The wagons were camped two miles north of Mineral, Oklahoma, on Cottonwood Arroyo—or Sweet Creek—and the men were holding a herd of beef cattle. A hard rain storm came up and lasted for two days, then it began to snow. A strong wind sprang up, and before the men hardly realized it one of the worst blizzards in history was upon them, the memorable Blizzard of 1889.

The cowboys, under the leadership of Billy Owens, tried to hold the herd, regardless of

113

"Moreno valley, Colfax county, New Mexico. Feb. 1943. George Mutz starting out on the range in a snow storm." Photo by John Collier. LC-USW 3-18901-E.

the blinding, stinging snow which beat upon them, until they could hardly see the cattle. Men changed horses often, as it did not take long to tire a horse out battling with the storm, but it was to no avail, after two days the cattle began to drift with the storm.

Wet, tired, and nearly frozen, the cowboys were still determined to hold the herd if possible. Orders were given to hitch the mules to the chuck wagon and follow the cattle. Away from the protection of the hills the storm grew worse, and the cowboys realized that they had lost all sense of direction as well as the cattle. It was then that "Nigger George" told the boss he believed he could find the way back. Billy Owens put him in charge of the outfit, and all followed George with little hope of ever getting to shelter again. Within a short time he had them back to the Harv Bramblet Ranch, one mile west of Mineral.

After the storm was over (it lasted thirteen days), the cattle were trailed by the frozen carcasses strewn over the prairie; the few survivors were found past Texline, Texas. All the horses, which had been ridden in the vain attempt to save the herd, were frozen to death. And fourteen men realized what their fate would have been if it had not been for the bravery and fortitude of the one Negro in the outfit.

After working for the Pitchfork Ranch for a number of years, George went to work for W. H. Jack, manager of the XYZ Ranch.

Mr. Jack later became owner of the ranch and changed the name to the Crowfoot Ranch. After Mr. Jack passed away in 1913, George became foreman of the ranch for Mrs. Jack. At one time he built up a small herd of cattle of his own; after selling these cattle he erected a nice cottage in Folsom.

He remained with Mrs. Jack as long as he lived, Mrs. Jack taking care of him in his last illness.

In April 1927, Nigger George passed away in Folsom and was buried in the Folsom Cemetery near several of his cowboy comrades, and not far from the ranches which he had given such faithful service for so many years.

"Street scene at Bean day festival." LC-USF 33-12417-M3.

Wagon Mound was founded by stockmen as Santa Clara and renamed for a nearby formation resembling a covered wagon. It was an important trade and shipping center when Russell Lee photographed the Annual Bean Day and rodeo in early September 1939.[16]

"Scene at Bean day festival." LC-USF 33-12416-M5.

"Placing a bar behind a bucking bronc to prevent his kicking while in the slot at the Bean day rodeo." LC-USF 33-12412-M4.

"Cowboys driving cows down the rodeo grounds, at the Bean day rodeo." LC-USF 33-12430-M1.

"Cowboys at the Bean day rodeo." LC-USF 33-12431-M1.

Genevieve Chapin also reported the biography of Clayton businessman J. H. Deam and described his cowboy-oriented trade:

"At the second door west of First Street, on the south side of Main Street in Clayton, we find the sign 'Harness and Saddles.' Here is the place of business of J. H. Deam, veteran harness and saddle maker, whose manufacturing interests are now confined chiefly to saddle making. . . . Most of his trade, however, is from out of state. His prices range from $55.00 to $95.00 and $100.00 per saddle. He states that the saddle business is better right at this time than he ever knew it to be in peace times before."[17]*

Bowie County, Texas, was the birthplace of J. H. Deam, now of Clayton, New Mexico. His father, A. D. Deam, was born in Bavaria and his mother in Alsace-Lorraine. This couple came to the United States and married later in Indiana. From Indiana the young immigrants went by wagon and ox-team to Kentucky, later moving by the same means of conveyance to Bowie County, Texas. The first night the A. D. Deams camped on Texas soil J. H. Deam, the subject of this sketch, was born to them in the big covered wagon.

The family located in Bowie County, where the father, A. D. Deam, worked as a wagon maker. There J. H. Deam grew up and got his schooling—not as much as he should have got and would have got, he says, if he had realized how useful it would have been to him later.

J. H. Deam served a three years' apprenticeship in the saddle making business under L. B. Howell at Lancaster, Texas. Since then he has made saddle making his trade, dealing also in harness. In 1889 he made the first saddle that was ever made in Oklahoma City, Oklahoma. Then after several months spent in different parts of Oklahoma in 1896 Mr. Deam came to Union County, where he bought the relinquishment to a homestead a few miles out of Clayton, New Mexico.

At the end of three years spent in Union County Mr. Deam returned to Bowie County on important business—his marriage to Miss Rebecca Jane Bailey of Bowie County. This occurred on October 9th, 1899. Then with his bride he returned to Union County, which has been his home the past forty years. Two children were born to them—a little girl who died at the age of three and a son, Arthur A. Deam, now of Stinnett, Texas.

After working for others for a while, Mr. Deam went into business for himself in Clayton in 1928, first in the Azar building but after one or two years later moved finally into his present location the second door west of First Street on the south side of Main Street. Here we find him making saddles and selling harness, although there is not much demand for the latter in this age of tractors.

Mr. Deam remembers with a smile the old sidesaddle days. At present his saddles are of the Western Stock Saddle type, which, with the hand-decorating he does on them, are real works of art. Most of his trade is from out of the state, his prices ranging from $55.00 to $100.00 each. He states that the saddle business is better right at the present time than he ever knew it to be in peace times.

Having been for years a dealer in harness,

---

*"Biography: J. H. Deam," coll. Genevieve Chapin; 400 wds., 3 pp., n.d. (A#239; LC38.3; LC47.1).

he has made himself familiar with the manufacturing and the harness business through frequent visits to the harness factories. But, he states, only twice in his experience has he seen horse collars made, as the fire hazard is so great in connection with this part of the work, on account of the material used for stuffing. This necessitates the collars being made in a part of the factory entirely separate and apart from the rest of the work.

Mr. Deam has watched Clayton grow from a small village of two or three hundred people to its present size with a population of about 2,500. He states that only two American women now remain in Clayton who were here when he came.

Ranchers and cowboys also needed footgear. In Clayton, Tony Spinelli provided it.*

Located on the south side of Main Street, well toward the west end of the block between Front and First Streets, we find the Clayton Boot and Shoe Hospital, whose proprietor is Tony Spinelli. As in all hospitals here, not only the aged and infirm are repaired and made as good as new but absolutely new specimens are sent forth to take their place in the world and battle valiantly to a good old age. Mr. Spinelli is a maker of anything that can be made in leather footgear, although most of his trade at present is in the form of boots and shoes for men.

He learned his trade in Italy, serving an apprenticeship under Frank Gata in St. Agata. He began this training at the age of eight years and finished it at the age of fourteen years, attending school during all this period of training. He began making footwear in 1909 and in 1916 established a business of his own in Walton, New York. Since that time he has been continuously in business for himself, except during his period of service in the World War.

Since 1927 Mr. Spinelli has been in business in Clayton. His work has become known in different places from coast to coast, his customers sometimes ordering by mail, sometimes making personal visits for orders. One man recently came from Cooper, Texas, purposely to get his feet comfortably shod.

Much of Mr. Spinelli's work consists in making to order expensive boots of the cowboy type; for these his prices range from $20.00 to $35.00. Men's dress shoes made to order are priced from $17.50 to $22.50 per pair. One of his most particular jobs, he states, is the making of boots for a man with an artificial foot. The material Mr. Spinelli uses is imported French calf and Australian kangaroo, which he buys from reliable wholesalers anywhere he can get it.

*From "Unusual Industries," coll. Genevieve Chapin from Spinelli; 25 July 1936 (A#238; LC47.1), pp. 2–3.

Two photos by John Collier featuring William Heck, a second-generation rancher in the Moreno Valley, Colfax County, New Mexico, February 1943:

"William Heck, straightening and fitting a 'cold forged' horseshoe." LC-USW 3-18641-C.

"William Heck shoeing a horse." LC-USW 3-18989-E.

THE LITERARY TULAROSA

Theodore Van Soelen at work on mural, "The Round Up."
Oil on canvas, 67″ × 151″, 1933–34. Grant County
Courthouse, Silver City, PWAP.[1]

White Oaks, as the old timers say, has "gone ghost." The little mining town that was once alive with frontier occupation, with the dreams and losses of those who ventured, with the labor and gains of sturdier pioneers, lies quietly today in the midst of one of New Mexico's most dramatic settings. Mountain ranges, one seeming to pile against the other with wide sweeps of desert flatlands between, each square mile with a story to tell. And appropriately enough, for out of little White Oaks in the latter nineteenth and the early twentieth centuries emerged some of the Southwest's finest literary talent—writers, story tellers, who unlike the town will never "go ghost."
—John L. Sinclair, *New Mexico: The Shining Land* (1980), p. 109.

Although in White Oaks today "a few homes still house the living, but very few," John Sinclair maintains that "the inspiration is still there in the loneliness" and the "lore and legend that fired the minds of Emerson Hough, Harvey and Erna Fergusson, Eugene Manlove Rhodes [and] Jack Thorp."[2]

Emerson Hough (1857–1923) and Harvey Butler Fergusson (1848–1915) arrived in White Oaks at approximately the same time—each, as Fergusson's novelist son Harvey (1890–1971) reports, "dead broke . . . hopeful, good humored and carefree" bachelors.[3] Hough stayed less than two years (1883–85), working as a lawyer, a reporter, and typesetter for the local newspaper, *The Golden Era*, and as an author for *American Field*.[4] Fergusson practiced law in White Oaks for about two years (1882–83), but, according to his son, "knew it was a mushroom town" and moved to Albuquerque:

But White Oaks always had a place in his life. He had friends and mining interests there as long as he lived and went back to it for frequent visits. He took me with him once, about 1900. I remember it very clearly as a beautiful quiet little place where graying men talked about great days that were over.[5]

It was Hough, of course, who later immortalized the gold mining boomtown in his 1905 novel, *Heart's Desire*.[6]

Although Nathan Howard (Jack) Thorp (1867–1940) was Eastern-bred, he arrived in New Mexico in 1886 and became a "sure-enough cowboy," who "for much the greater part of his life—for fifty years and more—. . . rode the range, lived the life, made his living out of cattle, and was an integral part of the cowboy scene."[7] He is best known for his 1908 collection, *Songs of the Cowboys* (printed at the News Print Shop in Estancia,[8] and expanded for Houghton Mifflin in 1921), and for his 1926 collection, *Tales of the Chuck Wagon* (printed by the New Mexican Publishing Company in Santa Fe). The former contains "Little Joe the Wrangler," the song he is most famous for having composed in 1898.[9] According to his biographer, Neil M. Clark, "Jack had little or none of the fictional skill of Eugene Manlove Rhodes—the two were contemporaries and fellow ranchers for a while in the San Andres Mountains, but his skill with a horse was greater than Gene's, and in the cattle industry he was the caliber of man who could, and did, serve as State Cattle Inspector."[10]

"The Bard of the Tularosa," as historian C. L. Sonnichsen calls Eugene Manlove Rhodes (1869–1934),[11] anticipated the task of Thorp (and of other NMFWP writers) in recording oldtimers in a brief article for *They Know New Mexico: Intimate Sketches by Western Writers* (issued by the Passenger Department of the Atchison, Topeka and Santa Fe Railway in 1928). Rhodes charged that "Santa Fe, herself so long neglected, is firmly incredulous of beauty, interest or charm to the southward; desports herself stepsisterly, as toward another Cinderella." However, Rhodes added, there was a human story here, waiting to be told.

Through the Cinderella country you can find old men, mild and frail, who tell of days when they were first-men in an untrodden land. Time was when they were less mild and frail, when two of them made a crowd. You will hear of Apache raiders, Victorio, Nana and Geronimo, of Kinney the outlaw, the Lincoln County War, the Tonto Basin. But these are old unhappy far-off things, gladly forgotten. Neglecting fractions, their tale is of work and not of war; of trail herds and roundups, roads, wells and ditches; of friendship and pleasant campfires, of hunger and thirst and weariness hardly to be borne. But not once do they voice regret for money lost, chances missed, herds that are no more. Their talk is of essential things; joy and laughter and all delight.

Bueno pues! These people are my people, their ways are mine. . . .

It is true that little happened in South New Mexico three hundred years ago. But something has changed here since 1865; the meeting of North, South, East and West; Latin and Saxon, Puritan and Cavalier. Three hundred years from now, Oliver Loving and his friends will be as far in the past as Onate is from today. But the inquirer of 2227 can not say, "Oblige me by referring to the files." There are no files. All that will ever be known of those stirring years is locked in a few gray heads. Old timers lived hard, rode hard, worked hard and drank easily. Worse than all, they breathed alkali dust around the herds. So they suffer from bronchitis, and upon slight provocation they die of pneumonia. Future historians will be grateful to any man with a gift of listening, who will listen now—not long—through Southern New Mexico.[12]

Eugene Manlove Rhodes was such a listener. Sonnichsen claims that Rhodes began working at Engle's Bar Cross in 1883, when he was thirteen. "For twenty-five years he rode the ranges of southern New Mexico and made himself known far and wide—not always favorably—among the cattle people. Then he began writing about what he knew and what he remembered."[13] Rhodes died in Pacific Beach, California, on June 27, 1934, and his body was buried in the San Andres Mountains near his ranch at Rhodes Pass, so named before his death. A group of friends and admirers placed a marker there in 1936. It is now within the White Sands Missile Range.

Prospectors Charles Baxter, John E. Wilson, Jack Winters and George Wilson discovered gold about a mile west of White Oaks in the late 1870s. They soon divided their mining claim into the South Homestake and North Homestake, and, as mining engineer Morris B. Parker recalled, "the customary new-gold-discovery followed."[14] Parker maintains that "White Oaks is said to have the deepest *dry* free-milling gold mines in the United States, probably in the world,"[15] and the seven main working shafts of the North and South Homestakes, the Old Abe and the Lady Godiva attracted a heterogeneous and quite cosmopolitan mix of speculators, miners, support personnel and families. The post office was established in June 1880, but the long awaited rail connection never materialized and so nearby Carrizozo, established on the El Paso and Northeastern Railroad in 1899, prospered while White Oaks gradually lost most of its 2500 or more inhabitants. Among those who stayed was May Lee Queen, wife of Edward L. Queen,[16] who was finally given deed to her beloved Leesville, White Oaks, property in 1936.*

My father, Captain John Lee, was born November 27, 1835, in Edinburgh, Scotland. His parents came to the United States when he was eighteen months old and lived in Moodus, Connecticut. When he was fourteen years old he ran away to sea. He followed the sea for many years and came to own his own sailing vessel. He traded extensively in the South Seas and dealt mostly in copra. He went around the world three times in a sailing vessel and discovered a small island that was called Lee's Island. When I was a small girl in school at White Oaks, New Mexico, this island was shown on the maps of my geography.

My father married Mary Purcell, who was a daughter of an English missionary of the Church of England and a graduate of Oxford. My mother was the granddaughter of King Mata Afa, who was king of the island of Samoa. My father and mother were married at Apia Samoa. They owned a plantation near Apia and lived there for several years. They had nine children, born on this island. Father decided that he wanted his children educated in the United States, so they left Apia Samoa on a sailing vessel for the States.

They were six months on the sea. They ran into "calms" and were delayed for days and weeks. Their water and food supplies got short and they were put on short rations. Just before the food was entirely gone they made the port of Honolulu and the vessel was restocked. They landed at San Francisco about the year 1879.

After visiting my father's family in Connecticut and traveling around a good bit they decided to settle in Richmond, Virginia. Father bought a farm near Richmond and lived there for about a year and a half. Mother and the children had chills and fever and were sick so much that they decided to move.

Father had always wanted a cattle ranch, so they moved down to southwest Texas and bought a cattle ranch about twenty miles from Brackettsville, Texas. The family came by train from Virginia to Texas and had been there only a short time when I was born on June 1st, 1882. About two years later my mother had another baby girl, and she and I were the only children born in the United States. While we were living there Father met a man named McBee, who had a ranch at White Oaks, New Mexico. He was always telling Father what a great country New Mexico was, so in 1886 my father sold out his place near Brackettsville and started for New Mexico.

Our family consisted of Father, Mother, and eleven children. My two oldest brothers and my oldest sister were married, so they and their families came with us to New Mexico. We were in five covered wagons drawn by horses. Father had about two hundred head of cattle and about sixty horses. The boys drove the stock and the ladies did the cooking. I was about four years old at the time, but one or two incidents stand out very clearly in my memory.

We were very much afraid of the Indians as we had heard of the terrible things that they had done to wagon trains. We were not molested by them at all, though we saw them on several occasions. I remember waking up

*"Pioneer Story," coll. Edith L. Crawford from May Lee Queen, age 56, of White Oaks; 1260 wds., 4 pp., 13 June 1938 (A#210; LC47.1).

one morning and hearing my mother crying. I looked out and it seemed to me that I saw piles and piles of dead stock all around us. The cattle and horses had died from drinking the alkali water. This happened where Seven Rivers emptied into the Pecos River.

My father was very much discouraged and took what was left of the cattle and horses and went up to Peñasco in New Mexico. He bought a farm and we lived there for about a year. We raised lots of potatoes that year and the boys sold them. Father decided to go on to White Oaks, New Mexico, to where the McBee's lived, so he sold out the farm and what cattle he had left and we moved to White Oaks.

My married brothers and my married sister and their families moved back to Texas. We went to the McBee ranch, which was about two miles from White Oaks. We lived on this ranch a year, and Father ran a dairy and sold the milk in White Oaks. At the end of the year Father got us a house nearer town, just above the Old Abe Mine pump station. He opened up a meat shop in town.

We children went to school and I remember one teacher especially, named Wharton. The geographies that we studied showed Lee's Island on the map, and the teacher often told the class that it was our father who had discovered this island.

My brother Bob married and worked in the South Homestake Mine. He drilled into a "dud" (a percussion cap that had not been exploded) and it blew up and killed him. This was about 1892.

There was such a big family of us, and all the married ones settled around my father and they called our place Leesville. There were about five families of us. Father used to drive the stage to Socorro. I remember

once that he did not get home when the stage was due and my mother got very uneasy. The stage was often held up and we were afraid it had been held up and my father killed. He was a night and day late, and just about the time my brothers and some friends got their horses saddled to go look for him we saw the stage coming over the hill into White Oaks. They had run into a terrible snow storm and the horses could not pull the stage through the storm. It was very cold and my father and the passengers were almost frozen. He stopped the stage at our house, and the passengers came in and got warmed up and drank some coffee before Father took the stage on into town. Father wore a beard, and I remember that it was all covered with ice and snow and you could only see his eyes.

I grew up with Edward L. Queen in White Oaks and we were married in the Methodist Church there on January 1st, 1902, by the Reverend Sam Allison, who now lives in El Paso, Texas. We have three children, two boys and one girl, all married, and one grandson and one granddaughter, who all now live in California.

Of my father's family there are only three left—myself, one brother, Jim Lee, who lives in Douglas, Arizona, and one sister, Mrs. Ray Lemon, who lives in Carrizozo. My father died in Douglas, Arizona, in 1920, at the age of eighty-five years. My mother died in Carrizozo at eighty-one years in 1925.

Mr. Queen and I leave White Oaks sometimes for years at a time, but we always come back. We have our home here. Judge Andrew H. Hudspeth, who owned the property in White Oaks known as Leesville, made me a gift of a deed to this property in 1936. I am very glad to own our old home.

John Sinclair remembers Jack Thorp as "the Princeton-educated cowboy . . . who rode the ranges of the Block Ranch east of White Oaks, and the Bar W to the west."[17] Sinclair was also familiar with the Block Ranch, but it was the Paterson place north of the Capitan Mountains which he bought in 1927. "It was fifteen miles from my fireside by way of Capitan Pass (not the Gap) to the town of Capitan on the Roswell-to-Carrizozo highway." When there, Sinclair "bought my meals at Mother Julian's Boarding House—table loaded with country-style food: 'eat all you can hold,' price of a sitting thirty cents."[18] When Jack Thorp submitted his description of Capitan and its oldtimers, including Mother Julian, in 1936, he was living "in a house beside the highway in Alameda, north of Albuquerque, a simple rustic adobe in his day—now modernized and stuccoed over like most of Jack Thorp's west."[19]*

Salau, or Capitan, is on Salado Creek, which empties into the Rio Bonito some six miles west of Lincoln, the old county seat of Lincoln County, New Mexico, where Billy the Kid and his gang carried on their petty thieving in the early eighties. Salau lies on the old highway over which freighters and mail coaches passed in years ago, and on account of the road following the canyon, which was heavily timbered and afforded the Indians ambuscades, was dreaded by those passing through. This town of Capitan lies in one of the most interesting sections in New Mexico, with Lincoln on the east, Fort Stanton and the Mescalero Apaches' reservation on the south, Nogal with its early mining boom on the west, and the old abandoned camp of White Oaks to the north. . . .

Waverly Johnson was one [of Capitan's interesting oldtimers], who together with his wife and son Clem—who could yell louder than an Indian when meals were ready—ran the first boarding house when the coal mines were opened at Salau some thirty-five years ago.

Sebe Gray ran the store and saloon and also was in the cattle business.

Then there was a young fellow who when he got drunk always threatened to commit suicide, and eventually did, and with all as medley a bunch of miners and cow-punchers as the West ever produced.

Surrounded as Salau was by big cattle outfits there was always a grown crop of punchers either there or at Lincoln. Among the cow outfits was the big Three Blocks and the V. V., while just past Nogal to the west lay the Bar W., or Carrizozo Cattle Company.

One of the great characters still living in Capitan is Mother Julian, who runs a hotel at that point. The oldtimers and cow-punchers stop with her whenever opportunity affords, and she is the friend of them all. You who do not know her and are interested in amusing anecdotes, hasten ye to Capitan, and arrange to stay a few days, then pin back your ears and listen.

I met her just after a car accident when the car insisted on leaving the road during a heavy rain storm, turning bottom side up in a deep arroyo. After kicking out the windshield I got my wife and niece out, and a passing car took us to Mother Julian's hotel. Her first greeting was a word of sympathy,

*"Salau or Capitan," coll. N. Howard Thorp; 1500 wds., 6 pp., 23 December 1936 (HC: Capitan; LC47.1).

and showing us a room, inquired if we were not pretty well shaken up, remarking, "I wish I had a drop to give you, but come to think of it when Tom Gray left this morning I saw him put something under the counter downstairs, and you"—pointing to me—"run down and see what it contains." It did! It contained a bottle of just the right formula to relieve shock and nerve strain.

Mother Julian is short and ample, with her hair cut close like a man's, no frills on the side that need curling. After supper and the necessary chores attended to, and usually surrounded by old cronies, a tactful question or two will get her started on a line of reminiscences, which if you can go without sleep, may last until morning.

Those recollections of hers, which I heard the first night while there, so impressed themselves that I shall try and retell them here. But in so doing they miss the gestures and expression which she alone is capable of. One of her stories concerns a marriage or two and how she handled her husband. Her first choice was a man named Julian, a man with a good education, but at last she lost him, and although later married to a prospector named Wells she thought so much of her former incumbent that she retained his name.

The man named Wells would borrow all the cash from her and his friends that was possible, load up his burros with food and whiskey—principally whiskey—and disappear to find the richest gold mine that was ever discovered.

As it afterwards proved, Wells would go a few miles from town to where there was a convenient spring and camp. When the supplies were gone he would return with some samples of ore he had picked up and spend the next week or so bragging about his mine.

On the strength of the samples brought in, he was able for some time to get grubstakes, but like all good things these eventually came to an end.

After his sources of supplies were cut off, Wells' days of prospecting ended, and he was perfectly contented to sit in an occasional game of poker, drink whiskey—when he could get it—and roost on the wood box behind the kitchen stove, his wife doing the cooking, making the beds, waiting on the table, and tending the hotel office.

Mother Julian never complained, until one time he became abusive and threatening. What happened she describes as follows:

"I had a full house as it was Christmas day, every room was taken, and I had to set the table three times in order to feed them all. At the last table were a lot of high-toned people, tourists I guess, who although nice enough, seemed a little fussy and I did not want anything to happen to spoil their dinner.

"My old man had been drinking all the morning, mostly the free Tom and Jerry's the saloons were furnishing, and when he came back to the hotel he was whiskey mean.

"I closed the door from the kitchen into the dining room and slammed him down on the wood box behind the stove, and told him to sit there and shut up. Then he begged me for ten dollars; again I told him to shut up. He then threatened if I didn't give him the money he would beat me, but I grabbed the ax and he sat down and kept quiet. Every time I'd pass him he'd whisper, 'Mother, give me ten dollars or I'll beat you.' As there was a dance on that night all the ranch people had left their babies with me to look after, and I was on the jump, waiting on the table and keeping the twenty odd babies quiet.

"For dessert I had served for the first and second tables three kinds of pie, but for the tourists I had in the oven a big egg custard. It was in a big pan that held some two gallons. I came downstairs from tending the babies and had taken away the empty plates, telling the folks I would bring in their dessert. After they all had been served I started to the kitchen with the container, which was still about half full of sticky egg custard. As I entered the kitchen and closed the door behind me, there stood Wells with a big stick of wood in his hand. 'Give me that ten dollars, you hear me? I want it right now.' Down I came on his head with that big pan custard and all, and crumpled him flat."

"What became of him?" I asked.

"Well, the last I heard of him," she replied, "he had taken his burros and left for the hills. Anyway, I divorced him and took back my first husband's name. God bless him."

"Reserve, New Mexico. June 1940. Uncle Bill, old-timer who claims to be the only man alive who was tried before the court of Judge Roy Bean." Uncle Bill owned Uncle Bill's Cafe, selling beer, wines, and liquor.[20] Photo by Russell Lee. LC-USF 34-36573-D.

Hinman and Julia Manlove Rhodes moved their family (twelve-year-old Eugene, Clarence, and Helen or Nellie) from Tecumseh, Nebraska, to the Tularosa Basin in 1881. Eugene Rhodes entered the University of the Pacific in Stockton, California, in 1888, but he was soon forced to return to New Mexico because of financial difficulties. There he took a variety of jobs, including mining, wagon freighting, and horse wrangling at the Bar Cross Ranch. His first published work, a poem, appeared in 1896, and on August 9, 1899, he married May Davison Purple of Appalachin, New York, a widow with two sons who had corresponded with him on literary matters. In 1902, his wife returned to her family's farm on New York's Susquehanna River, and Rhodes reluctantly followed in 1906. Much of his literary work was published or begun in New York, until ill health forced him to Los Angeles in 1919. The Rhodes family finally sold the New York farm in 1926 and moved to Santa Fe, and then to Pacific Beach, California, in 1931, where Rhodes died on June 27, 1934.[21]

In February 1937 Albuquerque NMFWP field writer Janet Smith began compiling a bibliography of works by and about Eugene Manlove Rhodes. Smith also conducted interviews with people who had known Rhodes. Mr. Robert Hopewell of 619 West Copper Avenue, Albuquerque, suggested Mrs. Jewett Fall Elliott, Tres Ritos; Johnny P. Dines, Winston; Lee Nations, Orrey (near Hot Springs); and Harry Benson and Leonard Goins, both bartenders at the Buckhorn Saloon, Hot Springs. James Threlkeld of Albuquerque's New Mexico Book Store thought she should contact Harrison Leussler of San Francisco, Houghton Mifflin's western representative.

Howard Roosa, "known as a collector of New Mexicana," of 1419 West Roma Avenue, Albuquerque, whom Smith interviewed on March 17, 1937, collected Rhodesiana and had met the author once in California. Roosa suggested that Smith contact his housekeeper, sixty-five-year-old Mrs. Bella Ostic, 104 Wilson Avenue, Albuquerque, who proved to be a rich living resource. The longer interview was in March 1937.*

"My, yes, I knew Gene Rhodes well," Mrs. Ostic answered. "Guess I hardly ever knew anybody any better than I did Gene. Come in. Sit down."

She walked over to a shelf and took down a photograph of a girl. From the back of the frame she removed several pictures, sorted them over, and handed me two of them. One

*"Interview with Mrs. Bella Ostic," coll. Janet Smith; 3400 wds., 10 pp., 22 March 1937 (A#140; H5–5–50#39; LC47.1).

was an old fashioned photograph in bad condition—a picture of a boy with a heavy determined mouth tightly shut, closely cropped hair, direct eyes, a slightly defiant air about him. The other was a snapshot of a man standing in profile beside a horse. He wore riding breeches and a Stetson hat. His features were clearly outlined against the horse's dark neck—the nose aquiline, the chin definite. He had the slightly protruding sag about the abdomen, unusual in a cowboy, of a man of forty or thereabouts.

"That old photograph is a picture of Gene when he was nineteen," Mrs. Ostic told me. "He got mixed up in some kind of a political scrape, and somebody threw him down a well. His scalp was all torn and lacerated and they had to cut his hair off short. It was just growing out in that picture."

"What was the scrape about?" I asked curiously.

"I don't remember, and I don't know as they ever did find out who was responsible for throwing him down that well. I know Gene was a Republican but that's all that I can tell about it now.

"I knew Gene for a good many years," Mrs. Ostic went on. "His father was agent on the Mescalero Indian Reservation, and my father was the blacksmith there. Gene was about seventeen or eighteen when I first knew him. He was born in Nebraska. His father's name was Hinman and he had been a senator from Nebraska. His mother's name was Julia. They had a ranch in the San Andreas and I believe came to New Mexico two or three years before I knew them. Anyhow, I know Gene was born in Nebraska and so was his little sister Helen—Nellie we called her. She was only a little girl when I first knew them so they couldn't have been in New Mexico many years before that.

"When Mrs. Rhodes needed something done she used to send for me to come over and help her. That's how I got to know Gene so well. His mother was a politician, always writing and going to Washington and doing things like that. She was a meddlesome kind of woman, always writing to somebody, telling this and telling that. She was just meddlesome, that's all there is to it, and she usually had her family in hot water of some kind. I liked her, though. She was splendid company.

"Mr. Rhodes was a quiet, serious man. He was a thoroughly honest man too, Mr. Rhodes was. So was Gene for that matter. I know the 'ring' at Las Cruces was always trying to 'get' Mr. Rhodes. William Riley—he died not so long ago—was a cattle man and politician, and he was the head of the ring. They didn't like it because Mr. Rhodes wouldn't accept poor beef from them and tried to cause him a lot of trouble. Colonel Fountain—the one who was murdered, you remember, and they never found his body—was an honest man too and was always on Rhodes' side.[22] The 'ring' never did succeed in running Mr. Rhodes out though. He stayed there until he was retired on a pension. I believe Gene got along better with his father than his mother. Though his mother was very fond of him, too. She always called him Genie.

"Gene couldn't ever talk just right—a kind of lisp. I don't know as you would call it a lisp either, but he couldn't pronounce 'R.' 'Odes' he would say instead of Rhodes. There were other words he couldn't say too which made it difficult for some people to understand him. Although to me—I understood him perfectly. Gene went to college in San Jose, California. One of his college friends was visiting him one time, and he told me that when the boys asked Gene what his name was he told them Eugene Manlove 'Odes.' They all called him 'Odes' until finally he wrote his name on a piece of paper and handed it to this boy and said, 'Here, tell these fellows what my name is.'"

Mrs. Ostic settled back in her rocking chair. "I suppose you want to know more about how he looked than you can see in that photograph. He wasn't a bad looking boy—not good looking either. His forehead was always a little too protruding for his other features. He had blue eyes and light hair and a reddish face. He was a little above medium height, not fleshy, rather slender. He always wore a brown suit, some coarse brown good with a big plaid. I never saw him with good clothes. Anything would do. I don't know how many shirts I patched for that boy. I remember, too, I made a harness for him to wear his gun under his shirt. He always seemed to think that people didn't like him and that somebody was going to shoot him or something.

"Gene was always kind of retiring. He lived at the Mescalero Agency for more than eight years, and I don't believe he ever had more than a bowing acquaintance with a few of the girls. He was no good at all as a mixer. He always seemed to feel that people didn't like him. And I guess they didn't very well. He was too far above the people that we had at that time. His mind was too good for our class of people. Except for his wife, I never knew him to have any women friends except the two Cassad [*sic*] girls in Mesilla Park.[23] I remember once those two girls and a Manlove cousin of his stayed at our house for two weeks and they all went fishing a lot. But except for them I don't think he was friends with any girls. I never heard him speak much of men friends either, except for one fellow, Charles Lummis.[24]

"Gene always had a kind of gloomy outlook on life. He hardly ever laughed, and I don't know as I ever did hear him tell a joke. He always liked sad things, sad poetry and sad songs. One thing he loved and that was to sing. But it was always some kind of a sad song. I remember he used to come over to my house. Maybe we'd be making bread, my sister and I. But Gene would call to my sister, 'Come on, you and Bella, I want you to sing La Golondrina for me.' And nothing would do but we'd have to leave our dough and come into the parlor where the organ was and sing songs. When Gene got a notion to hear something, he was going to have it. The words to that song were not the same as the words they sing to La Golondrina now. It was something about a man who would never

see the shores of Spain again. '*Nunca más, nunca más te ve.*' A very sad song and Gene loved it.

"He was really the strangest boy. He would go from one thing to another, just that changeable. We used to ride horseback together, and sometimes Gene would be telling me a story and suddenly burst out crying, for no reason that I could see. Just that changeable. He would come over to our house and sit down by himself and maybe I'd come into the room and there he'd be crying. He'd cry and cry and when I'd ask him what was the matter he'd just say, 'I'm so miserable, so unhappy.' But I never knew why. His mother always said it was because she was lonely and sad before he was born. Maybe that was the reason. Anyhow, I never could see any real reason for his being that way.

"Of course Gene was always scribbling. While others were talking in a room he was scribbling something most of the time. When I knew him he used to write poetry more than prose. His poems were always about something sad. I remember one—let's see—those poems are at home in Tucumcari with some letters from him in a receipt box. I wrote the boys to send them, but they never did. Well, anyhow, I remember the last line of one of them was 'that death is far more kind than love of life.' All of them were along that line.

"Before he left New Mexico Gene had quite a number of things published in a magazine called *Out West*. I remember he brought the paper over to me and wanted me to subscribe to it, because he said he was going to write for it. I did, but I never had much faith that Gene would ever publish anything much. Gene was usually considered a fool by everybody, poor fellow. I never thought he was a fool but he did seem to be awfully erratic.

"He would do the craziest things of any fellow I ever knew. I remember once he wrote me a letter at midnight from the top of a mountain peak. It was the peak where he is buried. They call it Rhodes Peak now. I had asked him to find the words to a verse by Mrs. Heeman for me.[25] He was on his way from Las Cruces to the San Andres and was camping for the night on the top of that peak when he sat down and wrote me a letter enclosing the poem I had wanted. I remember he said in that letter that there was not a lonelier man in the world than he was on the top of that mountain peak at midnight, but that nowhere else did he feel so near to God. Or Nature, I guess he must have said Nature instead of God. Gene wasn't a Christian. Anyhow I never knew him to go to church.

"Another thing about Gene, he was a great gambler. I guess that was the only thing Gene did that I didn't think was just right. I never did see him drink, but they used to say if he sat down to a gambling table there was no dragging him away. Even in gambling, though, he was always honest. A man told me once that he was a good card player, but the reason he didn't make a success of gambling was because he never would do anything the least bit dishonest."

I asked Mrs. Ostic if she knew why Rhodes left New Mexico for the East.

"He married the school teacher in Tularosa," she answered. "She was from New York state and she wanted to go back East."

"Didn't he get into trouble of some kind?" I persisted.

Mrs. Ostic looked at me sharply. "You mean something dishonest? Nobody could make me believe that Gene was not a distinctly honest man. He always was. If he didn't cheat at cards he certainly wouldn't cheat in the cattle business, or in any other way. He was always getting into a fuss over gambling things, debts and things like that, but I know he never did anything dishonest.

"I remember three days before he left New Mexico he came to our house for dinner, he and his wife and his mother. Like usual, he had a gloomy look. As I say he always had a gloomy outlook on life, but I'm sure there was nothing special bothering him. If there had been I would have known it.

"That was the only time I ever saw his wife. She was a big woman, rather pretty too. But she was a proud woman. I remember when Gene came in he kissed me the same as he always did, and he said, 'Bella, I'm going to leave New Mexico in three days and I want some of that good tapioca pudding you make, because I may never get any more of it.' I told him I didn't have any tapioca in the house, and he said, 'Well, we'll excuse you to get some then.' Gene was always fond of tapioca pudding. He hated green peas. I remember one day Mr. Roosa was reading a book by Rhodes and he looked up and asked me if I knew any kind of food that Eugene Rhodes especially disliked. Right away I said green peas. And it was green peas he had written about in that book. To get back to the last time I saw him, though, after dinner we all went for a walk around the sawmill. And all that time and during dinner I don't think his wife ever said a word. I guess she thought he was too free with us poor people and she didn't like it.

"That was in 1903 that he left New Mexico and I never did see him again. Some years after that I saw something about him in the paper, and I wrote to him. As I said, he had some stories published in *Out West* before he left and he had the manuscript of that story, 'Pasó Por Aquí' [published 1927], but I never did expect him to get much published or amount to anything. When I saw that in the paper I was glad he had made a success, and I wrote him care of his publishers, and told him there was still somebody in New Mexico who remembered him as 'dear Gene Rhodes.' He answered right back. He told me that his oldest son was named Percy Allen. 'Percy Allen' was the name of a song he was very fond of and we used to sing it together. It was supposed to be sung by a woman who said that if she had been able to marry her true love she would have had a son cradled under the wildwood tree. Her love was named Percy Allen.[26]

"Many years later he wrote me again from New York. He said he wanted to have a horse and a cow and live the way he used to in New Mexico, but he couldn't make it work out very well. He told me too that his nerves were all shot, and the reason was that one of his sons had been killed in the war.

"The next time I heard from him he was back in New Mexico. He wrote me from La Luz that he had come back to get color for some of his stories. After that he left for California."

Mrs. Ostic began rocking again and it seemed that her story was ended. Remembering the introduction to *The Trusty Knaves* [1934], I asked her if Rhodes liked cats. She smiled and said that he certainly liked her cat.

"He was always jumping up from the table to give that cat something to eat. We didn't have a piano in our house but we had an organ. When Gene would play that organ the cat would come running from wherever he might be and walk up and down in front of the organ dragging his tail on the floor. I always thought that cat believed it was his tail that made the noise. Anyhow, whenever Gene would start pumping the organ, in two minutes the cat would be right there, prancing up and down and dragging his tail.

"The cat was called Antonio Joseph. I taught school in Lincoln for awhile, and I took a kitten and a little dog away from some children who were abusing them. I named the cat Antonio Joseph and the dog Catron. They were the two big political figures in the state at that time. Both the cat and the dog seemed too weak and bedraggled to live long, and I said that whichever one died first, the man for whom he was named would be defeated. On election day the little dog Catron died, and Catron was defeated.[27]

"When I took the cat home and showed him to Rhodes he said, 'I like the cat all right, but I don't think much of his politics.' Rhodes was boarding at our house at the time. One morning I was sleeping late, and Gene woke me calling at the foot of the stairs, 'Bella, Bella,' he called. 'Hurry and get up. Antonio Joseph is Josie. She's had kittens.' That was one of the few times I ever heard

him say anything funny, and even then he didn't smile.

"Gene had a horse too that he was very fond of. Docre was his name and Docre was a mean animal. But Rhodes thought the world of him. Docre would throw him. Rhodes wasn't a good rider, and Docre knew it. That horse would dump him about every day, but Gene would stay with it. I've seen him ride a bronco and be thrown as much as three times and get up and ride him again."

Mrs. Ostic stopped again, and I asked her if she knew what kind of books Rhodes had been especially interested in.

"His people didn't have many books," she said. "We didn't either. People didn't have so many books in those days. But I do remember that he often told me the stories of Shakespeare's plays."

I remarked that I had heard that Rhodes hated the actual task of writing, that he even said he would never touch a pen or pencil again if he could think of any other way to earn a living.

"He might have thought that," Mrs. Ostic answered. "But he couldn't have kept from writing. He was always writing. When other people in the room would be talking and fooling, Gene would be over in some corner with a pencil, scribbling. I always wondered why he didn't write about the Indian people because he was very much interested in them and was always taking notes."

I realized suddenly that it was considerably past lunch time and rose to go. As I was pulling on my gloves, Mrs. Ostic said, "One thing about Gene Rhodes, he would stop anything anytime to help a person out. Once we had a diphtheria epidemic on the reservation. There was no hospital, no doctor even, and everybody was afraid to go near the people who had it. Gene sat up night after night with the sheriff's little boy who died of it. And Gene and my father laid out the little body, made the coffin and lowered it into the grave. The only people at the funeral were Gene and my father and my sister and I. Eight children in one Indian family died, one after the other, and every morning Gene stopped by to bring them water and see if they needed anything. Toward the end of the epidemic the government sent a doctor, a colored man. He was a good doctor and a fine gentleman, and we used to invite him and his wife to our house. But all the other white folks on the reservation would cut them. Except Gene—he used to come over to our house often and play cards with them. I guess that's all I can think of to tell you about Gene right now. I didn't know any of the important things about him, but I used to know him pretty well. Maybe if you come back some other day I'll think of some more things."

Janet Smith again interviewed Mrs. Ostic in April of 1937.*

"I've been thinking since you were here the other day about Gene Rhodes, and I thought of a few little things that don't amount to much but I thought I'd tell you anyhow. I found a poem Gene sent to me a long time ago, too. I've had it around so long it got torn, but you can have it if you want it. I wrote to Tucumcari for those others but they don't answer and I shouldn't wonder if my grandsons have gotten into them and destroyed them by this time." Mrs. Ostic rummaged in an old tin box and handed me a tattered piece of paper with some verses on it.

"I was thinking the other day about how a woman by the name of Mrs. Sutherland, from La Luz she was at that time, told me before I ever met Gene that some day he would be a great writer. She had been visiting at the Rhodes' and Mrs. Rhodes liked to show off her boys and showed her some of Gene's poetry. I sure thought Mrs. Sutherland had made a mistake when I saw Gene. He was the last person I would ever have expected to make something of himself. I guess I told you everybody used to think Gene was a fool. Even his mother used to say he was a fool, though she was fond of him, too. She always thought his brother, Clarence, would amount to more than Gene ever would.

"Another thing I was thinking about—I didn't tell you how he happened to call his horse Docre. Everybody thought that was such a queer name. So one day I asked him where he ever got such a name as that. He said, 'Well, his real name is Devil. But I thought if I went around calling Devil all the time, people would call me on it, so I named him Docre and I can call him Docre as much as I please.' That was the horse that used to throw him so much, and Gene thought the world of him.

"Then I was thinking, too, how Gene always kind of fancied himself as a private detective. He was always mixing up in things and raking up old arguments. Like that article of his, 'In Defense of Pat Garrett.' Gene was always mulling over old scraps, thinking he could be the one to discover something about them that nobody else had seen.

"The last time I ever saw Gene, we went to the railroad station with him and his wife. When he got on the train, he came back to the platform and sang 'nunca más te ve.' He was always doing some sad thing like that. Such things seemed to appeal to him."

*"Interviews on Eugene Manlove Rhodes," coll. Janet Smith; 500 wds., 2 pp., 5 April 1937 (A#140; H5–5–50#39).

SOUTHEASTERN SCOUTS, RANCHERS, AND HOMESTEADERS

Peter Hurd, "Sun and Rain." Fresco, 144″ × 207″, 1941–42.
Federal Building (formerly Post Office), Alamogordo; Treasury
Section of Painting and Sculpture.[1] Photograph by Peter
Bermingham and used with his permission.

The transcription on the Sun Panel reads: "Come Sunlight
after Rain to bring Green Life out of Earth"; on the Rain Panel:
"Ven Lluvia bendita, Ven a acariciar la Tierra Sedienta." According
to the *Alamogordo News*, vol. 45, no. 16, 1941: "The scene to
the left of the main entrance portrays the sunshine and the
green things that it brings from the earth—a beautiful scene of
trees and flowers from Peter Hurd's own home at Picacho in
the foreground, and the San Andreas Mountains and White
Sands in the background. The life-size woman in the picture is
Miss Edna Imhoff, teacher in the schools at Rebenton and the
child picking flowers is Della Joiner, daughter of the postmaster
at Hondo. At the right of the entrance is an old Mexican
shepherd praying for rain. This shepherd is Dorothel Montoya,
well known to the big sheep outfits in the Hondo Valley, and
back of him is the state flower with Sierra Blanca in the far
background."

In his novel of 1933 Depression-era Roswell, Paul Horgan (1903–   ) describes southeastern New Mexico as *Far From Cibola*.

It was a land where men had to conquer trial and treachery always, the area of New Mexico that shared the plains country and the mountain country, and men deciding to live there chose the small valleys of reluctant rivers, and planted their trees, making a shade over their houses that was the only kind thing for miles around. It was the land of the Seven Golden Cities of Cibola, that had wooed the northward Spaniards so long ago. The natural mystery of plains giving back to the sky a second sunlight and of mountains drawing the horizon up to blue pinnacles dazzled men through three hundred years, and led them up the dry beds of creeks and over the heat lakes toward the Cities of Cibola, whose yellow gates they never found. Crossing the very plains and mountains where the terrible wealth was promised to be, they were always far from Cibola; their hope had no strength in it but greed; and legend was only a powerful mockery. What wealth they ever found in that land was created by man with the earth, and toiled for in obedience to the seasons; just as the human graces of shade trees and windmills had to be brought and planted before the land gave any comfort.[2]

Lea County ranchwoman May Price Mosley, a field writer for the New Mexico Writers' Project, saw the buffalo hunters as the area's true pioneers, claiming: "Many had pronounced the desert-like Llano Estacado unfit for human habitation . . . but the buffalo hunters found . . . that they could travel all over the plains and rarely, if ever, be more than a day's drive or march from sufficient permanent water for camping purposes."[3] Their exploits were preserved in reminiscences like those collected by Georgia B. Redfield from two Roswell characters—exscouts and buffalo hunters William Kit Carson and "Old Hot Tamale" Charlie Fowler.

When the buffalo were exhausted, the hunters turned to antelope hunting and mustanging. They also began to sell their wells and watering places to incoming ranchers and then to engage in water hunting for the cattlemen. According to Mosley, the famous "Causey Brothers, of whom George was the chief hunter, and John the chief builder, were not satisfied with merely digging wells; they improved several small ranches which they sold to other ranchers, [and] John built many a rock 'chosey' beside the earlier dug wells of the plains . . . to sell, to use, for others, and it is said he 'built them for pastime.' "[4]

Thus did a few ex-buffalo hunters with their pick-axes and "dinimite" explode the long accepted theory of the Llano Estacado being a part of the "great American desert," and bit by bit uncover the fact that it was and is underlaid with one of the most remarkable and inexhaustible water supplies known to the continent. . . . water beneath all its prairies, which but awaited the perfection of the well drill, the windmill, and the pumping plant to make this desert bloom.[5]

By the late nineteenth century, there was a booming well-drilling and windmill business. James D. Shinkle reports: "Some hardware dealers had a windmill department and specially trained men did nothing but erect windmills for ranches and assure their operating condition. Large ranches soon had a man, or men, that were called 'windmillers' who did nothing but see that the windmills produced the necessary water for the range."[6]

Settlers in much of southeastern New Mexico were relative newcomers. Although Chaves County's enormous Corn family arrived in 1879, most homesteaders came after 1900, and they portray themselves as twentieth-century pioneers fresh from triumphs over deprivation, fire, blizzard, and drought. In this portrayal, the overall tone of their life stories and reports contrasts markedly with the pervasive melancholy for the "passing" of an old pioneer culture in many of the Hispanic folklife documents.

The eastern counties of New Mexico, part of the Dust Bowl of the Southern Plains,[7] were especially hard hit by drought. In 1978, Katheryn L. Fambrough recalled the "Depression Years in Lincoln County":

> Although my husband, Harvey Fambrough, was born and raised in Lincoln County, I never lived there until the early 1930s. This was just in time to witness the fierce dust storms we had to face during the "dust bowl" days, when there was no grass and very little water for the stock.
>
> My husband hauled cactus with a team of horses and a wagon. First he had to cut the treacherous stalks down with an axe, then load them into the wagon with a pitchfork, haul them to the corrals and burn off the stickers to enable the cows to eat them. The poor creatures were so hungry they couldn't wait until the cactus cooled and they often blistered their tongues trying to eat them while still hot. This was a very disagreeable job since the cactus plants were tedious to handle. Each plant had millions of tiny spines that actually seemed to turn loose of the plant and jump at the person handling them. These spines were very hard to remove from the skin because they were so tiny they were like fine hairs sticking into one's flesh—most irritating! The cows that were to eat the cactus were so thin and weak they sometimes had to be "tailed up" before they could eat. This was done by grasping a cow's tail and literally lifting until she had enough support to raise herself to a standing position. Some cotton seed cake was essential to supplement the cactus diet, else the cow would have "scourers" (diarrhea) so badly she would die from weakness. Many poor cows

survived the drought of the 1930s because of the plentiful crop of cactus and its food value.[8]

Unlike Alfonso Griego and Fabiola Cabeza de Baca, however, Fambrough does not see the end of a way of life but the testing of a new community.

That exultant sense of tempering is evident in a series of typed manuscripts written in 1938 by Mrs. Lena S. Maxwell, a school-teacher and manager of the Clovis Museum. The Curry County homesteaders she interviewed and the communities, including her hometown of Grady, whose history she compiled are truly settled, with schools and telephones and businesses tied to the railroads. In 1937, Mrs. Belle Kilgore interviewed Mrs. Maxwell at her Clovis home, and the stories the latter told then and subsequently in the 1938 manuscripts are like those known by Lea County's May Price Mosley, who documented *"Little Texas" Beginnings in Southeastern New Mexico*.[9]

Mosley recorded ranch and homestead life in towns like Eunice, Tatum, and Jal—late-blooming communities separated from older towns like Roswell by the Mescalero Sands. Early twentieth-century homesteaders like the Frank Thompsons and Walter McMillans crossed these sands into New Mexico by covered wagon. Joyce Hunter made the first automobile trip from Texas to Roswell in 1908. A quarter-century later, the route had become U.S. Highway 380, which became, like so many western roads, witness to caravans of cars filled with Dust Bowl refugees in search of work and subsistence. Their stories were perhaps best told in novels like John Steinbeck's *The Grapes of Wrath* (1939) and Paul Horgan's *Far from Cibola* (1936)—and in Dorothea Lange's famous FSA photographs, a few of which were taken in New Mexico and some included here.

Indian scouts were considered as colorful as the men and animals they used to hunt. Men like Roswell's William Kit Carson (who still rode in the parade of the Eastern New Mexico State Fair in 1955, at the age of ninety-eight, and who died in 1957) followed in the romantic Wild West tradition of ex-buffalo hunters and scouts like Captain Jack Crawford (1847–1917), New Mexico's famous Poet Scout.[10] Uncle Kit—the seventy-eight-year-old nephew of General Kit Carson (1809–68)—cheerfully capitalized on his Roswell reputation as "a relic of the old wild days" and, as he told Georgia B. Redfield in 1936, "the only living landmark New Mexico has left." Like his Indian scout friends, Pawnee Bill (G. W. Lilly) and Diamond Dick (Dr. Richard Tanner), and his father's friend Buffalo Bill (William F. Cody), Carson wore his hair long as a symbol of his former scout status.*

William Kit Carson is well known in Roswell. With his long white hair and beard, earrings and Indian costume, he is a colorful character of the past and Indian war days.

He has been for years a familiar and interesting rider in the Old Timers' annual parade during the Cotton Carnival in Roswell [in October].

The walls of his home are papered with pictures and newspaper articles of early days, in which he was the central character.

Many trophies and relics from the buffalo hunting trail, and Indian warpaths, hang from the rafters of his home at 619 W. 13th Street, Roswell, New Mexico.

"Yes, I am about the only living landmark New Mexico has left. I am a relic of the old wild days when a man's best friend was a fast horse and the quick straight shooting trigger of a six-shooter.

"I am seventy-eight years old, was born at Old Fort Union, New Mexico, at the foot of Turkey Mountain, in the northern part of the state on U.S. Highway 85.

"I am the son of William Carson and Maya Carson—an Indian woman—and am the nephew of General Kit Carson, who was the celebrated Indian scout and general of the southwestern district, during the Indian uprisings, and wars. My father was General Carson's First Lieutenant.

"The place of my baptism was at our Lady of Guadalupe Parish Church, Sapello, New Mexico.

"My height is five feet eleven and a half inches, weight 160 pounds.

"My Indian scout pals, 'Pawnee Bill' of Pawnee, Oklahoma, and 'Diamond Dick,' Dr. Richard Tanner of Norfolk, Nebraska, and I all wear our white hair long. The Indians have more respect for a man who had long hair, showing they were not afraid of scalping.

"'Pawnee Bill' was my blanket pal on the Indian trails. He is G. W. Lilly. After the Geronimo campaign ended in 1885, the Government sent him to be Indian agent of the Pawnees at Fort Supply. He still runs the old original log building trading post, at Pawnee, Oklahoma, and has the largest buffalo herd in the United States. You can buy buffalo meat there any time.

"The way and time Diamond Dick got

*"Indian Scout—William Kit Carson," coll. Georgia B. Redfield from Carson, 13 September 1936, Twitchell's *History,* and "Birth certificate of William K. Carson from Old Fort Union, Affidavits gathered by Case Aide, Mrs. Eva Joyner"; 1000 wds., 6 pp., 21 September 1936 (A#234; H5-5-50#32; LC47.1).

his name was in 1885 when we were both sent to hunt a troop of eighteen men who were lost in the White Sands in the country where Alamogordo is now. They had been sent after marauding Indians. We found the men riding in circles, their tongues swollen out of their mouths from want of water—five of the men and eight mules died. When we were carrying the lost men in, Dick found a diamond—one of those Pecos diamonds—and we commenced to joke him and called him Diamond Dick. The name stuck.

"I was here in Roswell often after 1878, when there wasn't anything but one store and a hotel in front of where the court house is now. I knew Van Smith who built both of those first buildings.

"I liked Roswell then and liked the climate and I came back here to live the rest of my days. I like the people here who call me 'Uncle Kit.' I want them to call me that. I have no relatives and I sit here at my door on this old log all alone, and watch the old captain [*sic*: Capitan] and White Mountains, and think about the days when there wasn't anything in all that country between here and there but Indian moccasin tracks.

"I was the scout sent by the Government in June, 1882, to protect an encampment of Missionaries, located right at that point you can see it from here, on Captain Mountain over there. Missionaries helped reduce the crimes 72 per cent in those days.

"North Spring River then was not the old bog hole it is now. It ran bank full. All these artesian wells took the rivers away.

"The Apaches I used to trail are right over here on the Mescalero Reservation. They come to see me sometimes. They are friendly and we don't talk about Indian fighting of the past, when there was murdering and pillaging. I was sent after many of them after uprisings and we always brought them in, and we lost more men from want of water, especially in the Arizona country, than we ever did from Indian wars.

"In the spring of 1883, the Chiricahuas killed the Indian Reservation policeman and let out seven hundred Indians to plunder and kill. They were roused up because settlers were coming in their country. They killed all the ranch settlers, miners and cowmen they could find. Captain [Emmet] Crawford's troops and about a hundred scouts protected the southern New Mexico people. We were at Fort Wingate at that time near the line between Arizona and New Mexico. We were ordered from post to post at each Indian uprising. We were ordered from Fort Wingate to Fort Grant [Arizona] when a band of Indians (between twenty-five and thirty Chiracahuas, led by their chief, Chato) broke through the guards and scouts and pillaged Grant County around Silver City. It was in March, 1883, they met Judge McComas and Mrs. McComas and Charlie, their little six-year-old boy, on the road to Silver City. They killed and scalped the Judge and left his body just at sundown, two miles out of Fort Grant, and left Mrs. McComas's stripped, horribly mutilated body in their buckboard. They took little Charlie into captivity, and he never was found.[11]

"We kept after Chato's band until we captured them about the middle of May between Fort Grant and Fort Apache [Arizona].

"My mother was an Indian and February 7, 1894, I married an Indian maiden, Wiewaks (the Indian maidens have only given names). She died in 1902 and left me and our beautiful daughter named Nuchie. This is Nuchie's picture in her Maiden Ceremonial dress. She caught cold and died a few months after this picture was made. She is looking at the sunrise and asking that the Great Spirit bring happiness for a new day. Everybody loved her. She and my wife are both buried in the Navajo burying ground near Taos.

"My uncle, 'Kit Carson' and his wife and six children are all buried there in our Carson burying lot. He married a Mexican. His last child, a son—Frank—died in 1934.

"W. F. Cody known as 'Buffalo Bill' was scout in 1862. He entered service at Fort Leavenworth, Kansas, and in 1863 was trans-

"Mescalero apache reservation, New Mexico Apr 1936. An Indian woman in front of her tepee. Many Indians live in such primitive tents." Photo by Arthur Rothstein. LC-USF 34-1910-E.

ferred to Old Fort Union, where I was born. In 1864 he was with my father, William Carson. They led the attack against the Cheyennes and Arapahoes at Cherry Creek in north Colorado. They lost heavily, but won the victory and rescued a white woman held captive by the Indians.

"My childhood days in the fort were happy. I played with the little Indian and Mexican boys around the fort. Horny toads and baby buffalo were some of our playthings. When I got to be a big boy we had to hunt the buffalo for our meat. They were plentiful

then. The soldiers at the fort were my pals, who taught me soldiering at an early age.

"I was allowed to ride and roam the prairies at will, for it was a time of peace, before the many Indian hostilities had begun.

"I sit here at my door and watch the mountains and the sunsets each day and thank the Great Spirit for peace which I helped bring to New Mexico. I ask the Guardian Angels to keep peace everywhere all over the world—always. . . .

"On July the fourth, the Mescalero Apaches hold their annual Devil Dances and during

"Mescalero reservation, New Mexico. Apr 1936. Indian tepee."
Photo by Arthur Rothstein. LC-USF 34-1669-E.

their celebration, the maidens who have become of marriageable age, have their own dances and feasting. . . .

"The Maiden Dances last three whole days. They are started off with a feast. This is a picture of my daughter, Nuchie, in her maiden ceremonial costume.[12] She is looking at the sun-rise—asking the Great Spirit to bring her happiness this new day. She was buried in a year with her ceremonial costume. The first evening of the maiden dances the bucks watch to see which wigwam their choice of the dancing girls goes to. The bucks then go twenty or thirty feet from her wigwam and sing or chant to their favorite. If the maiden likes him or his song when he turns to leave, she throws a few pebbles after him. That means she wants him to come back, so at the end of the next day he comes back and sings. The maiden comes out and gives him moccasins she has made for him to wear back to her, which he does the next night. He sings again, and she comes and sits beside him. He puts his blanket around her, and shoots his arrow and where the arrow falls he carries his maiden. The Indian tribe gathers around and they all talk to the Great Spirit and they are fast married, it is binding—no divorce there. When either of them do wrong they are whipped by some one of the tribe. This is meant to be a lesson to the entire tribe as well as to the married couple they punish.

"I did all those things when my wife danced when she had become of marriageable age. The old buck her father said to me—'We like you—how many ponies you got?'

"At death all personal things used by the Indians are buried with them to keep with them. Another reason for this is to keep their people from grieving over the things.

"Religious customs are not exactly like people think. They are not worshipping the sun each day when they spread their arms wide at the appearance of the sun. They are thanking the Great Spirit for another day. In the evening they thank him for his care during that day. The Great Spirit is the Great Maker who sends to us Guardian Angels.

"I don't know how to explain these beliefs, but I can dance them all."

Georgia B. Redfield also reported that the crochety, eccentric "Old Hot-Tamale" Charlie Fowler of Roswell's Chihuahua district had hunted Indians and buffalo on the Staked Plains during the 1870s.*

Many picturesque characters, of the Spanish American people, live in the district called Chihuahua, located in the southeast portion of Roswell.

Charlie Fowler—known as "Old Hot-Tamale"—lives in one of the many little adobe houses, of the Chihuahua district, which make this section of the city different with their clean swept dirt floors, whitewashed walls, and tiny fireplace tucked in a cozy corner—homes typical of the New Spain, which were built in New Mexico after the coming of Coronado in 1540.

Old Hot-Tamale insists that if there were a drop of Spanish or Mexican blood in his veins, he would let it out. He was married in his early years to a Mexican woman, who made her departure from his home leaving behind mysteries, lies and many unpleasant situations, for the man to battle with, alone, until a woman with a heart came into his life, married him—mothered him—and was a real companion for many years. "Now I am eighty years old and need her," said old Charlie, "and she has gone from me forever. Since she died I am helpless like a little child without her.

"After she was took from me I just went to sleep and didn't know anything for a long, long time. Now I can't pull my wagon of hot-tamales, like I used to do, and the Roswell people miss the ol' tamale man they say. They like me. Friends come to my door often to pass the time of day. Some men took my picture just yesterday, and the finest painters come from away off and paint me and my tamale wagon, and they want to write stories about me. I haven't told any of them what I am going to tell you, and you must get it all down good, for it's history, and they want to keep it here in Roswell, always.

"They are stories of things that happened, and things I saw, and heard in these parts long before you was born, when there wasn't

*"'Chihuahua' District Roswell: The Hot-Tamale Man," coll. Georgia B. Redfield; 890 wds., 5 pp., 24 December 1936, rec. 27 December (A#186; LC47.1).

nothing, any where 'round here closer than Fort Stanton.

"I guess now you must bear with me some, for my recollection gets to dodgin' roun' and roun' when I try hard to remember important places and times.

"I been burnt out here two times by a low Mexican, for revenge when he got mad at me. You're right, mam, I don't talk like Mexicans talk, for I ain't Mexican—thank God! I'm Indian mostly. My mother was a full blood Choctaw Indian. Don't make no difference what other blood I has. I am just a man of honor and of my word.

"The first man I ever worked for in my life, besides my folks, was John Chisum when he lived in Denton County, Texas.

"I was a leader of pack outfits on horses for him in 1867 and we would be gone five or six days at a time, working cattle. I had seven pack leading horses and five other packmen had six.

"We would lead some and drive some, when we came to New Mexico by way of Castle Gap east of pontoon bridge on the Pecos River, where the old T X ranch used to be at Horse Head Crossing. We came up from there on the west side of the river, to Bosque Grande, about thirty-five miles northeast of where Roswell is now, but it was all wide dry prairie then, and lots of coyotes and prairie dogs and nothing else living until you got to six mile hill west and found antelope. The Pecos River was the deadline for buffalo. I never saw one west of the river in my life.

"I was with General McKenzie's outfit in 1872. He was a great Indian fighter, even before the time Geronimo commenced his murdering and stealing. Geronimo was a terrible hard Indian and all New Mexico dreaded and feared him. But they say there's honor even among thieves, and I never heard of him harming a woman or child.

"He was a bitter old man after he was in captivity at Fort Sill. He would stand for hours facing his old hunting ground, with his arms hanging helpless never saying a word.

It ain't because I have Indian blood in me I say it, but the whites crushed the Indian people who were here in this country first. Do you know what become of the Lost Tribe which came up missing when Moses was leading them through the wilderness? Well they swung around that mountain (it was Mt. Ebo I believe)—and they wandered 'roun and 'roun and finally crossed the narrow channel in the Canada course. They was the beginning of the Indian people Columbus found when he came. Once a lawyer asked an Indian, where he got some of his Masonary [*sic*]. The Indian said, 'we always had it,' and I believe they did have it before the whites.

"In 1874 I was with General Davison in the U.S. 10th Cavalry trying to capture Lone Wolf, a bad Indian who raided with the Comanches. We had eleven companies of soldiers, 2v [*sic*] pieces of artillery (cannon), 78 head of cattle, and nine cowboys. We pulled in and fixed up for a camp at White Fish, where we were going to cross McClelland Creek, and here comes a stampede of buffalo. We fought buffalo from nine to eleven at night. We had to block the charging buffalo with the dead ones as we shot them to keep them from running through our camp outfit. We had been short on supplies, eating only one hard tack for a meal. After that we had plenty of meat.

"What with Indians and buffalo you had to travel with your eyes open those days.

"I was manager of the bull ox train, for L. B. Anderson, buffalo hunter on the Staked Plains in 1875. I was one of the fifteen skinners in camp. We worked over three and four hundred buffalo some days. In September the general course of buffalo traveling was southwest and in summer it was northeast.

"I have skinned buffalo, herded sheep, cooked, drove bull ox wagons, and barbered here in Roswell. The last three years have doubled up on me for I've had it so hard since my wife died. I am all tired now. Some day I will tell you more. We will write a book of all the things I saw and did, before I was the old hot-tamale man."

John L. Sinclair remembers Roswell of the 1920s as "Where the Cowboys Hunkered Down." Among those who could be seen in serious conversation at Second and Main was Charlie Corn from the Diamond A sheep headquarters at Walnut, west of Artesia: "History has it that there lived in Roswell, down by the stageline station, in 1880, a man named Martin V. Corn. That was about the time they labeled the new town after the postmaster's father Roswell Smith. But they'd better have called it Cornville, or Cornstown, because Roswell was no more than a giant hub, and out of this hub sprouted spokes, and at the end of each was a ranch owned and operated by a master stockman surnamed Corn. Now the Corn ranches are everywhere—far west into Lincoln county, north on the Macho at Eden Valley, and yonder toward the sunrise, anywhere that cattle graze the grama grass flats."[13]

In order to write the chapter on "Martin V. Corn [1841–1915]: Founder of Largest Family of Chaves County Planted Trees of Lovers' Lane" for her projected manuscript, "Pioneer Builders of Roswell in the Sunshine State of New Mexico," Georgia B. Redfield interviewed one of his sons, Robert Lafayette Corn of 812 North Richardson Avenue, Roswell, in April 1937.[14]*

"My father Martin V. Corn was born in North Carolina. He moved to Texas when a young boy. He was married in Texas April 25, 1867, to Mary Jane Hampton. He came with his wife (who was my mother) and the seven of us first children to New Mexico in 1879. I was five years old.

"We came in a caravan with four or five other families in covered wagons. Bill and Ed Hudson, Bill Holliman, Lon Spencer and Ike Teeters were some of the men. A man named Horn was leader of the Caravan, and he drove the cattle.

"I never will forget that trip. I remember we had tin type pictures taken, and after we got to New Mexico we made camp at Seven Rivers and most of the men went on to Ros-

well and Lincoln, prospecting. While they were gone Hudson killed Ike Teeters when they got into some kind of argument.

"My father liked this part of the country so we settled just east of Roswell, on South Spring River, five miles southeast of Roswell, just south of Lovers' Lane. Father set out the trees of Lover's Lane, on the south side, and Oregon Bell set them out on the north side, on what is now the L. F. D. Ranch, which Bell owned and afterwards sold to John W. Poe.

"Pat Garrett contracted to have the 'dobes and walls of our house made. The house is still there. You can see it looking south from Lover's Lane.

"While we were waiting for our house to

---

*"Martin V. Corn: Founder Largest Family of Chaves County (Given by Son R. L. Corn)," coll. Georgia B. Redfield, 14 April 1937; 384 wds., 3 pp., 15 April 1937, rec. 17 April (A#186; LC38.1; LC47.1).

be built, all nine of us lived in a dug out and one tent, and for a while in a sod house on the creek" (South Spring River).

"In 1881 I went to school to Judge Rogers. He was the first teacher in this part of the country and taught in this first school built three miles out East Second Street. The school was a one-room dirt-roofed adobe. I afterwards went to Miss Sara Lund, who is now Mrs. C. D. Bonney, who taught in a better and larger building, built in 1885 across the Hondo a half mile southeast of Roswell.[15]

"In 1900 I was married to Miss Maggie Bowden—a teacher—and we have six sons, Fred, Richard, Irwin, Alton, and twins—Donald and Roland. There are ranches enough for all of them spread all over the country.

"The Roswell people say the Corn men are bound to be ranchmen. No matter how much education they get they finally go back to ranching.

"The children born to Father's first mar-riage to Mary Jane Hampton were four girls, Mary, Minty, Eva and Sally who was a baby when we came to New Mexico and four boys, John, Bob (that's me), Mart and George. George was born after we came to New Mexico.

"Father's second marriage was to Julia McVicker on October 14, 1886.

"The children of the second marriage were three girls, Minnie, May, and Lillian, and eight boys, Waid, Lee, Charlie, Jess, Roe, Hub, Poe, and Clarence—nineteen children in all and a few extra ones our parents raised with us.

"The family has multiplied considerably and helped swell the population of this part of New Mexico.

"Father died at the age of seventy-six years. He was buried as he requested, at his 'Eden Valley Ranch,' twenty miles north of Roswell."

R. L. Corn's sister, May Corn Marley of 102 North
Kentucky Avenue, Roswell, told Georgia B. Redfield
about her father planting the trees of Lovers' Lane.[16]*

"I am May, the second daughter of my father's marriage to Julie McVicker. I was married to C. A. Marley March 4, 1906. We have a son and had a daughter Inez who died two years ago.

"There has been much discussion about who set out the trees on Roswell's old land-marks and place of interest—Lover's Lane—about five miles southeast of Roswell. I know who set them out and who cared for them for many years, and it should be written now as one of the important subjects to be pre-served in the records of Chaves County.

"Soon after my father settled on the old home site of the Corn family south of Lover's Lane—John Chisum came to him one day and said, 'Corn, I'll make you a proposition if you set out trees here along this ditch I'll get the trees. We need trees, lots of 'em on these hot dry prairies.'

"My father said he would plant them and care for them so Chisum sent two ox wagons to Alpine, Texas, in the Davis Mountains and got the cottonwood and willow trees. My father set them out and he and my sister Mary and the old darky we called 'Nigger Dick' whom everybody knew would watch and trim those trees and set the trimmings

*"May Corn Marley," coll. Georgia B. Redfield on 16 April 1937; 300 wds., 2 pp., 16 April 1937, rec. 17 April (HC:Roswell; LC38.1; LC47.1).

Martin V. Corn (#40916, WPA Collection, Persons Known, NMSRC).

out. They grew fast and soon made the beautiful lane which has been a favorite drive for young people, especially lovers, for nearly sixty years. Oregon Bell set some of the trees out on his land on the north side of the lane.

"J. P. White told me just before he died that every time he started to drive cattle through that lane my father would say, 'Be sure to keep the cattle from destroying any of those trees, White.' Mr. White said he would always promise to watch them and all of the thousands of cattle he drove through the lane, not one ever touched those trees that my father and John Chisum loved and tended so carefully.[17]

"When my father and family came to New Mexico they brought three or four hundred head of cattle and a hundred head of horses. He loved horses. He raised the horse that Billy the Kid made his escape on, when he broke jail in Lincoln after killing Brady. It was a black horse. Pat Garrett bought him from my father and named him 'Black Mart' after my father.

"My father loved his Eden Valley Ranch home, where he died and is buried.

"All of his sons like ranch life and have ranch homes scattered over all southeast New Mexico.

"I am like all the rest of the Corn children, I prefer my ranch home and only come for short visits to this nice home you see here in Roswell."

Many of the cowboys who "hunkered down" at Second and Main in Roswell purchased saddles and harness from E[lijah] T[homas] Amonett, who bought Max Goslin's Saddle and Harness Shop, the first of its kind in Roswell (started in the 1890s), on July 15, 1901. Operating first at 122 North Main Street and later at 210 North Main and then 211 West Third Street, the business eventually was given to Edd [Edwin Irvin] Amonett (died 1963) in 1913 by his father, who moved to El Paso and opened a saddlery and leather shop there.[18] Famous cowboy bootmaker Beecher Lank, who was interviewed by Georgia B. Redfield in 1938, worked for the Amonetts.[19]*

Beecher Lank, New Mexico cowboy bootmaker, was born at Lafayette, Indiana, on May 11, 1851. He has been making boots sixty-nine of the eighty-seven years of his life.

He was seventeen years of age when he first began making his way in the world by selling newspapers. He remembers selling over two hundred and fifty papers on the day, May 19, 1868, that General Grant was unanimously nominated for the presidency.

In 1869, when he was eighteen, he began making boots in Kansas City, Missouri, and while working continuously at bootmaking he gradually made his way west. He made cowboy boots for many years in Texas and for a while in Arizona before coming to Roswell, New Mexico, in 1914. He has made cowboy boots continuously for over twenty-four years at Amonett's, the oldest saddle and boot shop in Roswell and southeast New Mexico. For more than an average lifetime Mr. Lank has bent over machines patiently working out beautiful designs in decorative stitching and carefully shaping and building sturdy arches for as fine boots as can be made anywhere in the United States.

When he first began making boots in Kansas City Ulysses S. Grant was president of the United States. There was no Roswell in New Mexico and the Chisums were blazing the trails for the first herds of cattle that were brought from Texas to the Pecos Valley, and John Chisum had not yet established the famous Jingle-Bob Ranch at the head of South Spring River, six miles southeast of what is now Roswell. Mr. Lank cannot give even an approximate number of the thousands of boots he turned out during the years when a cowman was judged by the boots he wore.

"Things are different now," he said, "since the cattle business is not the most important industry in this part of the country, but I am still making lots of fine boots for the old cattlemen who want the real cowboy boots they can be proud of and that can be worn in comfort. I don't work as fast as I used to but I will show you I can still do a good job."

The boots he proudly brought out for inspection proved indeed that he not only could "do a good job" on their construction but that he was a master of the trade of which he has made an art anyone might be proud of mastering.

"I can make all kinds of boots," said Mr. Lank, "fancy ones like these or plain ones, and I make shoes too. I don't work as fast though as I used to when I was younger for I am getting old and slowing up. I like to

*"Beecher Lank: New Mexico Cowboy Bootmaker," coll. Georgia B. Redfield "from a personal interview with Mr. Lank himself"; 740 wds., 4 pp., 12 August 1938, rec. 15 August (A#186; LC38.1; LC47.1).

"Hobbs, New Mexico. Mar 1940. Stores in an oil boom town."
Photo by Russell Lee. LC-USF 34-35818-D.)

make them, like to think about who will wear them when they are finished and try to imagine what kinds of places they will be worn in, but I am getting tired. I would like to rest for the years I have left to live if I didn't have to pay for part of my keep. I get a little old age pension but it's just enough to pay my landlady. I board with Mrs. Long at 205 East Seventh Street."

When asked if he didn't have any relatives he replied: "I don't know. I was married and had a daughter Pearl. I don't know where she is now or if she's living or not. I married a girl named Jennie Moore but she died a long time ago, I don't remember when.

"No," he replied when asked if he could tell any stories of interest that have happened in his life. "I don't remember things very well any more. I saw Grant and heard him speak in Kansas City in 1880. I saw McKinley there too, and Teddy Roosevelt."

When asked if he liked Roswell he said: "Yes, and I like to work for Mr. Amonett. He is always good to me and all the other workers make it as easy for me as they can. Everybody I know is good to me."

His patient, kind eyes lighted up in appreciation as he talked of kindness shown him. He was gentle and pleasant and smiled all the time he talked during our interview, showing a mouth full of strong white teeth— all of his own, which is remarkable for a man of his age. He doesn't wear glasses either except for reading and close-up work.

"Oh, yes," he said. "I forgot I did have something interesting happen in my life. Just a month or two ago I got a letter from Governor Clyde Tingley, a birthday letter. Here it is. Read it."

I took it from him and read the few kind words that cheered and made happier the old man who had been alone for many of these last birthdays of his life that should have been happier.

"Now wasn't that a fine thing for our governor to remember an old man like me on his birthday?"

"It was indeed!" was my reply, and I truly thought it was. The letter dated May 11, 1938, is given below:

Dear Mr. Lank: Congratulations on your eighty-seventh birthday! Mrs. Tingley and I sincerely hope that you may enjoy many more happy birthdays. Cordially yours, Clyde Tingley.

The kind birthday wishes of Governor and Mrs. Tingley find an echo in the hearts of the many Roswell friends of Mr. Lank.

Until the early 1900s Roswell was county seat for a much larger Chaves County, which included future counties of Curry, Roosevelt and Lea.[20] Mrs. Lena S. Maxwell interviewed oldtimers and detailed the history of the Curry County settlements in a 1938 manuscript, "As It Happened in Curry County." She described natural abundance and disasters after homesteaders began arriving.*

In 1906 New Mexico was opened for filing. Emigrant cars lined the railroads. Prairie schooners, the covered wagons, made wider the then dim roads. The big six-inch rain that fell in seven hours caused such an underground moisture that brought grama grass waist high. Many farmers mowed it and stored it for a hay crop. Some sod forage crop was harvested too.

Then in 1907 vegetables grew quickly and to unbelievable size on sod. All this was heard back east by those who had come, filed, gone back to wind up business there and get here by the end of six months' filing to keep from being contested. Even a sweet potato as large as a pitcher raised on the Bill Mersefelder farm north of Texico was taken back east to prove the productiveness of New Mexican soil. The idea that all you had to do was to put anything in the ground and harrow it then it would grow to maturity without further effort. The settlers who came expected to prove up on the fourteen months' plan or to stay. Most of those expected hardships and met them in the true pioneer spirit.

But here ill winds do blow, and about November 15, 1906, a prairie fire started west of Melrose. The people in the Grady and Bellview country saw it coming for two nights and one day before it struck them about sunrise after the second night. Four hours more put this fire in Hereford. Then the wind changed. The fire [was] going [from the] south to [the] north side of the Santa Fe R.R. [when] a slight wind change sent the fire west traveling along the railroad to a

*From "As it Happened in Curry County," by Lena S. Maxwell (A#191).

plowed field west to Melrose where the set-tlers gathered with water to wet sacks with which to fight it. They won.

But the havoc wrought by this fire caused suffering to man and beast that winter. Nearly all the feed was destroyed and barns, corrals, chicken houses and houses burned. Many of the stock were burned too badly to recover sufficiently for working purposes.

Mr. J. T. Trapp northeast of Grady had an old mare that all the stock would follow. He loosed all his stock and had one of his boys ride this mare and drive the cows. The other horses followed to a big lake about one-fourth mile from the house. The cows were driven in, the mare ridden in. Other horses followed. This means saved unharmed all his stock. By Mr. Trapp's coolness he was able to save his barns and tent but lost most of his chickens.

Mr. Turner, a neighbor of Mr. Trapp, was less fortunate. He untied some of his stock, hoping they would escape. But when he went to help his son Euell untie two white mules from a wagon the worst was on. Mr. Turner's hands and arms were burned so he did not work for months. The two mules had all their hair and their ears burned off—they got well. Euell's face was so badly burned that today his right jaw lies open to his ear. Neighbors were kind to them, nursed them, and divided what they had left with them. This fire left prairies bare and the grass next year short. All range cattle was moved to Texas. The stragglers left ate loco and became worthless.

A blizzard that raged for forty-eight hours and heavy snow followed on the sixteenth of November. This put an end to the dumb brutes' misery. Some chicken, hogs and cattle were saved.

After all this did they go back east and sit down? No, they realized what had to be done and did it. Today they and their sons are some of the most substantial farmers of Curry County. When crops there failed, feed was hauled from south of Texico. Some years the southern farmers had to go to the north part of the country to get feed. This section of settlers did not give up.

They mixed a little fun along with their hardships. Mr. John F. Smithson, Grady's longstanding real estate man, helped out in so many ways. He was happy if he had some-thing to eat and a dollar in his pocket. Then you may look out for something from him. With all his tricks he wasn't smart enough to answer Mr. John Manning when he asked, "How would you know which way the emi-grants were going—east or west?" But Man-ning was obliging and told him that people going west left a trail of cans while those going east discarded packages found to be wrapped in jack rabbit hides.

Uncle Charlie Smith of Melrose told Mrs. Lena S. Maxwell about his life.*

I came here from Boliver [*sic:* Bolivar], Polk County, Missouri, forty miles north of Springfield, in January 1906. I've had the privilege of seeing every house in Melrose go up—every one of them. There was not a thing here when I came. Not a building, no railroad, depot, tree, barb wire fence or anything when I came. The townsite had been laid out and plowed in furrows with a horse and plow. The furrows showed the streets and alleys.

T. B. S. Denby was the United States

*"Told By Uncle Charlie Smith (Relation of Mr. C. C. Smith)" to Mrs. Lena S. Maxwell, 8 pp. (A#191).

Commissioner here. B. J. Norby was assistant to Denby. Denby was the man we all filed before and proved up before.

I know something about hard times in Melrose, New Mexico. We had lots of hardships. I hauled every drop of water I used for four and one-half years. For my stock, cows, hogs, horses, chickens and household purposes. Hauled all the water we had and paid ten cents a barrel, or three barrels for twenty-five cents and hauled some of it five miles.

When I landed here in 1906, we could go to Tucumcari, Texico or Portales as trading points. But when I came I brought an immigrant car and enough groceries to last me twelve months—all kinds of groceries.

I located three and one-half miles north of here when I moved in. I brought my wife and five children, and we lived for three months in a little box shack, 10 × 12, with a dirt floor. Finally I got to build more room and was just finishing the new room, nailing on the last shingle one Saturday afternoon when I saw a prairie fire coming. My shack was too small to get all of our furniture in that I brought out here, and I had part of it stored in another shack. I was afraid the fire would burn that, so I took my team and went and plowed around that shack to save my furniture. The fire did not come to my house.

This was on Saturday evening, about the seventeenth of November when the grass and everything was dead, and the fire swept quickly where it went. But before it reached my house a blizzard, the most terrible one I ever have seen, hit it and put out the fire. My cow and two horses suffered intensely. I brought the cow inside of our new room to protect her from the awful storm. I took some pieces of an old homemade carpet and spread over my horses, but one of them died anyway. Then I was left with one horse, and I had to haul water on a sled with it.

I bought an old mule to help make a crop the next summer. The old mule helped make two or three crops. I kept him till he died.

Two of my daughters, Mrs. Rosie Kennedy

and Mrs. Oscar McGruder, and one son, Carl Smith, and I still live in and around Melrose. My other two children are living— one, Rebecca Evans, in Stockton, California, the other, Omer Smith, in Cottage Grove, Oregon.

W. S. Turner was one of the first, if not the first peace officer here.

In 1906 and 1907 this land went like hot cakes. People came in here by the hundreds. About ten months after I came all the land close around town was taken up and people had to file out about McAlister. This country was going fast. Excursion trains ran every two weeks.

My first wife died during the World War, and our oldest boy was in France. He couldn't come home, and it took a letter thirty days to reach its destination. We had several letters on the road all the time.

Mrs. Norby's (Curless) father dug the public well. It was free water and people went to get water at all hours of the day and night, and each had to wait their turn, just like going to mill. I have climbed upon the windmill tower and turned the wheel by hand to get three and four barrels of water when there was no wind.

John Franklin from Boliver, Missouri, filed on land one mile west and four miles north of McAlister that looked good to him. He was the first to file on that section, so he went back home and came back on the next excursion in two weeks and brought three daughters, who filed on the other three quarters, as one quarter of a section was all one could file on. They built a four-room house right in the middle of the section. So each quarter had a building on it.

Melrose thought she was going to get the roundhouse. The Santa Fe spent over $100,000.00 on the roundhouse here and had it built up as high as the windows, then tore it down and moved it to Clovis. They had no inducements here.

When we filed here, the filing cost was sixteen dollars (ten cents an acre). Five years was the time given to prove up; but extension could be obtained to reach seven years to prove up. In eighteen months from date of filing, for $225 Uncle Sam would give a deed.

In five years, 1910, land sold for five dollars an acre. A Mr. Cooke filed three and one-half miles northwest of town. He and two sons and one daughter filed on one whole section No. 20. They lived here two years, made one crop, and sold out at five dollars an acre in 1907.

Fairplay, Missouri, was my home. It was near Boliver. I like this country. It is good all-around country. Every country has its drawbacks. Here we have high winds, sand storms, etc. Back east, we have damp rainy weather and fog so thick you could cut it with a knife. This is a healthful country. I've known dozens of people to come here with tuberculosis, come out of it and look red, rosy and healthful, and become dissatisfied, sell out and go back where they came from, and in eighteen months time be dead.

Dr. Bugg was a man of this type. He came here in 190? [sic] walking on two sticks. He filed out about four miles north of town, lived there about two years, I believe, relinquished his claim and moved to Melrose. He began to improve so fast that he gained in health as a fattening-hog gains when fed all he will eat. He began to practice and was a good physician. He was our doctor. Finally he went back to Kentucky on business. He started home, back to Melrose and for some reason he stopped in some of the low, swampy lands of Texas where the cottonmouth snake is. There was quite an opening there for one of his profession so he decided he'd locate there.

He wrote his wife, telling her his plans and asking her to sell the property here and for her and their two little girls to come to him, that he was too busy to stop and come after them, and for her to dispose of everything. So she did. She sold their house and everything, and she and her girls went to him. Mrs. Bugg had made many friends while here, and members of her friends [sic] wanted her to write back sometime and tell them how they were getting along. In the course

of around two months' time, she wrote to some of them saying Dr. Bugg was sick. The next hearing he was in the hospital. And in about six months, or less than a year, he was buried.

This is such a fine health country for those from the east who have tuberculosis. Lots of people get well. If not well, their lives are prolonged.

Melrose used to have lots more people than are here now. Just across the street, west, from Mr. Farrar's filling station is the foundation today where there was a big two-story hotel. It was a railroad hotel. When they moved the roundhouse to Clovis that hotel was torn down and moved to Clovis too. Lots of houses in our town have been moved out. Some to Clovis, some out in the country.

Dr. Swearingen who used to be here is at Roswell. He and Dr. Lynch practiced together.

The principal crops when we first came out were Indian corn, kafir corn, maize, sorghum, beans, millet and broomcorn. I planted one crop of broomcorn, about fifteen or twenty acres. I didn't know anything about it and got it too thick. It only made some feed. I never did fool with broomcorn any more.

I planted corn that made fifty bushels to the acre. One year I planted some kafir corn and only got about a half stand. I didn't know what to do but finally decided I'd burst the middles and replant in something else. So on the Fourth of July I replanted in sorghum. There came a good rain and it came up good. I went over it with a harrow and it was as clean as could be. It kept raining along and in ten days it was a foot high. I went over it again with the harrow. Two cultivatings and that with a harrow was all that sorghum got. Oscar McGruder cut it the first of October. The rows were nearly a quarter of a mile long, and he cut forty bundles to the row. Some was in head, some in boot. I sold these bundles for ten cents a bundle. One man from up north bought $200.00 worth.

He came by the field and bought it and paid me $100.00 down. This land produced sorghum at forty dollars an acre and the land itself was worth about five dollars.

I sold headed maize for forty dollars a ton in the early days, in 1905, 1909, 1910. We got good prices for our farm products.

Mr. Pickens, the husband of the late Mrs. Pickens, used to run a tin shop here and made galvanized water tanks and galvanized casing for wells. I cased my well with deep well Artesian casing and it is still there and will be there when Gabriel blows his horn. That well is one of the best in the country and was known by everybody far and near. Travelers would make it a point to stop there and get water. Its supply was inexhaustible. Can't be pumped dry. One day Oscar McGruder decided he'd pump that well dry but he couldn't. He pumped for fourteen hours with a gasoline engine and it was still throwing as good a stream when he stopped as when he had been pumping for thirty minutes.

In 1910–1911 a good many people left. I couldn't leave, but I had to borrow money to stay. We had some pretty hard, dry years. The best I recollect, I made enough feed, my first crop in 1907, to do me. I never did make a complete failure. Sometimes I only made about enough feed to do me, sometimes I had to buy some. But I always made something.

One thing that was so bad in the early days was people could hardly shelter themselves. Some difference then and now: Now people have good shelter for themselves and also good shelter for their stock. So many of the stock froze in the cold snowy times back yonder.

In 1929 the biggest wheat crop I've ever seen in this country was raised. Lee Wrinkle, W. K. Hollifield, and C. L. Tennison bought wheat and piled it out on the ground in great big piles. We had some rains and the wheat got wet and lots of it was lost. I've seen trucks lined up from the post office to the depot, waiting their turn to get unloaded.

And when they could unload, they would drive up to a place and scoop the wheat out on the ground. There was some difficulty in getting railroad cars.

I've known newcomers to go north of here and buy wheat land, all on credit. And the first crop would pay for the land and have half of it left.

The basement under Cal Mathey's store I dug with teams and scrapers. We took hoes and shovels and straightened up the walls. Cal Mathey's wife and my mother were sisters.

This is a strange thing and seldom known: My father and my mother were each of a family of fourteen children, seven girls and seven boys, equally divided in each of the two families.

We made all of our clothing. I never bought a ready-made shirt until I lost my first wife. I lost her on the eighth of September, 1918. I bought material and my wife did all our sewing. You couldn't get "ready-to-wear" like you can today. We could get some things ready-made, but not everything.

Money is never wasted when invested in good books for the home. Children can be greatly benefited by the proper kind of literature in the home. Anything that tends toward infidelity should not be allowed where they can get it.

I remember one family; the mother was a Christian and the father an infidel. The father brought his literature and the mother hers for the children to read. One daughter, who was grown, had a long, lingering spell of illness. The time came when she realized she was not going to live. She called her infidel father to the bedside and asked him one very pointed question. She said, "Papa, you all have kept from telling me of my condition, but I know I can't get well. I've got to go. Now, whose God must I rely upon?" The father was put to a very serious test. He sat there a while without a word. Then he says: "Daughter, rely on Mother's God."

I also remember another family where both the father and mother were infidels. No

Christian literature or influence in the home. One daughter wanted to go to church but was forbidden. She would ask to spend nights at the homes of different girl friends, and she would go with them to church. She heard the preaching and was converted. She went to the altar and her parents heard about it. They didn't chide her roughly; they knew it would not do, but they tried to reason with her.

They were wealthy, had everything money could buy. They kept talking and working with the girl, and finally she yielded to them.

Her father promised anything she wanted, such as the finest of clothing. They wanted her to stay in society. She bought the finest piece of silk that she could find and was going to have it made up in the most elaborate way to wear to a ball. But before she got it made she was taken sick. She called for her father and told him to go to her drawer and bring her the new dress. He went and got it. She fingered the beautiful material, tenderly talking to her father as she did so, saying: "Isn't this pretty? Isn't it fine? But father, this is the price of my soul."

Clyde Stanfield told J. Vernon Smithson about early difficulties with water.*

There were more families on the territory in 1907 than there are today, but these families did not stay here throughout the year. In the early fall they would pick cotton under the east caprock. After cotton picking time, however, they would return to their homesteads. In the winter the chief employment of the settlers was the securing of wood and posts from the "brakes." Wood was very essential to withstand the severe blizzards to which this country is subjected.

All groceries and merchandise were secured from Texico, for this was long before Clovis was begun. Three days were required to make the trip: one day to go, one day for the team to rest and purchases to be made, and one day to return. Mr. Stanfield was engaged in the freighting business for seven years, and he had many interesting experiences on the road.

The way in which water was secured is an interesting story in itself. The only windmill for miles around was the 3T mill, situated in what is now known as the Pettigrew Lake and owned by a syndicate whose headquarters

were at Prairie View. Prairie View was the first post office near here and was located northwest of Grady.

Each day twenty or thirty wagons came to the well for water. Some of them drove many miles and sometimes had to stay all day to fill their containers. The method of getting water was this: the men lined up with their twelve-quart buckets and took their turns at the windmill.

One day there were about thirty wagons waiting for water at the 3T mill. All the men except one had twelve-quart pails, and this one had a bucket that would hold half a bushel. The other men became angry because he was getting more than his share of water, which had to be caught from the pipe. The mill was pumping very slowly and each man was jealous lest another should get more than he.

The anger of these men finally resulted in a fight. The man possessing the large bucket was hurt quite badly. He was forced to give up his big pail and used a twelve-quart pail thereafter.

*"Old Timer's Tales," coll. J. Vernon Smithson for S-240-Folk-Ways from Clyde Stanfield; 400 wds., 2 pp., 26 October 1936 (A#191; H5-4-5#7; LC47.1).

"Magdalena, New Mexico. April 1940. Windmill which furnishes water for private residences. Magdalena is the trading center for nearby ranchers." Photo by Russell Lee. LC-USF 34-35869-D.

Clovis businessman C. V. Steed was interviewed by
Mrs. Lena S. Maxwell before his death in 1938.*

The first telephones and telephone wires in Curry County were built by Mr. C. V. Steed, who filed on what is now the Andy Moore place south of Clovis stock yards. But at that time Mr. Steed was living with Mr. Clayton Reed on Mr. Reed's filing where the monument now stands.

Mr. Steed built this line from Texico to Riley's Switch, which was where the underpass on Prince Street now is. The wires were strung on the "Right of Way" posts. The first box was put in the post office. A Mr. Palmer was postmaster. Later the post office was moved across the track to where the Citizens' Bank now stands. The telephone went right along with the post office.

Late in the spring of 1906 Mr. Steed extended the telephone line to Melrose. He put in boxes all along the line.

Mr. Steed in his modest way related to Mrs. Lena S. Maxwell two weeks before his death the building of this line but she gathered from other sources the following:

Mr. Steed had served Clovis twenty-nine years and had been in the undertaking business at 112 West Grand Avenue twenty-five years. He died Sunday, June 5, 1938. His was the largest funeral ever in Clovis. This alone speaks for the man who, in the spring of 1906, came to Clovis from Kansas City, Missouri, to seek a place in the newest of the new countries of the Southwest. Born in the blue hills of North Carolina, the Great Plains country was far different from anything he had seen, and he frankly admitted that its endless stretches brought many a lonesome moment to him.

As it had drawn him, the Southwest was beckoning to hundreds of others, and Steed soon found he was in the midst of a clamoring crowd seeking new homes in the new country. This offered him the first business opportunity, and he formed a real estate partnership with Clayton Reed, who, by the way, yet resides in this region and is operating a farm.

Steed and Reed opened their real estate offices in a little frame shack on the site of the present Montgomery Ward building on Main, and for several months they spent their time locating newcomers on land adjacent to Clovis. Reed owned a farm which included that portion of the city east of the First Baptist church. Reed's farm became part of the townsite when the railroad planned its new cut-off between Texico and Belen, with Clovis scheduled to be a division point.[21]

Those were real frontier days, filled with privations, hardships and hopes. Clovis was just a shack town in the midst of seemingly endless prairies. But it was in new country, and new country meant opportunities. Steed took his chance, and for twenty-nine years had made this city his home and his pride.

*"The First Telephones and C. V. Steed," by Lena S. Maxwell, 2 pp. (A#191).

Mrs. Lena S. Maxwell described "Curry County's Inland Towns" of Grady, Hollene, Pleasant Hill, Claude, Ranchvale, Bellview, Field, and Fairfield. "Each has an interesting history, but Grady being about the oldest and best known back east—also the home of the writer—will be dwelt upon first."*

This little town founded December 13, 1906, is thirty-six miles northwest of Clovis. Mrs. Pearl Grady, now of Texico, named this town. She owned much land in and around Grady. She gave a lot as a present to the first child who was born at Grady. Grady Box was the lucky baby.

A dugout to shelter the people who came to file was made on the site where Dr. John Hale's home is now. In boom days Clovis was hardly known back east, but you would hear Grady spoken of as the future railroad center of the prospective railroad north to connect with the Rock Island. Even large tracts of land and many a bonus was subscribed to finance this road. Today there is no prospect of a railroad through the Grady country, for the good highways have filled the needs of a railroad.

Grady has not grown. About two hundred inhabitants now, but the consolidation of surrounding school districts has resulted in Grady having a large high school which was held in new buildings this year.

The agricultural district has enabled many of the original filers to become permanent citizens. Among these are: John F. Smithson, Johnny Hamilton, Dr. John Hale, the Stanfield brothers, the Carters, McIntoshes, Bryants, Warrens, W. I. Simms, Boxes, Graus, Vandevenders, and Bordens.

The first three years were the hardest for the settlers in all parts of Curry County. Their clothes were worn out, patched and repatched. Very little funds to buy new ones. Provisions they brought along were gone. The little debts owed them back East had

been paid. They no longer could look to the East for money, but "a willing mind finds the way."

Cows shipped with their goods had increased. This supplied some families with milk. A few gardens were made, some corn for roasting ears and hominy and Mexican beans stored for winter helped to supply the table. But always some are not thrifty.

One family north of Grady ran out of food. All they had was crushed maize made up with salt and water for bread. A neighbor learned this. He sent them a two-bushel sack of black-eyed peas that he had shipped here to plant. When these were gone they still needed food and this same neighbor sent them another two bushels, but this time it was crowder peas. Before these were all eaten, two of the grown boys were stricken with erysipelas.[22] Mr. C. J. Kempf, the same neighbor, had a fresh jersey cow. What milk was not needed for the calf was taken to these sick boys. They recovered. When Mr. Kempf and his wife moved back to Kentucky years later, this unfortunate family mourned at their going almost as much as they did several years later when this old couple passed away.

After the third spring, gardens and feed patches were made. Some food for man and beast was stored. Chickens, tame cattle and hogs had multiplied. The people had learned to farm in this country. They began to see their way. They were kind to neighbors and visitors, were a happy people. They made Grady a town that will always be on the map.

Claude [sic] was first located on the Claude Kelley filing west of Pleasant Hill and over

*From "Curry County's Inland Towns," by Lena S. Maxwell, 1938 (A#191).

"Claud (vicinity), New Mexico. June 1938. Great Plains homesteads and a sheep barn." Photo by Dorothea Lange. LC-USF 34-18270-C.

twelve miles north of Clovis. Here Mr. Kelley, now of Clovis, built a store and had a flourishing business. Claude was the town's postmaster. A $12,000 school building was erected two miles east of this store. Today it supports two teachers.

Claude became noted for wheat crops. In 1910 Cyclone Jones raised such a crop of wheat that wheat raising began all over Curry County. He got a yield of twenty bushels to the acre. Some farmers have raised more. Some years wheat is a failure. Some crops are good. This town once aspired to be county seat of Curry County but according to law the county seat must be on a railroad. Then Claude threw her votes to Clovis. Claude today does not have even a business house. She exists in name only.

"June 1938. Dust Bowl farmer driving tractor, with young son. Near Claud, New Mexico. 'I left cotton-growing east of Wichita Falls to come out here to get to grow wheat. (The superior status of wheat over cotton farmers is traditional.) I guess I've made 1000 miles right up and down this field in the dust when you couldn't see that car on the road, and had to use your headlights. This soil is the best there is anywhere, but it sure does blow when it's right. If you stay in the house and wait for the dust to stop, you won't make a crop. But I've seen only one year since I came here in 1920 that I didn't make *something*.'" Photo by Dorothea Lange. LC-USF 34-18267-C.

Mrs. Maxwell wrote an autobiographical manuscript entitled "Schools and Teachers of Curry County," in which she claimed: "Then and now I'm welcome in the old homes left and the new ones made by my pupils of that day. There is a time perhaps when I draw my Teacher's pension—(The Attn. Gen. has ruled I am eligible)—and do not have to work so steady, then I can visit my old pupils and have our love feasts and dream of those dear old days."[23] Mrs. Maxwell also told her story to Mrs. Belle Kilgore of Clovis in 1937.*

Mrs. Lena Kempf Maxwell [*sic*] was born in Adamsville, Logan County, Kentucky, in 1874. She came with her father C. J. Kempf in 1908 to New Mexico and took up land according to the fourteen-month plan at that time. They could take up only 160 acres. They filed four miles north of Grady, New Mexico, west of State Highway Number Eighteen.

"Yes, I have had sorrow and privations mixed with the pleasant things that come to the life of a pioneer. I had been a bride, a mother and a widow all within the space of one year. I came with my father, C. J. Kempf, and settled near Grady in 1908.

"I had been prepared for a teacher and had taught four years when we came to New Mexico. I was a high school graduate, had training in the teacher normals in Kentucky and attended Bethel Female College and held a sixteen year's state certificate from Kentucky, but I had to begin again to prepare for teaching in New Mexico, for nothing but work from accredited colleges from other states will be recognized in this state. I entered the college at Las Vegas and continued my work until I acquired a college degree and thereby a lifetime certificate. I have taught sixteen years in New Mexico and have been principal of some of the best rural schools in New Mexico and incidentally in the United States. The equipment for these schools was purchased by money made from pie suppers, tackey parties and festivals common in this state. There were also some private donations.

"Yes, we have had 'hard times'—cold weather, hot weather, storms, snows, and fires and other inconveniences common to people on the frontier. There have been years when people were compelled to use a great deal of ingenuity to be able to stick to their claims.

"One story is told of a family after years of dry weather who ground maize in a coffee mill because there was not enough of the maize to pay the toll if it was taken to the mill to be ground. At one time there was no fuel, so the mother soaked her beans several days in water and then they ate them without seasoning or salt. But these were rare instances, for the homesteaders were thrifty people and even instances like the above were caused by circumstances and not because the people were thriftless.

"I remember about the prairie fire that swept everything from the face of the earth reaching from the southwest of Grady and Belleview [*sic*] to the northwest and as far as Clayton, New Mexico. One boy was caught out with his mules. The child's face was burned so badly and only his teeth on one side was left. The mules were so badly burned that they had to be killed.

"Storms! An electric storm where we lived, four miles south of Grady and six miles directly south of the edge of the caprock. It was sometime in August. A big cloud stretched from east to west, which was the blackest

*"Mrs. Lena Kempf Maxwell, School Teacher & Museum Manager, Clovis, New Mexico," coll. Mrs. Belle Kilgore; 1150 wds., 6 pp., 26 June 1937 (A#192; LC47.1).

and angriest that I have ever seen. The horses had come up and waited across the road. I knew that something had to be done to get them away from the wire fence. The cows were against the fence too. My daughter and I got buckets of grain maize heads and went across to where the horses were. After flashes of lightning we crawled under the wire and ran down to the other end of the pasture and scattered the heads of grain. After the horses began to eat we went back to the house, leaving the bars of a lot down. When we went into the house and closed the doors there were little sparks of electricity all through the room just like sassafras wood sparks from an open fireplace popping from the fire. The lightning got continually worse. We took the metal hairpins out of our hair and I took off my corset which had steel staves in it. We put on our night dress and crawled into a fifty-pound feather bed. My daughter put her arms around me. I said, 'Do not do that dear, if I am struck and killed it will kill you too.' She cried, 'Mama if you are killed I do not want to live.' So we lay clasped in each other's arms until the electrical display had passed over, which seemed at least an hour. That is the most terrible experience that I have ever gone through with. That was perhaps in 1914 or '15.

"I think that it was in 1910 that we had a very severe snow storm. It was necessary for my father to send some money to the bank. He saw a man who was going to Clovis from Grady so he gave the money to him. That night after he had given the money to the man he heard of some of his dishonest dealings, so he awoke me about twelve o'clock and told me to get a horse from the stable and lead him to my brother-in-law's about three quarters of a mile and tell my brother to go to Grady and get the money and take it himself. The snow had been on the ground for seven weeks and the reason I had to lead the horse was because the ice was so slippery that my father was afraid for me to ride. I had to go across the pasture and open the gates. I was nearly frozen when I arrived. I awakened the family and my brother-in-law set out for Grady at once. My sister begged me to stay until morning, but I knew that my father would be uneasy, so after resting a half hour and drinking some coffee I started home. Just outside the yard gate I heard the wolves, but I went on. I found a stick and waved them back, but they came to within fifteen feet of me. I waved the stick and flung my bonnet around my head several times and hallooed at them. I was at the pasture gate and I thought that they would get me, but as I went through I yelled at them and threw the stick and ran with all my might to the house. The wolves were famished for they could find nothing to eat in the two or three feet of snow. They had eaten several young calves and colts in the pastures and human flesh would taste just as good to them. They attacked some school children at San Jon, a small school not far away, but the older children fought them off.

"During the same time my sister and I climbed a snow bank fifteen feet high to reach a feed stack on the other side. At one end of the stack the snow was not very deep. We would tie a rope around the bundle of feed and draw it up. I would hold the feed and she would climb a little farther up.

"During the snow storm a ferocious jersey bull that was chained in a pen was covered up in about five feet of snow except just a breathing hole. We had to dig down and get the chain and turn him loose. We shoveled the snow from around him and by the time we got him out of the snow some of the fight was taken out of him. Stock suffered a great deal that year and several different times we have had some severe snows. I taught school several miles from home and often I have had to shovel two or three feet of snow out of the schoolroom before I could even get a fire built.

"My brother-in-law, W. I. Simms, [who married her sister Mabel], was offered some lambs from the DeOliveria ranch near Grady. There was not much feed for the sheep and the snow was so deep that the sheep could not graze, so if the owners kept the lambs they ran the risk of losing both ewes and lambs. So they gave the lambs to Mr. Simms if he wanted them. He took a number home with him. He had five good cows, and letting these lambs milk the cows was easier than to milk them himself or to try to feed the lambs. So he built two platforms far enough for the cows to walk between and just right for the lambs to stand on and he would drive the cows between the opening and then turn the orphan lambs in on the platform. I have always been sorry that I did not have a Kodak. Each lamb knew its place at the table. In this way the cows got a milking about three times a day. I am not sure, but the wagging of the lambs' tails would have frustrated the camera

man. He had a flock of twenty of these lambs that spring.

"Yes, I enjoy the work in the museum. There is a great deal to do, but it is interesting and I am classifying the different sections and have a great deal of information written about the different archaeologic finds, especially those of recent discovery in New Mexico. Some of the out-of-state visitors say that it is the best one (museum) they have ever seen in a town of this kind."

Mrs. Maxwell is a very interesting person and is glad to give any information that she has concerning the Clovis Museum, which is located in the Public Library on 8th and Pile Street. Her address is 402 Connelly Street, Clovis, New Mexico.

In 1936, May Price Mosley described similar Lea County "blizzard happenings."*

If there is one word sure to evoke the recounting of early-day experiences from South Plains pioneers, that word is *blizzard*. And whether they tell you of the blizzard of '84, '88, '96, 1903, 1906, 1918, or of the big freeze in 1933, memories are suddenly stirred to keenness, while eyes take on the faraway look of one remembering, and words often reflect a sense of awe.

The story may have to do with a lone rider, lost in a blizzard and snowstorm, riding continually for three days and two nights, over uncounted and unfenced miles—without food or fire or sleep—and without coming upon human habitation, person, or landmark during that time.

Or it may be about cattle—piles of them— drifting for miles in a storm, along the old drift fence, and at its end stumbling blindly

off the edge of the cliff to death two hundred feet below.

Or the herding of sheep flocks toward the caprock, seeking to get them "under the hill" for shelter; and how the snow whipped into banks many feet over their heads; and that for fourteen days owners and herders, guided by small air holes melting through, were taking out live sheep.

A few can tell you of the thousands of cattle, of open range time, drifting with a blizzard for days—some, for three hundred miles—in an unbroken stream across the plains to the Pecos.

Others will tell of the two cowboys, strangers, lost and partially frozen, who were saved by one woman's humane custom of keeping lamps burning in her windows on such nights.

*From "Blizzard Happenings (Lea County)," coll. Mrs. Benton Mosley of Lovington from "the personal knowledge of the writer; occurring to friends, acquaintances, or well known people in the vicinity"; 850 wds., 5 pp. 20 July 1936 (A#208).

And the story of the young rancher who brought cattle here from a milder climate, in winter, and when spring came he had not a tenth part of them.

Or of drifted, frozen cattle piled so high in the southwest corners of pastures that other cattle walked on over dead cattle, fences and all—as bridges from one pasture to another—not from a few pastures, but from many.

One hears of the traveling camper and his young son, who seeking their team—during a breathtaking blizzard, with visibility no more than an arm's length—lost their way and perished only a few yards from their camp.

And of frozen herders (most of them Mexicans) running into the 'teens from one blizzard—for a herder must stay with the flock, regardless of death risks.

The "fortunate" ones in 1918, whose fat cattle and those in sand pastures, were at first apparently unharmed, but many of which later lost their feet and had to be shot.

Some one is sure to recall the homesteading woman who lost her way between home and the barn.

And that the evening before the big freeze (1933) was the warmest for weeks: a fire and the usual bed coverings being uncomfortable; yet before dawn the lowest recorded temperature of this section (around 30 below) had been experienced. This freeze destroyed many of the prettiest landmarks in the country—huge weeping willows, many of them a quarter-century old, and this the first proof that they could not survive here.

Before U.S. Highway 380 connected Roswell with the Texas line through Caprock and Tatum in what became Lea County, the Mescalero Sands east of the town posed tremendous difficulties to homesteaders like the Thompsons and McMillans, who journeyed to New Mexico from Texas by covered wagon in 1902 and 1903.*

I was born in Adamsville, Texas, January 15, 1880. My father, Frank Thompson, was born in Alabama, February 28, 1852. When he was quite young his parents moved to Texas. My mother was Elizabeth Richardson and was born in Hamilton, Texas, June 5, 1857. My father and mother were married at Adamsville, Texas, in 1872. My father owned a large farm and raised fine blooded horses and registered jersey cattle. My mother and father had ten children, John, Fannie, Whit, Lemmie, Mary Ellen (myself), Guy, Hattie, Thomas, Elizabeth, and Belle.

When my father was about nineteen years

*"Pioneer Story," coll. Edith L. Crawford from Mrs. Mary Ellen Thompson McMillan, age 58, Carrizozo; 1993 wds., 7 pp., 10 October 1938 (A#210; LC47.1). Crawford sent corrections on October 19: "My mother and father had ten children, John, Fannie, Whit, Lemmie, Mary Ellen, Guy, Hattie, Thomas, Elizabeth and Belle, all born in Adamsville, Texas"; and "The five children that came to New Mexico with my mother were my two brothers Whit and Guy and two sisters Fannie and Belle and myself. The rest of the children, three boys and two girls, were married and had homes of their own in Texas."

old he helped drive a herd of cattle from Adamsville, Texas, to someplace in Colorado. (I do not remember the name of the place.) He came back to Texas by way of Lincoln County, New Mexico, and was so much impressed with the country that he always wanted to come back to Lincoln County to live. His mother never would consent for him to move his family to New Mexico, as she thought it was such a wild country, but in May 1902 he decided to sell his place in Texas and come out to New Mexico.

My father and a friend of his named Bill Lane and Tom and Jack Dooley, who were my father's nephews, came out to New Mexico to find a place to locate. They stopped at Nogal, New Mexico.

About two months after my father left to come to New Mexico I was married to Walter H. McMillan on July 10, 1902. My husband and I wanted to come to New Mexico too, but we stayed on with my mother until the crops were all gathered. My mother and sisters and I put up around two hundred gallons of fruit and vegetables that fall. We were very busy getting ready to join my father in New Mexico.

On October 24th, 1902, my mother, two brothers, two sisters, my husband and I started from Adamsville, Texas, for Nogal, New Mexico. We had three covered wagons, each wagon drawn by two horses. My mother and my youngest sister rode in one wagon, my brother Guy drove one, and my husband and I had our own wagon. My mother had decided to bring out some of our fine horses and had about twenty head. My brother Thomas and my sister Belle rode horseback and drove the horses.

The three wagons stayed together for about six days until we got to Crews, Texas, where my husband's father lived. We decided to stay there for a while (my husband and I), but my mother decided that they would go on and so she, my brothers, and sisters took the two wagons and the twenty head of horses and went right on through to Nogal. They got there about the middle of November

1902, and joined my father. My mother and father stayed at Nogal about a year and went to Ancho, New Mexico, and filed on a homestead there and lived on this same place until their death many years later.

My husband and I stayed with his father in Crews, Texas, until January 1903. It had gotten so cold that we decided that we would wait until spring to go on to New Mexico. We left Crews, Texas, and went up to Guion, Texas, about twenty miles south of Abilene, Texas, where we stayed until March 27, 1903, when we started out for New Mexico in our covered wagon. We had two horses, a gentle one and one that was not well broken. When my husband would get the team hitched up the unbroken horse would immediately start to run. I would always get in the wagon and hold the lines and my husband would have to run and catch the wagon as it moved off.

We had our chuck box on the back of the wagon and carried two water kegs tied on the side. We had a pair of springs in the wagon with our bed on it and we slept in the wagon. We used a lantern for light. We had a coop tied under the wagon with six hens and a rooster, full blood white leghorns, that kept us in eggs all the way out to New Mexico. We used wood for fuel until we got on the plains and then we used cow chips.

We struck the plains at Gail, Texas, and the very first day on the plains we ran into the worst sand storm that I ever experienced in my life. The sand filled up the ruts in the road and made it very hard to travel. We were facing the wind and late in the afternoon we came to a large water tank. It was a dirt tank and full of water and while we were still about a quarter of a mile away from it we thought it was raining for we could feel the water, but it was just the wind blowing the water against the dam with such force that it threw the water up in the air. We stopped at the tank for the night and the wind was so very strong that we were afraid that the wagon would be blown over. We could not cook any dinner or supper that day but we had all our provisions with us. We had to open some canned fruit but it got so full of sand that we could hardly eat it at all.

We traveled the old Chisum Trail and there was not a store or a post office from Gail, Texas, to Roswell, New Mexico. We saw a lot of antelope, coyotes, and prairie chickens. One day my husband decided that he would shoot some prairie hens as we had only bacon for meat. I stayed in the wagon and my husband got out to shoot them. He had a shot gun and when he fired at the prairie hens the team of horses got frightened and ran away with me. They ran for about a half mile before they stopped. We were so excited that we forgot to get the prairie hens, although we knew that he had gotten two of them, and we did not get any fresh meat after all.

After we left Gail, Texas, we came to the Fish Ranch. This ranch was about twenty-five miles northwest of Gail. The cattle were dying by hundreds. It was very dry and grass was poor. When my husband went up to a windmill to see if he could water the team and get water for our water kegs he found one of our old friends from Adamsville, Texas, a man by the name of Virgil Piper. We were so glad to see him and he ate dinner with us that day. He worked on the Fish Ranch.

From the Fish Ranch the road followed up what was known as Sulphur Draw. The next place we came to was the L. F. D. Ranch. The headquarters ranch house was at Mescalero Springs, near what is now known as Cap Rock, Texas. Not far from Mescalero Springs we came to some alkali sands which were twelve miles across. My father had already written us about these sands and did not think that we could make it across them with just the one team of horses. He had told us that he would send one of my brothers to meet us at Mescalero Springs with another team of horses, but when we got there my brother had not come so we decided to try to cross anyway. The sand had piled up into ridges and was so fine that the wagon wheels sank almost to the hubs. It was very hard for the horses to pull and every time that

they would get to the top of a ridge the horses would have to stop and blow. It took us one whole day to cross these sands and just after we got on the other side we met my brother coming with the extra team. He was very much surprised that we had made it across as well as we had.

Not very far from the Mescalero Springs we came to a small ranch where there was a big prairie fire. The man on the ranch (I have forgotten his name) asked my husband if he would take one of our team of horses and go round up a saddle horse for him as all of his horses were out in a big pasture and he could not get them on foot. The man had a number of baby calves out on the flats and he was afraid that the fire would trap these baby calves. My husband was glad to help him out by getting his horses for him, and the man and his wife gave us some fresh milk and butter and eggs.

Not very much happened from this ranch on into Nogal. I saw my first burros between Roswell and Nogal. They had water kegs strapped on their backs. I thought it looked very queer.

We reached Nogal, New Mexico, on April 15, 1903. We stayed there for a short while with my parents and then we moved to Ancho, New Mexico, where my husband had work at the cement plant there. There was only one house in Ancho at that time. We lived in a tent. My first child, Ruth, was born on July 31, 1903. She was the first American child born in the town of Ancho. While we were living at Ancho, New Mexico, my father filed on a homestead near Ancho and moved there.

In October 1903 my husband decided to work for the railroad company and we moved to Carrizozo, New Mexico. My husband worked as pumper for the El Paso, Northwestern Railroad Company and stayed with this company for about ten years. When we moved to Carrizozo there was one store, a saloon and post office, all in one long building under one roof. There were very few people in Carrizozo then and even as late as 1905

"Las Cruces, New Mexico. Aug 1936. Former inhabitant of the land use project." Photo by Arthur Rothstein. LC-USF 34-2965-E.

there were not enough children here to have a school. I had to go to White Oaks, New Mexico, for my dry goods. That was a real nice town at that time.

After leaving the railroad company my husband went to work for the New Mexico Light and Power Company and he stayed with this company for ten or twelve years. In 1929 my husband filed on a homestead eight miles south of Ancho, New Mexico. We lived there until 1937 when we traded our homestead to our son-in-law, Walter Burnett, for a house and two lots in Carrizozo, New Mexico, where we still live.

My mother and father lived on their homestead at Ancho until their death. My mother died in 1922 and my father in 1933. About five years before my father died he lost his

eyesight. He lived with me while we lived on our homestead near Ancho. I have a sister Belle, Mrs. J. T. Johnson, who with her husband and two children live on their homestead about three miles from Ancho. Of all my father's family there are only four living. My brother Whit Thompson lives near Adamsville, Texas. My sister Fannie is Mrs. Carter and lives at Hot Springs, New Mexico, and my sister Belle, Mrs. Johnson, is at Ancho, and I am at Carrizozo. Both of my parents are buried at Ancho, New Mexico.

My husband and I have six children—Ruth, Bonnie, Euda, Walter, Mary Ellen, and Corrine. All were born in New Mexico and all live in New Mexico now. For the past four years my husband has driven a school bus from Ancho to Carrizozo.

❋

Joyce Hunter rode the first automobile to cross the Mescalero Sands from Texas to Roswell in 1908, over what would become U.S. Highway 380.[24]*

To those who are skeptical as to the advantages of good roads, if there are any such, the following incidents may be enlightening. Passing over US 380 east of Roswell and on to the Texas line the present day traveler seldom realizes when he passes over the "Mescalero Sands." To the old timers, however, the building of the modern road across this stretch is little short of miraculous. Where the crossing of the sands once took half a day, today the same crossing is made in less than ten minutes. Where horses toiled and heaved for hours pulling a light load, now cars and trucks speed by with never a thought of the hardships endured by man and beast here a quarter of a century ago.

Good roads bring traffic; traffic brings trade; trade brings people. Good roads are now taken as such a matter of course that perhaps it will be of interest for the present generation to learn what experiences their parents had to undergo to reach the plains from Roswell.

"The Sands" stretching north and south between the Pecos River and the cap rock used to be the nightmare of those crossing east to the Texas line. A stretch of sand not more than seven miles in width was a killing distance for horses pulling a light load. With a heavier one, part had to be left to be carried across on a second trip. The "road" was a trail made by wagons through the dunes, traveled until the ruts were too deep even for wagon wheels; a new trail was then started approximately parallel to the former one, which soon became filled with loose sand and covered again with shin oak. It was the belief at that time that no road could ever be built across the sands. Several attempts had been made in a crude way but the first wind storm usually covered this roadwork so deep in sand that finally it was considered a hopeless task.

This was the state of affairs in 1908 when the first auto crossed the sands, a trip which had been looked upon as impossible of achievement. Mr. Herbert FitzGerald of Roswell bought a Pope-Toledo, one of the heaviest cars made and at that early day somewhat of a curiosity as it was not of the buggy shape and chain drive class. In this Mr. FitzGerald and a driver started on their trip to the T 2 Ranch owned by Mr. FitzGerald and which was just over the Texas line.

In September of 1908 Mr. FitzGerald had moved his family to the Texas ranch from Roswell to a home he had built in the I N K basin. The house was modern, had running water and a complete bathroom, all fixtures having been hauled by team from Roswell one hundred miles west. One of the older cowmen who was being shown through the house, on seeing the bathroom eyed it rather doubtfully and remarked, "Yes, it's handy, but isn't it unhealthy to have all that water running under the house?"

The car made the trip from Roswell to the T 2 without accident, arriving in the afternoon of the same day on which it had left the city, a distance of one hundred miles, an astounding feat!

The FitzGerald home was on the north side of the I N K basin partway up on the slope and a clear view was obtained past the two I N K wells and up over the hill toward the west where the road from the foreman's home, four miles away, was located near the

---

*"First Automobiles to Cross the Sands: The Pope-Toledo," 1160 wds., 5 pp., n.d.; "The Second Car across the Sands," 640 wds., 3 pp., 17 July 1937; both coll. Joyce Hunter (A#185; H5–5–61#19; LC47.1).

edge of the ranch on the New Mexico–Texas line. Those coming from Roswell came over this road.

One afternoon just before sundown the children were scattered around the house looking from time to time toward the road as they were expecting their father to return within a day or two. All at once a shout went up, "Here he comes," and then, when all had gathered to see the team and buggy, one of the boys shouted, "It's a car!" There topping the rise, silhouetted against the setting sun, appeared the car. It looked monstrous in size on the hill top but descending the slope grew smaller until it assumed its normal appearance. The excitement was intense and when the car finally reached the house it was immediately surrounded by children who stood in awe around it, hardly daring to believe their eyes. The first trip across the sands had been made in a car!

It was my "privilege" to be a passenger on the return trip as it was nearing Christmas and about time for me to begin my Christmas vacation. We left in the morning, about ten as I remember. When the traveling was good we must have made at least twenty miles an hour, when it was not so good, much less. We stopped and had our lunch on the open plains and then resumed the journey. At this time there were no gates to open, no fences even to be seen after leaving the T 2 until one came to the L E pasture west of the sands, two days' travel with horses.

But we were now above such slow transportation and were to make the whole trip in less than a day. The tonneau was rather large for a hundred-pound school teacher but not too uncomfortable, especially when I realized that I would have something to brag about on reaching home. An auto ride anywhere then was an exciting experience but an auto ride across the sands was beyond belief. We descended the caprock through what was then known as Clark's Gap, causing much excitement as we passed the house, the first on the road since leaving the T 2, and approached the sands.

Soon we were in them; there was no doubt of this fact to the one in the back seat, a seat wide enough for three persons. I tried holding onto the seat, without the least effect; I still bounced. Next I grasped the robe rail with both hands and a deathlike grip. No good; my arms were almost torn from their sockets. Mr. FitzGerald, looking back to be sure that I was still there, asked how I was making it, and my pride would not let me acknowledge that at each bump I expected to be left behind (lucky for me that the car had a top). Finally I found that the best way to bump was just to bump and trust to luck that if I became limp enough my neck would not be broken and my arms and legs would still be of some use if we ever got across the sands. Those seven miles were the longest I ever passed over but as with all things they were at last behind us and from there on such affairs as chuck holes and other minor irregularities of the road were too insignificant to be noticed.

Roswell was finally reached and I was taken to my home feeling that I had been pounded with a heavy mallet from head to foot. It took several days to unloosen the kinks in my anatomy which had been placed there by my auto trip across the sands.

Returning to my teaching duties after the Christmas vacation I went by buggy and team as the Pope-Toledo was laid up for repairs. On the way in with me in the back seat and no other load, nine of the eleven leaves of the springs were found to have been broken. If a genuine heavy weight had been in that seat on that trip what would have happened? However, the car had been put in commission and started on the trip back with Christmas tree and gifts—but that is a story in itself—and that was the trip which really did put it out of running order.

Pioneer motorists underwent experiences unknown to those of the present day, whose cars glide along the oiled highway on US 380 and whose greatest inconvenience in running out of gas is to wait a few moments for a passing auto or to walk the short distance to one of the many filling stations. In 1910 it was quite different. In those days no motorists were passing to loan a gallon or give a lift to a nearby filling station. Only in towns could gasoline be purchased unless some ranch headquarters had a supply for pumping purposes.

The second car to cross the Mescalero Sands, also owned by Mr. FitzGerald, was a Franklin, air cooled. Mr. FitzGerald believed that an air cooled motor would make the sands trip with less trouble than one which was water cooled. Several trips were made with little or no incidents of importance until the spring of 1910. In May of that year Mr. and Mrs. FitzGerald, accompanied by two of their daughters, the younger being only six years old, left the ranch for Roswell to take the train for Colorado where their oldest son was to graduate from the Colorado College of Mines.

Leaving in the afternoon they expected to arrive at Roswell that evening. As usual, trouble did not develop until the sands were reached. After passing through two miles on the sands the car stopped. This time it was not because of mechanical difficulties but for a reason that often causes motorists even of the present day to be stranded in the most unforeseen spots, lack of gas. It was sometime before the trouble was located, as at that time sudden stopping of the motor was attributed to some breakdown of the machine. Dark was upon them when it was finally discovered there was no gasoline in the tank. There was not a filling station then between Roswell and the Texas line. There were no houses or ranches within miles of the sands on either side so the little party was literally stranded in a desert.

Toward nine o'clock it was becoming so cold that the one blanket in the car was not enough to keep them warm. Mr. FitzGerald wished to walk to the L E Ranch, but as Mrs. FitzGerald did not want to be left in the car alone with the two girls it was finally decided that they would all walk to the ranch house, nearly twenty miles west.

Walking in sand is difficult as anyone who has tried it knows, but walking in the Mescalero Sands, sinking ankle deep or more at each step, at night when it is difficult to see where one's foot would land, was a wearisome task. At intervals the party would stop to rest, wrapping the one blanket around them, and then continue for a few hundred yards before taking another breathing spell. The start was made at nine o'clock at night and at six the next morning the pilgrims arrived at the L E where there was a telephone and where they were received with true cowboy hospitality.

Roswell was reached by phone and later in the day a car arrived with gasoline. This was taken to the sands where the Franklin had been abandoned, and it was not long before the two cars returned to the L E ranch house and the trip to Roswell was concluded—a day late.

About this time several other adventuresome ranchmen bought cars to travel across the sands. It was soon proved that light cars were better suited to this travel than the heavier ones and within a few years Model T's were bouncing gaily over the trail until at last the highway was completed and cars no longer felt the jars and jolts of the early days.

"Roswell, New Mexico. May 1937. Migratory family travelling across the desert U.S. highway 70, in search of work in the cotton." Photo by Dorothea Lange. LC-USF 34-RA16718-E.

A Final Portfolio

According to Van Deren Coke, "Dorothea Lange, a former portrait photographer in San Francisco, photographed for the FSA the stream of ancient cars laden with people and household goods that moved across southern New Mexico roads on their journey to California from the drought-stricken area of Oklahoma and Texas. She had first photographed in New Mexico in 1931 and returned in 1935 to Albuquerque. There she married the University of California economics profes-

"Lordsburg, New Mexico (vicinity). May 1937. Three related drought refugee families from farms near Claremore, Oklahoma. Have been working as migratory workers in California and Arizona, now trying to get to Roswell, New Mexico for work chopping cotton. Have car trouble and pulled up alongside the highway, near Lordsburg, New Mexico." Photo by Dorothea Lange. LC-USF 34-16671-C.

sor Paul Taylor, with whom she had been associated in 1934–35 in work with farm labor documentation for the California Rural Rehabilitation Administration. Her pictures in the mid 1930s caught the poignancy of the people's plight as their cars broke down and they ran out of gas and money. She photographed their caravans and made pictures of individuals that clearly convey the erosion of the people's hopes. We can sense that her photographs were real, that they were a reaching out gesture to those unfortunate people."[25]

"August 1936. Part of an impoverished family of nine on a New Mexico highway. Depression refugees from Iowa. Left Iowa in 1932 because of father's ill health. Father an auto mechanic laborer, painter by trade. Tubercular. Family has been on relief in Arizona, but refused entry on relief rolls in Iowa, to which state they wish to return. Nine children, including a sick, four-month-old baby. No money at all. About to sell their belongings and trailer for money to buy food. 'We don't want to go where we'll be a nuisance to anybody.'" Photo taken near Deming by Dorothea Lange. LC-USF 34-9749-E.

"May 1937. Three related drought refugee families from farms
near Claremore, Oklahoma. Have been working as migratory
workers in California and Arizona, now trying to get to Roswell,
New Mexico, for work chopping cotton. Having car trouble and
pulled up alongside the highway, near Lordsburg, New Mexico.
'Would go back to Oklahoma, but can't get along there. Can't
feed the kids on what they give you (relief budget) and ain't
made a crop there, you might say, for five years. Only other
work there is fifty cents a day wages, and the farmers can't pay
it anyways.' One of these families has lost two babies since they
left their home in Oklahoma. The children, seventeen months
and three years, died in the county hospital at Shafter,
California, from typhoid fever, resulting from unsanitary
conditions in labor camp." Photo by Dorothea Lange. LC-USF
34-16676-C.

BIOGRAPHICAL SKETCHES
of Project
Workers Represented

The architects, artists, photographers, and writers who provided this portrait of New Mexicans are very much a part of the documentation process. Whether famous or not, their lives and works have been encapsulated in the following sketches.

Each entry gives a minimum of the worker's name and the project(s) worked on. (For a description of each project nationally and in New Mexico, see Glossary.) In the case of FWP writers, at least their place of residence and the inclusive dates of their known NMFWP submissions are noted. Some workers did submit autobiographies, which are transcribed here, and occasional personal facts included in their various submissions are also noted.

Additional references are appended where possible. Unless otherwise noted, most art projects data come from Peter Bermingham, *The New Deal in the Southwest: Arizona and New Mexico,* an undated catalogue for the University of Arizona Museum of Art, Tucson; and FSA material from F. J. Hurley, *Portrait of a Decade: Roy Stryker and the Development of Documentary Photography in the Thirties* (Baton Rouge: Louisiana State University Press, 1972). Other quotes are preceded by the following notations:

Baumann 1934: Comments on PWAP artists by Regional Coordinator Gustave Baumann in a 1934 report to Jesse Nusbaum, Director of Region 13, "A Retrospect of Work and the Artists Employed in the Thirteenth Region under the Public Works of Art Project" (A#155).

Haskell 1936: Muriel Haskell, Supervisor of District One (northeastern counties), "Narrative Report: February 7th to 27th 1936" (H5-5-57#6).

1940 NM: Santa Fe writers Margaret Lohlker and Alison Dana, with help from Edgar L. Hewett, Alice Corbin Henderson, Will Shuster, and others, assembled a thirty-eight-page special Artists and Writers supplement to *The Santa Fe New Mexican* of June 26, 1940. Many of the 150 or so New Mexico artists and writers included provided their own biographies, and because this was an important contemporary document these have been quoted below. Supplement reprinted in Marta Weigle and Kyle Fiore, eds., *New Mexico Artists and Writers: A Celebration, 1940* (Santa Fe: Ancient City Press, 1982).

"Women and the NMFWP": Marta Weigle with Mary Powell, "From Alice Corbin's 'Lines Mumbled in Sleep' to 'Eufemia's Sopapillas': Women and the Federal Writers' Project in New Mexico," *New America* 4, 3 (1982): 54–76.

ADAMS, KENNETH MILLER (1897–1966): PWAP; Section. Baumann 1934: "A representative artist to head the long list—Adams is a good painter whose forte is portraiture. For some reason he spent most of his time on a landscape that now hangs in the President's Office, New Mexico University, Albuquerque. A portrait of a Mexican farmer and lithograph of a Mexican woman complete his contribution under the project."

1940 NM: "Born August 6th, 1897, at Topeka, Kansas, son of Charles and Susan Miller Adams. Began the study of fine arts at the age of 16 with George M. Stone of Topeka. Studied at the Art Institute of Chicago during 1916 and 1917. Served as a private in the army during part of 1918. Resumed study at the Art Students League of New York in 1919, entering the classes of Kenneth Hays Miller and George Bridgeman. Studied in the League summer school at Woodstock, New York, under Andrew Dasburg. In 1920 studied at the League under Maurice Sterne and Eugene Speicher.

"Went to Europe in 1921 and spent two years in France and Italy, studying and painting. Settled in Taos, New Mexico, in 1924 and has been a resident of the state ever since. Elected to the Taos Society of Artists in 1927. Married Hilda Brann Boulton in July, 1929. Taught art at the University of New Mexico in 1933.

"Invited to compete for the mural decorations for the new post office in Washington, D. C., in April 1935. Was awarded a commission to paint a mural, 'Rural Free Delivery,' for the post office at Goodland, Kans. Executed mural decorations for the Colorado Springs Fine Arts Center in 1936. Was commissioned to paint a mural for the post office at Deming, N. M., in 1937.

"Appointed artist in residence at the University of New Mexico, September, 1938, through a grant from the Carnegie Corporation of New York. Grant renewed 1939. Principal work being the painting of four murals for the new Coronado library at the University and teaching of a class in painting. Elected as associate of the National Academy, March, 1938 . . ." (p. 36). Retired from teaching at University of New Mexico, 1963. Died in Albuquerque, 1966. Ref.: *Kenneth M. Adams, N. A.: 1897–1966* (Albuquerque: Western Art Gallery, 1972).

BROWN, LORIN WILLIAM (1900–1978): FWP; WP. Born Elizabethtown, New Mexico, November 22, 1900, of Lorin W. Brown, Sr., a newspaper editor and printer, and Cassandra Martínez de Brown of Taos, a schoolteacher. Raised in the Taos area and schooled there and in Sterling, Kansas, where he attended one year of Sterling College. After World War I he did various jobs, including with Albuquerque newspapers. Became the schoolteacher and lived in Cordova, where his mother had moved and remarried to Margarito Lopez, 1922–33, and returned there periodically while employed on the NMFWP, 1936–41. In 1933 moved to Santa Fe and bought a house on lower Agua Fria Street. Married Frances Juanita Gilson, August 31, 1939, and lived in Tesuque and Santa Fe until joining the Office of Postal Censorship after Pearl Harbor. After World War II he worked at various jobs in California, Idaho, Washington, Mexico, New Mexico, and Alaska, where his wife died on December 26, 1969. In the 1970s divided his time between California, his children's home, and New Mexico. Working on "Tales of Taos" ms. at time of his death in Oakland, California, January 17, 1978. Buried in Cordova, January 21, 1978. Ref.: Lorin W. Brown with Charles L. Briggs and Marta Weigle, *Hispano Folklife of New Mexico: The Lorin W. Brown Federal Writers' Project Manuscripts* (Albuquerque: University of New Mexico Press, 1978).

BURNS, JAMES A. (1875–1951): FWP. Born Sauk Rapids, Minnesota, 1875; educated through high school in Stillwater, Minnesota. Left home in 1900 and became a railroad and road surveyor in Montana, Washington, Oregon, British Columbia, and by 1920 in Colorado. Came to Santa Fe, 1924–25, and to Taos to survey roads in 1927 and remained. NMFWP, February 1936–January 1937. A noted Taos character according to Rebecca Salsbury James: "Perhaps no figure seen in the Plaza during the past twenty-five years aroused more curiosity and interest than Jim Burns. Who is that mysterious man with the beard who seldom speaks? Why does he carry that big stick? Is he an old prospector? Is it true that he speaks Greek—that he is a Harvard graduate?" Died in Taos, June 1951. Refs.: James, *Allow Me to Present 18 Ladies and Gentlemen and Taos, N. M., 1885–1939* (Taos: El Crepusculo, 1953), p. 47; Claire Morrill, *A Taos Mosaic: Portrait of a New Mexico Village* (Albuquerque: University of New Mexico Press, 1973), pp. 143–44.

CARTER, MARIE: FWP. Resident of Anthony. "I am the widow of a veteran of the World War in need of immediate work. I began my career as a writer twenty years ago, but due to poor health, was forced to give it up at intervals.

"Three years ago I collaborated with an editor, and completed quite a number of short stories and articles. Unfortunately, I was sent to the hospital, and following my recovery was advised to give up writing.

"Since my husbands's [*sic*] death I have resumed my work and hope to carry on. Since I am trying to support myself and fourteen-year-old son, I am appealing to you to give me an opportunity to make a living. Who has a better right than the widow of a veteran who died to make this a better world for the present generation?" (Carter to George W. Cronyn, 4 December 1936. Record Group 69, National Archives). NMFWP, March–July 1937.

CHAPIN, GENEVIEVE: FWP. Haskell 1936: "In Clayton . . . Mrs. Genevieve Chapin . . . has done considerable writing and lived for many years in the community. . . . Mrs. Chapin is doing fairly well, altho [*sic*] there seems to be no great continuity or follow through in her work." NMFWP, February 1936–October 1939.

CHAPMAN, MANVILLE (1903–?): PWAP; FAP; FWP. Of his father, Kenneth Fordyce writes: "Mr. William Albert Chapman, a native of Massachusetts, entered New Mexico as a lad of sixteen years of age. In 1877, spent two summers in New Mexico, and after completing his schooling in the East, returned to New Mexico and made his home permanently. He has held many public offices in Raton and Colfax County; has held offices in the many fraternal orders, and since 1900 has engaged in the insurance business in Raton. He has kept many historical records of early day happenings, has lectured before audiences in New Mexico and Southern Colorado on early day history and is conceded to be an authority on what happened in the settlement years" ("Place Names, Colfax County: Corrections, Biographical Sketches of Informants," n.d., A#15).

Manville, 1940 NM: "Born Raton, N.M. November 20, 1903. Educated Raton schools, Iowa State University, Art Institute of Chicago. Divides time at present between Taos and Raton. Member Taos Artists Association. Has Murals in Shuler Auditorium, Roundup Tavern, El Portal Bar and private homes in Raton and superintended Children's mural painting in Raton Public Library for Federal Art Project. Has illustrated with wood block and pen and ink for several New Mexico publications. Has made wood and linoleum blocks for Federal Art Project. Has designed Southwestern greeting cards. Author of a few published New Mexico stories" (p. 38).

Baumann 1934: "One of the younger group—we managed to find for him a series of narrow oblong panels in the lobby of Shuler Auditorium of Raton where he lives. Not a major project but his paintings will look

well hidden among the plaster ornaments of a cove ceiling."

NMFWP, February–June 1936, when address was 444 South 3rd St., Raton. Haskell 1936: "In Raton, Mr. Manville Chapman, artist, and his father W. A. Chapman, insurance man, have both offered to cooperate to the best of their ability in writing up material which is already available to them as well as doing research."

COLLIER, JOHN, JR.: FSA. Formative period in San Francisco Bay area where he attended California School of Fine Arts. He studied mural painting with Maynard Dixon, Dorothea Lange's first husband, and was influenced by her documentary work. Joined Stryker's staff, September 1941. Upon Lange's recommendation, his photographs of Hispanic New Mexico were taken early in 1943, after the FSA had become the Office of War Information. In 1943 left to work with Stryker on the Standard Oil Project for four years. Moved into anthropology and photography with studies of the Maritimes of Canada, the Navajo Reservation, and Peru. Taught anthropology in California schools in 1960s. Refs.: John Collier, Jr., *Visual Anthropology: Photography as a Research Method* (New York: Holt, Rinehart and Winston, 1967); Van Deren Coke, *Photography in New Mexico: From the Daguerreotype to the Present* (Albuquerque: University of New Mexico Press, 1979), p. 31.

CRAWFORD, EDITH L.: FWP. Of Carrizozo. NMFWP, May 1937–July 1939.

DELANO, JACK: FSA. Studied drawing and painting at Pennsylvania Academy of Fine Arts, Philadelphia, and in Europe. Joined FSA, May 6, 1940. With his wife Irene photographed New England and southern states. Joined Roy Stryker's Standard Oil project after World War II, then continued work in documentary photography. Directed government television service in Puerto Rico. Refs.:

Arthur F. Raper, with FSA Photographs by Jack Delano, *Tenants of the Almighty* (New York, 1943); Greg Day and Jack Delano, "Folklife and Photography: Bringing the FSA Home," *Southern Exposure* 5 (1977): 122–33.

DICKENSHEETS, DONALD W.: HABS photographer.

DUNTON, W. HERBERT ("Buck") (1878–1936): PWAP. Baumann 1934: "Since President Roosevelt selected one of Dunton's pictures, gloom has left Dunton's studio and I hope he has seen the last of hard luck at its worst—an O. K. by the President supercedes any further comment." FDR selected "Fall in the Foothills," ca. 1933–34, oil on canvas, 34 × 42 1/8, for his offices. It is now in the National Collection of Fine Arts, Washington, D. C.

Born August 28, 1878, Augusta, Maine, of William Henry Dunton and Anna Katherine Pillsbury. Studied at Cowles Art School, Boston; Art Students League, New York; in Taos with Ernest L. Blumenschein and Leon Gaspard. Traveled throughout West as illustrator and artist. Married Nellie Hartley of Waltham, Massachusetts, 1900–1920. First came to Taos, June 1912; charter member, Taos Society of Artists, July 1915 until resignation in 1922. Died 1936, Albuquerque. Refs.: Mary Carroll Nelson, "William Herbert Dunton: From Yankee to Cowboy," *American Artist* 42 (January 1978): 60–63, 100–101; Patricia Janis Broder, *Taos: A Painter's Dream* (Boston: New York Graphic Society, 1980), pp. 163–76.

EMERY, WILLIAM M.: FWP. Grandson of Madison Emery, who settled Madison, first town in Union County, in 1865. Son of Matt Emery, oldtime cowboy in northeastern New Mexico. Resident of Clayton and probably married to Roxie Thompson, daughter of Mr. and Mrs. George Thompson. Mr. Thompson was an early settler who had freighted over the Cimarron Cut-off of the Santa Fe Trail

and who died in Las Animas, Colorado, February 8, 1934, at age 97 (W. M. Emery, "Old Timers Stories: Captured," 9 September 1936; A#238). NMFWP, February 1936–July 1937. Haskell 1936: "Mr. William M. Emery . . . has been appointed a sort of foreman over the work in that section [eastern part of district]." He "seems to be very conscientious and working hard. An effort is being made to turn to him for all of the most important material to be collected in the Eastern part of the district," and he is going to keep "a more careful supervision of work" by Mrs. Genevieve Chapin and Mrs. Carrie Hodges.

FORDYCE, KENNETH: FWP. Of Raton since January 1922. NMFWP, December 1936–March 1939.

GRANT, BLANCHE ("Blanchie") CHLOE (1874–1948): FWP. Born Leavenworth, Kansas, September 23, 1874; raised Indianapolis, Indiana. B.A., Vassar College, 1896; studied Boston Museum Art School, Pennsylvania Academy of Art, Philadelphia, and Art Students League, New York. Became an illustrator in Wilmington and then New York in 1911, when she studied portrait painting.

1940 NM: "Burning the candle at both ends was interrupted finally by the World war and then life swung away from New York to Lincoln, Nebraska, but there were no mountains near. She was just in the west. There, in 1918 [1916], a very welcome telegram summoned her to New York and she went to France as an overseas Y. M. C. A. secretary whose work was to plan color cheer in the "Y" huts in the Le Mans, Sarthe, area. Six months' service gave her the coveted gold stripe on her gray-green uniform sleeve. Like many a soldier, she returned to work [she] thoroughly disliked and that last year in Lincoln was filled with the strain of the wish to break her bonds.

"June of 1920 found the painter in Taos where she expected to stay a few weeks. Letters flew from her to the good uncle who had backed her, years before, and now, to her unbounded happiness, he stood ready to let her follow her own trail once more. After the trip to California planned for that summer she left the train at Pueblo, Colorado. On the platform, a red-coated band was playing a sharp march of welcome to someone. She appropriated the music to herself and stepped in time, smiling because she intended to write her mother about the band awaiting her that day when she was to take the train and the bus to Taos. In 1940 she is still here!

"The twenty years brought opportunity to paint, win recognition and send one-man shows to New York City. In 1922, the editorship of the Taos Valley News came her way as did also the suggestion from Bert G. Phillips, the artist, who had been in the village since 1898, that she write the story of the various artists who had followed him and find out what had brought them hither. Out of that experience arose ... the desire to write a history of Taos, the quaint old place, once the northernmost outpost of Spanish life and trade. The work was begun but did not appear until 1934, and then under the title 'When Old Trails Were New; The Story of Taos.' Other books came to the light of day. Writing and painting engrossed Blanche Grant for she was content that her anchor had dragged and caught 'out west in the mountains'" (p. 34). In her biography Helmut Gusdorf writes that "in the course of her activity in civic matters, Miss Grant played an important part in the meetings which resulted in the establishment of a Taos fire department, in 1933" (A#234; LC47.1; LCms#6). Died in Taos, June 19, 1948.

Baumann 1934: "Miss Grant puffs through art or literature with equal facility—she brought fame to some obscure genius of the fifties whose portrait painted by Miss Grant after a daguerreotype will be hung in the room of the State Historical Society in Santa Fe." Baumann refers to her portrait of Lewis H. Garrard.

NMFWP, January–October 1936. Has-

kell 1936: "Miss Grant is turning in fairly good wordage—but has nearly finished all material on 'cities, towns and villages of Taos County.' It is difficult to get her to write anything outside the county. It has been suggested by this office that she do a series of oldtimer stories, interviewing those people whom the office suggests. This has not been greeted enthusiastically, altho [*sic*] not flatly refused.

"A more serious problem faces the office here; it has been definitely established that certain material collected has not been written up and turned in to the office but kept for private publishing later. This of course is not 'cricket' and the supervisor took it up with the worker. However without direct advice from the State office on the situation the District Office did nothing besides issue a warning. Two or three technicalities enter into this picture: Is this information obtained by Miss Grant as an individual or as a worker on the Writers' Project? Nothing can be done if while on a trip (which she is paying for herself) she is told information without soliciting it. Of course there is no question but what the thoroughly *honest* thing would be to turn in all interviews and all oldtimers stories that come her way. Miss Grant definitely mentioned in this office having obtained a good Indian story in Questa and promise of good photos—and stated she did not intend to turn them in. There is no possible way to check on these workers. The supervisor has thought out many schemes for checking up but every one leaves a loophole where people can be interviewed and information obtained which may be withheld. This situation follows on the heels of opposition on her part to publicity in the local paper concerning the Writers' Project." Ref.: Robert B. McCoy, "Publisher's Preface," in Blanche C. Grant, *Taos Indians* (1925; reprint, Glorieta, N.M.: Rio Grande Press, 1976).

HASKELL, MURIEL: FWP. Supervisor for District One, NMFWP, January 1936–February 1937. "Haskell, described by [Ina Sizer] Cassidy as 'an experienced newspaper woman of a number of years experience in the east, now making her home in Taos [and] for two or three years . . . head of an advertising agency in the middle west, handling the publicity of several large firms,' was hired in January 1936 at a non-relief wage of $86.25 per month. According to Cassidy, when she and her new supervisor travelled throughout the district in February they were welcomed enthusiastically everywhere—even by 'rabid Republicans'!" ("Women and the NMFWP," p. 59).

HENDERSON, WILLIAM PENHALLOW (1877–1943): TRAP; FAP. Baumann 1934: "Sometimes affectionately called Windy Bill— a tough hombre unless you let him drone on about himself, Valázquez and dynamic symmetry. Judging from his panels for the Federal Building at Santa Fe, he is oblivious to the fact that the art world has turned several times since he took to building houses and carving furniture about ten years ago—the slump in building decided him to be off'n the new love and on with the old—thinks he did a slick job, but the supervising architect may not agree."

Born Medford, Massachusetts, June 4, 1877, to William Oliver Henderson of Thomaston, Maine, and Sallie Augusta (LeGallee) of Biddleford, Maine. 1940 NM: "Spent childhood on father's cattle ranches in Texas and Kansas. Educated Massachusetts Normal Art School and Boston Museum of Fine Arts. Three years in Europe, 1900–1903, on Paige Traveling Scholarship from Boston Museum of Fine Arts. In 1904 painted in Old Mexico and Arizona. Lived in Chicago from 1904 and taught several years at the Chicago Academy of Fine Arts. In 1910–11, painted in Italy, France and Spain. Represented in Chicago Art Institute, Denver Art Museum, private collections, and PWA murals in Federal Building, Santa Fe. Came to Santa Fe in 1916, where he has since painted and practiced architecture. As ar-

chitect of the Museum of Navajo Ceremonial Art, also designed the permanent and symbolic panels in the building" (1940 NM, p. 14). Died in Tesuque, October 15, 1943. Ref.: *Catalogue for William Penhallow Henderson Retrospective Exhibition,* July 21 through August 20, 1963, Museum of New Mexico, Fine Arts Museum, Santa Fe.

HODGES, CARRIE L.: FWP; HRS. Of Clayton. Haskell 1936: "Has done considerable writing and lived for many years in the community." NMFWP, February–December 1936. Haskell 1936: "Mrs. Hodges is officially assigned to work on the Historic Document [Records?] Survey but is assisting in the gathering of material for the Writers' Project as well." She "does not have a news sense and often leaves out facts which are essential to the accuracy and completion of the story. However, the supervisor is taking the matter up with Mr. Emery and by a more careful supervision of work on his part and by outlining in advance certain subjects for both Mrs. Chapin and Mrs. Hodges this may clear up. Only time will break in these people, who have had no experience on such a project, and an effort to speed them up will be made in order to get what is needed." However, "Mrs. Carrie Hodges has started a series of articles on 'Women Who Have Pioneered New Mexico.' This material is being held in the District Office until completed or very nearly so, in order that it may be pulled together."

HOGNER, NILS: PWAP. Of Albuquerque. Baumann 1934: "Oh! Mr. Hogner!—if he had only painted as well as he talked. He had C. C. C. workers chopping a tree with the cut on the far side, pick axes poised to brain a neighboring worker before taking effect in the ground and other humorous inaccuracies to prove him a bear for all sorts of technical punishment."

HUNTER, JOYCE: FWP. "Born in Milwaukee, Wisconsin. Daughter of Elizabeth

Porter Hunter, born in Milwaukee of Scotch-Irish parents, and Henry B. Hunter, born in Orange County, New York of Revolutionary War descent. Lived in Milwaukee and Wauwatosa, Wisconsin. Came to New Mexico in 1906 and has resided in that state since that time at Roswell, Chaves County. Attended private schools, Milwaukee-Downer Seminary, University of Wisconsin. Graduate of the Ancient Classical course with degree of Bachelor of Arts. Took course in book-keeping at Roswell Business College, Roswell, New Mexico. Taught in rural school District No. 7, Chaves County; in Roswell High School, teaching English; Clovis High School, teaching English, History and Latin. Had experience in teaching in private school for girls, 2 years, in Milwaukee and in private tutoring for a number of years. Book-keeper for W. T. Clardy, Clardy's Dairy, 1924–1927. Manager of Roswell Photo Copy Co., 1928–1931, both in Roswell, New Mexico. Served as typist and clerk in ERA work at ERA office and State Employment Service, and typist on Library Project WPA and investigator on Writers' Project (65-1700 E) WPA. Still employed on Writers' Project" ("Autobiography of Joyce Hunter," n.d., A#22; LCms#6). NMFWP, April 1936–July 1937.

HURD, PETER (1904–1984): Section. Born in Roswell. 1940 NM: "Peter Hurd's father spent considerable time and money trying to turn a naturally gifted artist into a soldier. After graduating from the New Mexico Military Institute (where he was chief bugler, and drew cartoons for the cadet publications), young Hurd was shipped off to West Point. But he spent so much time sketching and painting that he flunked math in his second year and was dropped.

"Next, young Hurd was sent to Haverford College in Pennsylvania, where he met the noted mural painter and illustrator, N. C. Wyeth, who was so impressed with his talent that he took him on as an apprentice. In his spare time Hurd attended Pennsylvania Academy of Fine Arts.

"Hurd has painted murals for the New Mexico Military Institute; for the post office at Big Springs, Texas (a Treasury Department commission); and for the post office annex at Dallas, Texas, also a federal project. One of his paintings was recently purchased by the Metropolitan Museum" (p. 8). Ref.: Robert Metzger, ed., *My Land is the Southwest: Peter Hurd Letters and Journals* (College Station: Texas A & M University Press, 1983).

KIDDER, J. T. MORSE: HABS.

KILGORE, BELLE: FWP. Of 718 Wallace St., Clovis. NMFWP, January–July 1937.

LANGE, DOROTHEA (1895–1965): FSA. Born Hoboken, New Jersey. Apprenticed to Arnold Genthe, studied with Clarence White, New York. Worked in San Francisco, 1918. Opened portrait studio, married painter Maynard Dixon, became popular photographer. In early 1930s met University of California economics professor Paul Schuster Taylor (1895–?) and with him began documenting social conditions of poor in California for California Division of Federal Emergency Relief Administration. They moved to Washington to work with the Resettlement Administration and by June 1935 Lange was field investigator, photographer, with Information Division and Taylor was regional labor advisor for California, Arizona, Nevada, Utah, and New Mexico. Lange was hired by Stryker for the Historical Section on September 1, 1935. She married Taylor in December 1935. Lost her FSA job in 1939. Exhibited widely, and a retrospective of her work was exhibited at the Museum of Modern Art in 1966. By Lange: "Draggin'-Around People," *Survey Graphic,* March 1936, pp. 524–25; and Paul Schuster Taylor, *An American Exodus: A Record of Human Erosion* (1939; rev. ed., New Haven: Yale University Press, 1969); "Documentary Photography," in *A Pageant of Photography,* ed. Thomas J. Maloney, Grace M. Morley, and Ansel Adams (San Francisco: Crocker-Union, 1940); *Do-*

rothea Lange Looks At the American Country Woman (Fort Worth, Texas: Amon Carter Museum; Los Angeles: Ward Ritchie Press, 1967). Refs.: Milton Meltzer, *Dorothea Lange: A Photographer's Life* (New York: Farrar, Straus, and Giroux, 1978); Howard M. Levin and Katherine Northrup, eds., *Dorothea Lange: Farm Security Administration Photographs, 1935–1939*, 2 vols. (Glencoe, Ill.: The Text-Fiche Press, 1980); Karen Becker Ohrn, *Dorothea Lange and the Documentary Tradition* (Baton Rouge: Louisiana State University Press, 1980).

LEE, RUSSELL (1903–   ): FSA. Born Ottawa, Illinois; educated as a chemical engineer at Lehigh University; married artist Doris Emrick (divorced 1938); left his manufacturing plant manager's job in 1929 to study painting at California School of Fine Arts for two years; eventually moved to Woodstock, New York. Taught himself photography by 1935. Hired by Stryker at FSA in fall 1936 and photographed in Midwest, Ohio Valley flooding, Texas, New Mexico, and elsewhere. Married journalist Jean Smith, who wrote FSA captions for him, during this time. Joined Air Force and made aerial photographs during World War II. Documented Appalachian coal mines for U.S. Department of the Interior, 1946. Joined Stryker's Standard Oil project then became freelance photographer for major magazines. Taught photography at the University of Texas. Refs.: Russell Lee, "Pie Town, New Mexico," *U.S. Camera*, October 1941, pp. 39–54, 88–89, 106–107; idem, "Autobiography," *Russell Lee: Retrospective Exhibition, 1934–1964* (Austin: The University Art Museum of the University of Texas, 1965); F. Jack Hurley, *Russell Lee, Photographer* (Dobbs Ferry, New York: Morgan and Morgan, 1978); William Wroth, ed., *Russell Lee's FSA Photographs of Chamisal and Peñasco, New Mexico* (Santa Fe: Ancient City Press; Colorado Springs: Taylor Museum of the Colorado Springs Fine Arts Center, 1985).

LOVELADY, RAYMOND: HABS.

LYNN, BRIGHT (?–1939): FWP. A student at New Mexico Normal (now Highlands) University, Las Vegas, who apparently had known folklorist Benjamin Botkin from the national FWP office. NMFWP, June 25, 1938–July 1939. "I regret to have to report the death (suicide) of Bright Lynn, one of our most promising young writers. . . . On the stipend of a Senior Writer, he put himself through the last year, of his three, at the Las Vegas Normal University. He would have been a senior this coming year. He was an honor student and an outstanding athlete. His work with this project was noteworthy" (Aileen Nusbaum to Henry G. Alsberg, 2 August 1939). Ref.: Marta Weigle, "Guadalupe Baca de Gallegos' *Los tres preciosidas* (The Three Treasures)': Notes on the Tale, Its Narrator and Collector," *New Mexico Folklore Record* 15 (1980–81): 35.

MARTÍNEZ, REYES NICANOR (1885–1970): FWP; WP. Born and raised in Arroyo Hondo, where he lived off and on throughout his life until illness forced him to move permanently to California in 1963. During the early 1930s, Martínez, his wife Matilde Anaya, and the first six of their ten children (the other four were born later) lived in Kit Carson's house in Taos. Martínez then worked in different city offices. Before and after his FWP and WP employment, he held various jobs in New Mexico, Wyoming, California, and other states, always returning to Arroyo Hondo, where he continued to own land and where his brothers Onécimo and Tomás lived. Among his many jobs was work at the roundhouse of the Union Pacific Railroad in Green River, Wyoming, and as night clerk at Anderson's Inn in Buellton, California.

From his family history: "On January 20, 1851 . . . Julian Antonio Martínez was born in the little village of Arroyo Hondo, in Taos County. . . . A descendant of two of the principal Spanish families of the province, he . . .

received the rudiments of his education in the village schools of Arroyo Hondo and later attended Saint Michael's College at Santa Fe. . . .

"The Luceros, Martínez and Anayas intermarried among themselves. Don Vicente Martínez, who first came to Abiquiu, an Indian village in Rio Arriba County, later moved to Arroyo Hondo. There he married Salomé Lucero. From this union was born four sons, Rómulo, Félix, Julián and Bonifacio, and one daughter, Lorencita. Don Vicente became a wealthy trader, establishing the first outfitting post in northcentral Taos County, from which trading expeditions journeyed into Kansas and Colorado. . . . Don Vicente died before he reached an advanced age. His wife died a few years later and his children, ranging in age from sixteen to thirty-two years, continued to live in the old home; with the exception of Lorencita, who was already married and had moved to her husband's home.

"Rómulo, the oldest, directed the business affairs of the family. He carried on the trading business established by their father, managing, also, the herds of cattle and horses and their farm lands. In his charge was left also their considerable cash inheritance, which he kept in the old family safe, the combination of which no one else knew. After a time he discontinued the trading expeditions into Kansas and sent the ox-wagon caravans into Colorado a few times, then ceased outside trading altogether, as Taos became the center of distribution of merchandise. Then Rómulo married Cirila, a daughter of Don Juan Santistevan, prominent merchant and banker of Taos. He died a short time thereafter. At this time the family fortune (in cash) disappeared in some mysterious manner. Rómulo was a well educated man. The books that he left, on philosophy and higher mathematics, gave evidence of his profound learning. He was versed also in matters of law, and was consulted by many persons from Taos and surrounding counties.

"After the death of Rómulo, Félix married and separated from Julián and Bonifacio, who remained in the old home. Don Julián, as he later came to be known, started a small general-merchandise store and saloon in one of the rooms of the old home in Arroyo Hondo in 1880—groceries at one end of the room and liquor at the other end. He had previously acquired the sum of two thousand dollars, his share of the sale, as one of the heirs, of the extensive Tierra Amarilla land grant to Thomas B. Catron, wealthy attorney of Santa Fe. Luck seemed to accompany him from the start, as in 1881 a placer mining boom started in Arroyo Hondo and continued for two years thereafter, during which period all the men of the village who were willing to work were employed by the mining company at good wages, and Don Julián had all their trade. His rigorous bringing-up stood him well in his business, as many a night he went without sleep in order to attend his customers in the saloon. His business increased by leaps and bounds and he acquired large holdings of lands and became the owner of extensive herds of sheep and horses, owning also a fair number of cattle. He sent a petition from the people of the village to the Post Office Department at Washington for a post office and was appointed the first postmaster of Arroyo Hondo, a position he held till 1904, when he retired from business and moved to Santa Fe. A significant fact is that the post office has remained in the old Martínez home and family since its establishment more than fifty-five years ago.

"A stern but loving father, Don Julián gave his children the best of an education, among the schools they claim as their Alma Mater being Denver University, Regis College (both in Denver), the New Mexico Military Institute at Roswell, and the higher schools of Santa Fe.

"Don Julián, together with José Eulogio Lacome, Alexander Gusdorf and other contemporary politicians, directed the political affairs of Taos County, for many years with absolute sway. The county was overwhelmingly Democratic, and not till after Don Julián moved to Santa Fe did the Republican party ascend to the majority in Taos County.

"Of conspicuous prominence in the life-history of Don Julián may be mentioned the wedding of his daughter, Cleofas, to Colonel (he was a member of Governor Miguel A. Otero's staff) Venceslao Jaramillo, a prominent young politician and scion of one of the most wealthy and cultured Spanish families of New Mexico. The ceremonies of this prominent couple lasted several days. The bridegroom rented the whole Barron hotel in Taos for the use of the guests. . . .

"Don Julián, now nearing 86 years of age, lives in Santa Fe. His seven children, five sons and two daughters, also are living. His wife died in 1931" (Reyes N. Martínez, "Spanish—Pioneer: The Martinez Family of Arroyo Hondo," 11 December 1936; BC420; A#234; H5-5-47#22; LCms#6). A brief biography of Julián A. Martínez by Santa Fean John Looney notes that he lived in Arroyo Hondo until 1902, when he came to Santa Fe and "engaged in the Real Estate and Loan business . . . and resides at 125 Grant Ave." ("Biographical Sketch," 14 July 1939; H5-5-51#8; LCms#6). At the time of Cleofas M. Jaramillo's death on November 30, 1956, her sister, Mrs. Mae M. Raizizun of El Paso, and all five brothers—Onécimo G. and Thomas J. of Arroyo Hondo, Reyes N. of San Francisco, and Ben L. and Alfonso D. of Santa Fe—survived.

NMFWP, February 1936–May 27, 1941. Haskell 1936: Martínez "has lived in the same village since boyhood and is peculiarly able to gather material on the northern villages, folklore and customs—and additional oldtimers stories. [He is] very willing to cooperate in any way—however [his] wordage is not entirely satisfactory." Martínez submitted more than three hundred contributions, many of which were sent to Washington in their original, handwritten form. At the time of his firing from the Writers' Program he was working on a collection of alabados from Taos County. Refs.: Robert L. Shalkop, *Arroyo Hondo: The Folk Art of a New Mexican Village* (The Taylor Museum of the Colorado Springs Fine Arts Center, 1969); Marta Weigle, "About Cleofas Martínez de Jaramillo," in Jaramillo, *The Genuine New Mexico Tasty Recipes* (1942; reprint, Santa Fe: Ancient City Press, 1981), pp. 19–20; Carol Jensen, "Cleofas M. Jaramillo on Marriage in Territorial Northern New Mexico," *New Mexico Historical Review* 58 (1983): 153–71.

MOSLEY, MAY PRICE (1891–1970): FWP. According to Martha Downer Ellis's foreword to *"Little Texas" Beginnings,* a collection of Mrs. Mosley's NMFWP pieces, May Price was born in Midland, Texas, in 1891, and grew up on ranches in west Texas and eastern New Mexico. Educated at home, "a year or so boarding in Midland, a little at Knowles, and . . . one year at Western College in Artesia, New Mexico," she married Benton H. Mosley, "son of an early merchant at Knowles, New Mexico [in 1917], and they engaged in the ranching business in Lea County most of their lives" (p. vi). She died in Portales in August 1970 and is buried in Lovington Cemetery.

NMFWP, April-December 1936. According to her biography, written when she lived in Lovington: "Born in Midland, Texas, eldest daughter of Mr. and Mrs. Eugene H. Price, who at that time made their home on the Quinn ranch in Terry County, Texas. Mrs. Mosley was the only child in that county for some time, and her mother [Lily Kirby] often the only woman. The family first moved into what is now Lea County (N. Mex.) in 1896, moving to the old E Ranch, which was located some twenty miles northeast of where Lovington now is; and since that date this section has been home to her most of the time. 'Education,' writes Mrs. Mosley, 'in those days and circumstances, was necessarily a very fragmentary affair and mine acquired by an especially patchy process.' She learned her letters reading the various brands on cattle that drank at the ranch water trough during open range. Later, her parents usually managed to sandwich in a year's schooling (far away from home) for her between each year of home study. So much alone-ness made of her an omnivorous reader, and so much reading seems early to have given her the desire to put the drama of life into written words. 'Leisure,' she declares, 'was the only thing on the ranch of which there was plenty.' She had two years at a freshwater college, but spent most of her time there on music. She is married and spends her time as do most housewives, save that she often substitutes study for parties, and for pastime prefers piecing colorful words into paragraphs rather than gay scraps into patchwork quilts. 'The only thorn on the rose of writing for pleasure,' she writes, 'is the alone-ness of the game; just like sol: no partners—and so much happens, while you write, that you are left out of.' Due to early environment, she declares, she will always be instinctively a little afraid of people—interesting as she finds them—and feels much freer with animals, of which she and her husband are equally fond" ("Biography," 1 June 1936; A#208; LCms#6). Refs.: May Price Mosley, *"Little Texas" Beginnings in Southeastern New Mexico*, ed. Martha Downer Ellis (Roswell, N.M.: Hall-Poorbaugh Press, 1973); Eugene H. Price, *Open Range Ranching on the South Plains in the 1890's* (n.p.: Clarendon Press, 1967).

REDFIELD, GEORGIA B.: FWP. According to James D. Shinkle: "The *Roswell Daily Record* of October 7, 1937 printed an article written by Mrs. Georgia B. Redfield that is especially interesting. It is the only account that has been found, giving the impressions of a sensitive teenage girl to the Roswell area in pioneer days.

"Mrs. Georgia B. Redfield came to Roswell in January of 1893. She came from Louisiana with an older sister. The sister, Mrs. R. H. Parsons, was coming to this country to join her husband at Picacho, New Mexico, where he had purchased a combination store and small hotel located on the stage route west from Roswell. Mrs. Redfield was to make an extended visit of about eight months, but she stayed approximately one-and-a-half years.

Here is Mrs. Redfield's interesting story.

" 'I came to this section of the country by way of the slow stage coach, which took from daylight until long after dark to make the trip from Eddy (now Carlsbad) to Roswell.

" ' "You had better stay away from that wild woolly western country," was the advice Louisiana friends gave the young girl—just a scrap, that was I, who weighed only about eighty pounds, which fact prompted them to say:

" ' "You'll blow away in one of those terrible prairie wind storms, or be bitten by rattlesnakes or stung by scorpions, and there are no good schools out there like you have here." These were just a few of the discouraging points used in arguments against my coming to New Mexico with my sister, Mrs. R. H. Parsons, and W. C. Marable.

" ' "You'll freeze out there in winter, for they have to dig roots from the ground for fuel to keep warm when there is a blizzard, and they have to buy every drop of water they drink, and it's roasting hot in summer out there"—as if this particular spot was shut off from the rest of the world, in a perfect inferno of heat in summers and blizzards of the North Pole in winter' " (p. 186).

"Native of State of Louisiana. Public Schools Bastrop and New Orleans, La. Private French school, Bayou St. John, New Orleans, La. Came to New Mexico, 1893. Attended public schools two years. Substitute teacher, at age of 15 years, for one year. Met S[idney] I. Redfield in 1894 [when he was owner and editor of *Roswell Register*] in Roswell, New Mexico. Married in Louisiana in 1900. After marriage lived a part of the time in Roswell, but after 1910, it was permanent home. Have two children, a son and a daughter. Appeared in numerous magazines and newspapers, in descriptive articles and poems, and in Henry Harrison's Anthology, 1930. Assistant Editor 'Morehouse, Clarion,' Bastrop, La., on news, social, and poems, 1898–1899, and part of 1900. Author of 'Our Mammy,' songs and stories of Christmas" ("Georgia B. Redfield," 16 May 1936; A#22;

LC38.1). Attached is an unidentified newspaper clipping dated 16 March 1938: "The appointment of Mrs. Georgia B. Redfield as historian of the Chaves County Archaeological and Historical Society was announced today by Justice C. R. Brice, president."

NMFWP, December 28, 1935–August 1939. Initially upset about her designation as a "non-laborer" because "no matter what prejudiced opinion may be, at Santa Fe, I think I should be classed as a writer, and have made a living in the past as a writer" (Redfield to Gov. James F. Hinkle, 1 September 1936; in "Women and the NMFWP," pp. 60–61). Was collecting biographies for a book to be entitled "Pioneer Builders of Roswell in the Sunshine State—New Mexico" (outline dated December 19 and 21, 1938) to be sponsored by the Chaves County Archaeological and Historical Society for the Coronado Cuarto Centennial in 1940. Ref.: Georgia B. Redfield, "Coming to Roswell in Stagecoach Days," in James D. Shinkle, *Reminiscences of Roswell Pioneers* (Roswell, N.M.: Hall-Poorbaugh, 1966), pp. 186, 195–99.

REICH, BETTY: FWP. Mrs. Reich lived in Deming. NMFWP, April 1936–July 1937.

REUTER, BERNHARDT A.: FWP. Foreman for repair and restoration of the old Acoma mission, a project sponsored by The Society for the Restoration and Preservation of New Mexico Mission Churches, 1926–29. Resident of Pecos while on NMFWP, October 1938–August 1939. Most of his submissions describe Acoma Pueblo in considerable detail, but there are a few on Spanish customs in Pecos and historical matters there, especially on members of Governor Donaciano Vigil's family and their descendants.

ROLLINS, WARREN E. (1861–1962): PWAP. Of Farmington. Born Carson City, Nevada, 1861; raised in San Francisco, trained at San Francisco School of Design. Traveled throughout the West as an itinerant sign painter and eventually painted for the Santa Fe Railroad. Was painting in Taos when he decided to become Santa Fe's only artist and convinced Governor Bradford Prince to let him hang the first one-man show in the Palace of the Governors about 1893. "He stayed on to found and become the first president of the Santa Fe Art Club, and to teach art classes in a studio at the Palace—although he felt that 'great art is precisely that which never was nor will be taught'" (Robertson and Nestor, pp. 22–24). Was in and out of Santa Fe throughout his long life. Ref.: Edna Robertson and Sarah Nestor, *Artists of the Canyons and Caminos: Santa Fe, the Early Years* (n.p.: Peregrine Smith, 1976).

ROTHSTEIN, ARTHUR: FSA. In the fall of 1934, as a senior at Columbia University, worked with Stryker on National Youth Administration money to help him copy pictures for a source book on American farming for the Information Division of the Agricultural Adjustment Administration. Joined Stryker in the Resettlement Administration in July 1935 and set up the darkroom by the end of 1935. Documented Shenandoah Valley, Oklahoma dust bowl, western plains, Midwest and South in 1938. Left in 1940 to work for *Look Magazine*. Returned to work with Office of War Information but joined Army Signal Corps as photographer in 1943. Returned to *Look* after war and became technical director until its demise in 1971, after which he taught photojournalism at Columbia University and began a major national documentary project on pollution sponsored by the Environmental Protection Agency. Refs.: Rothstein, "The Picture That Became a Campaign Issue," *Popular Photography*, September 1961, p. 42; idem, *Photojournalism: Pictures for Magazines and Newspapers* (Philadelphia, 1965); idem, *The Depression Years, As Photographed by Arthur Rothstein* (New York: Dover, 1978).

RUSINOW, IRVING: BAE. Of Albuquerque. Photographed El Cerrito, 10–16 April

1941, for the Bureau of Agricultural Economics. Ref.: Richard L. Nostrand, "El Cerrito Revisited," *New Mexico Historical Review* 57 (1982): 118.

SIMPSON, HELEN F. GAGE (1873–1954): FWP. Of Farmington. Fourth wife of Indian trader R. T. F. (Dick) Simpson (1863–1945), whom he met after selling his Gallegos Canyon store in 1927 and moving to Farmington. According to McNitt: "Here he married Helen F. Gage of Durango and operated a small grocery store until his death April 15, 1945" (p. 299). NMFWP, April–October 1936. Ref.: Frank McNitt, *The Indian Trader* (Norman: University of Oklahoma Press, 1962).

SMITH, DUDLEY T.: HABS. A Yale graduate in architecture, he was laid off such work in Denver by the Depression and started the Acoma work in 1934 at age thirty-two. Ref.: Peter Nabokov, *Architecture of Acoma Pueblo* (Santa Fe: Ancient City Press, 1985).

SMITH (Kromer), JANET: FWP. Of 1216 East Central, Albuquerque. NMFWP, March 1936–March 1938. Apparently she married Tom Kromer of Albuquerque by early 1937, when the first submissions are signed Janet Smith Kromer. He has submissions dated 1936–39. Ref.: Marta Weigle and Kyle Fiore, *Santa Fe and Taos: The Writer's Era, 1916–1941* (Santa Fe: Ancient City Press, 1982), p. 207.

SMITHSON, J. VERNON: FWP. "Born October 8, 1912, near Carnegie, Washita County, Oklahoma. Parents, George K. and Stella B. Smithson, Anglo-Saxon. Moved to Curry County, New Mexico, in 1914, went to grade school at Grady, New Mexico. Moved to Clovis, New Mexico, in 1926, finished High School at the Clovis Public Schools. After finishing High School in 1931 traveled over the western and southern states, employed at various trades which included lumbering, photography, advertising, newsreporting and construction work. Employed by the Evening-News Journal of Clovis,

New Mexico, in 1934. Worked in the advertising department of the Church Lumber Co. of Alabama in early part of 1935. Employed as investigator for the American Guide, covering Curry and Debaca counties of New Mexico, February 10, 1936" ("Autobiography of J. Vernon Smithson," 5 and 18 May 1936; A#22; LC38.3). NMFWP, 10 February 1936–July 1937.

THORP, ANNETTE HESCH: WP. Widow of N. H. (Jack) Thorp, living in Santa Fe. Born of Austrian father who was a sheep rancher near Palma, New Mexico, and an Irish mother. Married Thorp in 1903. NMWP, September 1940–July 1941. Thorp was interviewing old Hispanic women for a collection of life stories to have been entitled "Some New Mexico Grandmothers." Ref.: Marta Weigle, "'Some New Mexico Grandmothers': A Note on the WPA Writers' Program in New Mexico," in idem with Claudia and Samuel Larcombe, eds., *Hispanic Arts and Ethnohistory in the Southwest* (Santa Fe: Ancient City Press; Albuquerque: University of New Mexico Press, 1983), pp. 93–102.

THORP, NATHAN HOWARD (Jack) (1867–1940): FWP; WP. Born June 10, 1867; raised in New York City and Newport; educated St. Paul's School, Concord, New Hampshire. First western experiences on his brother Charles's ranch near Stanton, Nebraska. Went West while in his teens due to his father's losing his money. First New Mexico employment as superintendent of Enterprise Mining Company, Kingston. Ran his own cattle in San Andres Mountains, then began working for Bar W ranch in Lincoln County.

1940 NM: "N. Howard Thorp, widely known as 'Cowboy Jack,' died June 4, 1940, at his home in Alameda, N.M. He had lived in New Mexico for more than half a century, as engineer, cattleman and cowboy poet. He made his home Santa Fe for many years before moving to Alameda five years ago. Thorp's first volume, 'Cowboy Songs' [1908], was published many years ago as a private edition, and is now out of print. 'Songs of the Cowboy' was published by Houghton-Mifflin in 1921, and was followed by 'Tales of the Chuck Wagon' [1926], and many smaller items for the publications of the Texas Folklore Society" (p. 13).

NMFWP, February 1936–August 1939; briefly afterward. Most of his work after July 1938 was on a juvenile book entitled "Cowland: A Story of New Mexico Ranch Life," seventeen chapters plus a glossary. Although rewritten during the Writers' Program after Thorp's death, the book, which was illustrated by NMFAP workers, was never published. Ref.: Neil M. Clark, "Introduction," in Thorp with idem, *Pardner of the Wind* (1941; reprint, Lincoln: University of Nebraska Press, 1977), pp. 13–20.

TOTTY, FRANCES E.: FWP. Mrs. W. C. Totty of Silver City. NMFWP, May 1937–November 1938. "I have been in the hospital as my husband stabbed me in the back. I have been working on my data and am trying to get my work all straightened out, and will send in all of my stories as soon as I gain more strength. Speaker Alvan White has my case now sueing for a divorce, and I hope will soon have everything straightened out for me. I'm sorry that my work has gotten into such a tangle" ("Women and the NMFWP," p. 61).

VADEN, CLAY W.: FWP. Of Quemado. NMFWP, March-December 1936.

VAN SOELEN, THEODORE (1890–1964): PWAP; Section. Born St. Paul, Minnesota, 1890. Studied St. Paul Institute of Arts and Sciences; Pennsylvania Academy of the Fine Arts, Philadelphia. Died Tesuque, 1964.

1940 NM: "In 1916 Mr. Van Soelen stepped off a train in Albuquerque and for nearly twenty years he was seldom outside this state. Before settling down in Santa Fe he lived in Albuquerque, San Mateo, and San Isidro. During those years of wandering around New Mexico he met and knew most of the old timers, among them Gene Rhodes, Vic Culbertson, red-whiskered Red Morley, Uncle Lou Gatlin, Tom Talle, Ed and Manuel Otero, Dick Wooten. He says he could fill pages with the names of cowboys, miners, sheepmen, trappers and so on. He and Uncle Lou lived up on the side of Mount Taylor one summer when Lou was riding for the Fernandez Co., and Van Soelen was trying to imitate him. Old Lou was a type no longer seen around the Plaza in Santa Fe. He was the type who worked for Charles Goodnight, John Chisum, the Matador outfit and many others. He painted a portrait of Lou and he wished that he could have done a dozen" (p. 40).

"During his first years in the west, he acquired a nom de plume when a clerk at an employment agency could not understand his name and wrote him down as 'T. Dan Sullivan.' He didn't bother to correct him when he found it a pretty good name to his companions in the wide open spaces" (p. 44).

"After Virginia Morrison Carr left a cattleman's home for an artist's studio he and Mrs. Van Soelen lived in Santa Fe for several years, then moved to Tesuque Valley, which is still their home. From Santa Fe and Tesuque he sent pictures east which won Bronze medals. . . . Besides landscapes, he has painted portraits more or less steadily during his entire career, as well as murals for the Grant County Court House, Post-Office at Portales, N. M., P. O. at Waurika, Okla., and one he is now working on for the P. O. at Livingston, Texas. In most of his murals he has used some of animal life as the motif" (p. 40).

Baumann 1934: "A painter of established reputation—he not only put a great deal of study into his two decorations for the Grant County Court House, Silver City, New Mexico, they also indicate a fine regard for the wall and warrant more than passing attention. He is one of the few that outdid himself and whose interest never lagged. A Major project."

NOTES

Introduction:
Government-Issue Grass Roots
in New Mexico

1. Tamara Hareven, "The Search for Generational Memory," *Daedalus* 106 (Fall 1978): 137–49; reprinted in David K. Dunaway and Willa K. Baum, eds., *Oral History: An Interdisciplinary Anthology* (Nashville, Tennessee: American Association for State and Local History in cooperation with the Oral History Association, 1984), pp. 248–63. The quote here appears on p. 258.

2. Ibid., p. 260.

3. Ibid., p. 259.

4. The quotations in this paragraph are cited in William F. McDonald, *Federal Relief Administration and the Arts* (Columbus: Ohio State University Press, 1969), pp. 103, 104, and 129, respectively. A fifth sub-project of Federal One, the Historical Records Survey, directed by Luther H. Evans, was not established until November 16, 1935.

5. Ibid., p. ix.

6. Marta Weigle, "Appendix: Notes on Federal Project One and the Federal Writers' Project in New Mexico," in Lorin W. Brown with Charles L. Briggs and Marta Weigle, *Hispano Folklife of New Mexico: The Lorin W. Brown Federal Writers' Project Manuscripts* (Albuquerque: University of New Mexico Press, 1978), p. 240. These "notes" were based on scant administrative records preserved in Santa Fe and have been considerably modified after two NEH-sponsored research trips to Washington repositories.

7. For photographs and a description of El Parian Analco see Sarah Nestor, *The Native Market of the Spanish New Mexican Craftsman, Santa Fe, 1933–1940* (Santa Fe: The Colonial New Mexico Historical Foundation, 1978), pp. 35–55. Hereafter, all quotations and citations not otherwise identified in this introduction are from Record Group No. 69: Records of the Work Projects Administration, National Archives, Washington, D.C. Because of their relative inaccessibility, they have not been further specified here.

8. Nusbaum was born in Las Vegas, the daughter of an Irishman and Marie Josephine Otero O'Bryan, sister of ex-Governor Miguel A.

Otero. She studied art and drama at the Sorbonne and first married musician Alfred Baehrens, with whom she had a son, Deric. After a stint of nursing in France, 1914–15, she and her son returned to New Mexico, where she married Jesse L. Nusbaum in 1922. The couple spent ten years at Mesa Verde National Park, then returned to Santa Fe, where he became director of the Laboratory of Anthropology. See biography of Aileen Nusbaum in Marta Weigle and Kyle Fiore, comps. and eds., *New Mexico Artists and Writers: A Celebration, 1940* (Santa Fe, New Mexico: Ancient City Press, 1982), p. 39.

9. Brown, with Briggs and Weigle, *Hispano Folklife,* pp. 25, 26, 247.

10. This view was originally set forth in Marta Weigle, with Mary Powell, "From Alice Corbin's 'Lines Mumbled in Sleep' to 'Eufemia's Sopapillas': Women and the Federal Writers' Project in New Mexico," *New America* 4, 3 (1982): 54–58. For an alternate view more sympathetic to Cassidy, see Andre Dumont, "Ina Sizer Cassidy and the Writers Project," *Impact: Albuquerque Journal Magazine* (19 January 1982), pp. 12–14.

11. NMFWP districts followed those of the NMWPA. District One was the northeast quadrant (Taos, Colfax, Union, Harding, Quay, Guadalupe, San Miguel, and Mora counties); District Two, the southeast quadrant (Curry, Roosevelt, Lea, Eddy, Otero, Lincoln, De Baca, and Chaves counties); District Three, the northwest quadrant (San Juan, Rio Arriba, McKinley, Sandoval, Santa Fe, Torrance, Bernalillo, and Valencia counties); and District Four, the southwest quadrant (Socorro, Doña Ana, Luna, Hidalgo, Grant, Catron, and Sierra counties).

12. Monty Noam Penkower, *The Federal Writers' Project: A Study in Government Patronage of the Arts* (Urbana: University of Illinois Press, 1977), p. 31.

13. Ibid., p. 32.

14. "Works Progress Administration Handbook, Federal Writers' Project, State of New Mexico," prepared by Ina Sizer Cassidy, 1938 (A#71).

15. On the literary aspects of the NMFWP, see Marta Weigle and Kyle Fiore, *Santa Fe and Taos: The Writer's Era, 1916–1941* (Santa Fe: Ancient City Press, 1982), pp. 49–56.

16. Penkower, *The FWP,* pp. 84–85.

17. Ibid., pp. 94–95.

18. Idaho beat all forty-eight states and the District of Columbia in publishing the first guide, edited by Vardis Fisher and printed in January 1937 by Caxton Printers Ltd. of Caldwell, Idaho. The last state guide, Oklahoma's, was published by the University of Oklahoma Press in 1942. For a useful checklist see Arthur Scharf, "Selected Publications of the WPA Federal Writers' Project and the Writers' Program," in Jerre Mangione, *The Dream and the Deal: The Federal Writers' Project, 1935–1943* (Boston: Little, Brown, 1972), pp. 375–96.

19. Minor revisions were made on this guide in 1953 and 1962. It has recently been completely redone as *New Mexico: A New Guide to the Colorful State,* by Lance Chilton, Katherine Chilton, Polly E. Arango, James Dudley, Nancy Neary, and Patricia Stelzner (Albuquerque: University of New Mexico Press, 1984).

20. For more on folklore and the FWP, see Susan Dwyer-Shick, "Review Essay: Folklore and Government Support," *Journal of American Folklore* 89 (1976): 476–86.

21. The pamphlet is in A#47. Also see the introduction to T. M. Pearce, assisted by Ina Sizer Cassidy and Helen S. Pearce, *New Mexico Place Names: A Geographical Dictionary* (Albuquerque: University of New Mexico Press, 1965), pp. vii–xv.

22. See, e.g., *These Are Our Lives as Told by the People and Written by Members of the Federal Writers' Project of the Works Progress Administration in North Carolina, Tennessee, and Georgia* (Chapel Hill: University of North Carolina Press, 1939); Tom E. Terrill and Jerrold Hirsch, eds., *Such as Us: Southern Voices of the Thirties* (Chapel Hill: University of North Carolina Press, 1978); Leonard Rapport, "How Valid Are the Federal Writers' Project Life Stories: An Iconoclast Among the True Believers," *Oral History Review,* 1979, pp. 6–17; James Seay Brown, Jr., ed., *Up Before Daylight: Life Histories from the Alabama Writers' Project, 1938–1939* (University: University of Alabama Press, 1982). Ann Banks presents a

geographical range of life histories in her collection, *First Person America* (New York: Alfred A. Knopf, 1980), including Annie Lesnett's account of the Lincoln County Wars given to Edith L. Crawford in 1938 (pp. 23–26).

23. The most recent assessment and bibliography of this extensive material is Norman R. Yetman, "Ex-Slave Interviews and the Historiography of Slavery," *American Quarterly* 36 (1984): 181–210.

Chapter One:
Rebozo and Resolano:
Old Hispanic Lifeways

1. NMSRC WPA-PWAP #5409. One of six large federal courthouse paintings (with "The Old Cuba Road"; "Monument Rock—Cañon de Chelly"; "Taos Mountains"; "Cabezon—Puerco Valley"; and "Sand Trail Up Acoma Rock") by Henderson started under the Public Works of Art Project and completed for the Treasury Relief Art Project. William Henry Spurlock, II, "Federal Support for the Visual Arts in the State of New Mexico: 1933–1943" (Master's thesis, University of New Mexico, 1974), p. 75. Also, see Peter Bermingham, *The New Deal in the Southwest: Arizona and New Mexico* (Tucson: University of Arizona Museum of Art, n.d.), pp. 23–24.

2. For an overview, see Marta Weigle, *Hispanic Villages of Northern New Mexico: A Reprint of the 1935 Tewa Basin Study with Supplementary Materials* (Santa Fe, N.M.: Lightning Tree, 1975).

3. "El Inocente," coll. Lorin W. Brown, 20 September 1937; transcribed in Lorin W. Brown, with Charles L. Briggs and Marta Weigle, *Hispano Folklife of New Mexico: The Lorin W. Brown Federal Writers' Project Manuscripts* (Albuquerque: University of New Mexico Press, 1978), pp. 123–24, and listed as no. 72, p. 262.

4. "The Passing of the Tapalo," coll. Reyes N. Martínez, 10 April 1937; transcribed in Marta Weigle, with Mary Powell, "From Alice Corbin's 'Lines Mumbled in Sleep' to 'Eufemia's Sopapillas': Women and the Federal Writers' Project in New Mexico," *New America* 4, 3 (1982): 71–72.

5. Cleofas M. Jaramillo, *Shadows of the Past (Sombras del pasado)* (1941; reprint, Santa Fe: Ancient City Press, 1980), p. 97.

6. Fray Angelico Chavez, *My Penitente Land: Reflections on Spanish New Mexico* (Albuquerque: University of New Mexico Press, 1974), p. xiv.

7. Fabiola Cabeza de Baca (Gilbert), *We Fed Them Cactus* (1954; reprint, Albuquerque: University of New Mexico Press, 1979), pp. 177–78.

8. Alfonso Griego, *Good-bye My Land of Enchantment: A true story of some of the first Spanish-speaking natives and early settlers of San Miguel County, Territory of New Mexico* (n.p., 1981), pp. 67, 69.

9. William deBuys, "Fractions of Justice: A Legal and Social History of the Las Trampas Land Grant, New Mexico," *New Mexico Historical Review* 56 (1981): 72.

10. According to Van Deren Coke, Collier's "well-composed pictures reflect his training as a painter. His earlier assignment in the [Pennsylvania] coal mines had given him experience with synchronized flashbulbs. He used this technique to light interiors in which there were people and to create a sense of drama in some of his pictures. There is usually an upbeat feeling to his work that separates it from many other FSA photographs. Strong faces that fill the frame are common. These frequently were taken with a flashbulb or flashbulbs arranged to illuminate one side of a subject's face more than the other so as to create a feeling of roundness and record skin textures in detail. Collier's photographs . . . are very humanistic, and also strong as pictures, for he had a sensitivity to pleasing arrangements of bold shapes that were distinctive." Coke, *Photography in New Mexico: From the Daguerreotype to the Present* (Albuquerque: University of New Mexico Press, 1979), p. 31.

11. Marta Weigle, "'Some New Mexico Grandmothers': A Note on the WPA Writers' Program in New Mexico," in idem with Claudia Larcombe and Samuel Larcombe, eds., *Hispanic Arts and Ethnohistory in New Mexico* (Santa Fe: Ancient City Press; Albuquerque: University of New Mexico Press, 1983), pp. 93–102. "Catalina Viareal" is listed as no. 3, p. 100.

12. The first 1835 Las Vegas settlers from San Miguel del Bado included several named Ulibarri and Baca. However, a search of F. Stanley [Crocchiola], *The Las Vegas (New Mexico) Story* (Denver, 1951); Milton W. Callon, *Las Vegas, New Mexico ... The Town That Wouldn't Gamble* (Las Vegas Daily Optic Publishing, 1962); and Lynn Perrigo, *Gateway to Glorieta: A History of Las Vegas, New Mexico* (Boulder, Colo.: Pruett Publishing, 1982) yielded no references to Santiago Ulibarri, María Ignacia Gonzales or Severo Baca. Before the American administration Hilario Gonzales served as local *juez de paz* and with others in 1855 filed a claim with the surveyor-general for confirmation of the Las Vegas Land Grant. Perrigo, ibid., pp. 67, 103, 104. Callon reprints a notice of Santa Fe Trail wagon and goods belonging to Ilario (Hilario) Gonzales. Ibid., p. 41.

However, Fabiola Cabeza de Baca's remembers Don Hilario Gonzales as one of the richest men in the 1870s, running both cattle and sheep on the Llano. Cabeza de Baca, *We Fed Them Cactus*, pp. 31, 57, 68, 70. He and Don Francisco López purchased part of the huge Pablo Montoya Grant from the Montoya heirs (p. 69). In 1860, he built the chapel at San Hilario (pp. 31, 68). Cabeza de Baca also notes that "I knew his two daughters, Doña María Ignacia Baca and Doña Juanita Martínez" (p. 68), but she does not mention Severo Baca, Santiago Ulibarri or Guadalupe Baca de Gallegos.

When the young priest Jean Baptiste Salpointe first arrived in New Mexico in October 1859, he and his companions dined at Las Vegas with Father Francisco Pinard: "The Rev. gentleman was an ex-officer of the French army, who, after his ordination to the priesthood, had come to New Mexico to devote himself to the work of the missions." Salpointe, *Soldiers of the Cross: Notes on the Ecclesiastical History of New Mexico, Arizona and Colorado* (1898; reprint, Albuquerque: Calvin Horn, 1967), p. 218. On April 2, 1864, a correspondent described Pinard as a "Frenchman from France [who] has seen his sixty years of this world ... a man [who] seems kind, liberal and hospitable and much respected by his parishioners." Callon, *Las Vegas*, p. 27.

13. HABS NM-12, Library of Congress. See Alicia Stamm, "The Checklist of Buildings, Structures, and Sites," in *Historic America: Buildings, Structures, and Sites* (Washington, D.C.: Library of Congress, 1983), p. 514. For a photo and guide to the house today, see Marc Simmons, *Following the Santa Fe Trail: A Guide for Modern Travelers* (Santa Fe: Ancient City Press, 1984), pp. 177–79.

14. For one of Sra. Gallegos's magic tales see Marta Weigle, "Guadalupe Baca de Gallegos' *Los tres preciosidas*' (The Three Treasures): Notes on the Tale, Its Narrator and Collector," *New Mexico Folklore Record* 15 (1980–81): 31–35.

15. Father Joseph Maria Coudert came to New Mexico in 1856. His officiating at an 1865 Las Vegas wedding seems problematic, since he was traveling with Bishop Jean Baptiste Lamy in 1863–64 and 1866–67, and apparently did not become parish priest at Our Lady of Sorrows Church until the 1880s. Salpointe, *Soldiers of the Cross*, pp. 240, 273; Perrigo, *Gateway to Glorieta*, p. 163.

16. Sostenes may represent the blurring of two legendary figures. Billy the Kid's "gang" involved Tom O'Folliard, Charles Bowdre, Dave Rudabaugh, Billie Wilson, and Tom Pickett. Stephen Tatum, *Inventing Billy the Kid: Visions of the Outlaw in America, 1881–1981* (Albuquerque: University of New Mexico Press, 1982), p. 30. Vicente Silva arrived in Las Vegas in 1875, opened the Imperial Bar on the plaza, and by 1890 became openly known for his nefarious activities. His "band" included the twins Tomás and Juan de Dios Lucero. The latter had a son named Sostenes, who became a noted criminal in Mora County. Tom McGrath, *Vicente Silva and His Forty Thieves* (Las Vegas, 1960), pp. 6, 13–14.

17. Mary Elba C. De Baca is the daughter of Mr. and Mrs. F. C. De Baca, 105 Taos Street, West Las Vegas. In his "Brief Biography of Mary Elba C. De Baca" (139 wds., 1 p., 27 March 1939, rec. 29 March; BC138; H5-5-51#6; LC47.1), Lynn notes: "Mary Elba C. De Baca was born in Las Vegas, New Mexico, September 14, 1917. ... Except for a short time spent in Los Alamos, New Mexico, when she was seven years old Mary Elba has lived all her life in Las

Vegas. She attended the Las Vegas High School and is now a sophomore in the New Mexico Normal University where she is majoring in education."

18. In 1869 Rumauldo Baca lent the Sisters of Loretto a three-room adobe in which to start a girls' school and about 1878 built a four-story building west of the Exchange Hotel on the plaza in anticipation of the railroad depot. Instead, the station was built across the river in East Las Vegas and his building came to be called "Baca's Folly." Perrigo, *Gateway to Glorieta,* pp. 18, 19, 133. Fabiola Cabeza de Baca refers to Don Romualdo Baca, who lived on the plaza and donated land for the church and school. Cabeza de Baca, *We Fed Them Cactus,* pp. 81–82. An Isador V. Gallegos dealt in land and livestock and figured in various land claims in the early 1900s. Ibid., pp. 116, 124. However, it may be that neither of these figures are indicated in Mary Elba C. De Baca's account of her grandmother's life.

19. In 1870 Kansas City millionaire Wilson Waddingham purchased the Pablo Montoya Land Grant and began combining other tracts into the Bell Ranch of nearly a million acres in the Canadian River Valley. Manuel Cabeza de Baca is Fabiola Cabeza de Baca's uncle, and she describes him as an elegant gentleman and well-educated lawyer for years employed by the Atchison, Topeka and Santa Fe Railway. In 1896 he published *Historia de Vicente Silva, sus cuarenta bandidos, sus crimenes y retribuciones* at La Voz del Pueblo Press in Las Vegas. An undated English version, *The History of Vicente Silva and His Forty Bandits,* was later published at Las Vegas by the Spanish-American Publishing Company. Ibid., pp. 96, 120. According to Cabeza de Baca, her Uncle Manuel "was a very proud man, but after his death [in 1915], we found out that he was quite a humanitarian. His books were filled with the cancelled debts of poor people who were unable to pay him for his services as a lawyer." Ibid., p. 96. Don Manuel's son Florencio was married in 1905. Ibid., p. 119.

20. The description of Chihuahua is from "Roswell," coll. Georgia B. Redfield; 230 wds., 2 pp., 8 December 1936, rec. 10 December (A#187; LC38.1).

21. Lynda A. Sánchez uses NMFWP materials and interviews with old residents to portray the Hispanic view in "Recuerdos de Billy the Kid," *New Mexico Magazine,* July 1981, pp. 16–19, 68, 70–71. For a contrasting Anglo viewpoint, see N. H. Thorp's "Billy ('The Kid') Bonney," in idem with Neil M. Clark, *Pardner of the Wind* (1941; reprint, Lincoln: University of Nebraska Press, 1977), pp. 168–93. Also, see Tatum, "Introduction to Billy the Kid's Legend and Bibliography," *Inventing Billy the Kid,* pp. 3–14.

22. For more on Lucien Bonaparte Maxwell (1818–75), his grant, and the legendary Cimarron mansion, see Jim Berry Pearson, *The Maxwell Land Grant* (Norman: University of Oklahoma Press, 1961); Lawrence P. Murphy, "Master of the Cimarron: Lucien B. Maxwell," *New Mexico Historical Review* 55 (1980): 5–23; and idem, *Lucien Bonaparte Maxwell: Napoleon of the Southwest* (Norman: University of Oklahoma Press, 1983). The concrete statue photographed by Lee can be seen in a park next to the Cimarron City Hall. Simmons, *Following the Santa Fe Trail,* p. 140.

23. Costilla had a vocational training school under Brice H. Sewell and the State Department of Vocational Education by March 1936, so this may have become part of the WPA by 1939. See William Wroth, "New Hope in Hard Times: Hispanic Crafts are Revived during Troubled Years," *El Palacio* 89, 2 (Summer 1983): 22–31.

24. G. Emlen Hall calls Octaviano Segura "smart, cagey, and progressive." He worked with two Pueblo Lands Board employees, Mark W. Ratcliffe and Joe W. Sena, in 1929, cooperating "in agreeing that each East Pecos resident's individual claim ran from the Pecos River almost two miles east, to the grant boundary itself. As the northernmost resident of the area purchased by his father-in-law [Donaciano Vigil] from Preston Beck, Jr., sixty-five years before, Segura found himself in a position to suggest to the board surveyors that almost three hundred acres at the north end of East Pecos, above the community irrigation ditch, now belonged to him, for lack of any other owner." Hall, *Four Leagues of Pecos: A Legal History of the Pecos Grant, 1800–1933* (Albuquerque: University of New Mexico

Press, 1984), pp. 263–64.

25. Irving Rusinow, *A Camera Report on El Cerrito: A Typical Spanish-American Community in New Mexico*, Miscellaneous Pub. No. 479, United States Department of Agriculture, Bureau of Agricultural Economics, January 1942, p. 3. El Cerrito has been studied several times since the visits of BAE social scientists Olen E. Leonard (October 1939–May 1940) and Charles P. Loomis (February-April, June, October, and November 1940). For an overview and recent study, see Richard L. Nostrand, "El Cerrito Revisited," *New Mexico Historical Review* 57 (1982): 109–22. Negatives of Rusinow's photographs are in the National Archives.

Chapter Two:
Miners, Merchants,
Homesteaders, and Indians:
Western New Mexicans

1. NMSRC WPA-PWAP #5489. According to Gustave Baumann, in "A Retrospect of Work and the Artists Employed in the Thirteenth Region under the Public Works of Art Project" (1934), "Warren E. Rollins, Farmington, New Mexico [was] one of the old timers to whom working on the project is the high moment—his decoration for the Gallup Post Office depicts an Indian Ceremony—inappropriate anywhere excepting in a town that capitalizes on these ceremonials" (A#155, p. 21).

2. "Bill Warner," coll. Frances E. Totty from Leo Schiff and Ed Cooney; 1 p., 2 May 1938 (A#203.)

3. From "Joe Griggs, Amateur Naturalist," coll. Mrs. W. C. Totty from Joe Griggs; 2 pp., 19 June 1937 (A#203).

4. James A. McKenna, *Black Range Tales: Chronicling Sixty Years of Life and Adventure in the Southwest* (1936; reprint, Glorieta, N.M.: Rio Grande Press, 1965, 1971).

5. Norman Cleaveland with George Fitzpatrick, *The Morleys—Young Upstarts on the Southwest Frontier* (Albuquerque: Calvin Horn, 1971), p. 242.

6. Agnes Morley Cleaveland, *No Life for a Lady* (Boston: Houghton Mifflin, 1941), p. 331.

7. Ibid., p. 333.

8. On Lilly, who was buried in Silver City, see: J. Frank Dobie, *The Ben Lilly Legend* (New York, 1950); H. A. Hoover, *Early Days in the Mogollons (Muggy-Yones): Tales from the Bloated Goat*, ed. Francis L. Fulgate (El Paso: Texas Western Press, 1958), pp. 57–58; Bill [William] Rakocy and R[osamond] S. Jones, eds., *Mogollon Diary, 1877–1977* (El Paso, Texas: Superior Printing, for Rio Bravo Press, 1977), pp. 118–40. On Stevens, see: Montague Stevens, *Meet Mr. Grizzly: A Saga on the Passing of the Grizzly* (Albuquerque: University of New Mexico Press, 1943); Sharman Apt Russell, "Dan Gatlin and Montague Stevens: A Friendship of the Old West," *New Mexico Magazine*, January 1984, pp. 63, 69–71; Marc Simmons, "Stalking Grizzlies," in *Ranchers, Ramblers and Renegades: True Tales of Territorial New Mexico* (Santa Fe: Ancient City Press, 1984), pp. 73–75.

9. Michael Jenkinson, "Tales of the Gila," *New Mexico Magazine*, April 1979, pp. 40–41.

10. Caption on LC-USF 33-12703-M3. J. Frank Dobie surveys the personal and printed sources on "Where I Dug for Adams Gold" in his *Apache Gold and Yaqui Silver* (1928, 1931, 1938, 1939; reprint, Albuquerque: University of New Mexico Press, 1976), pp. 357–62.

11. Erna Fergusson, *New Mexico: A Pageant of Three Peoples* (1951, 1964; reprint, Albuquerque: University of New Mexico Press, 1973), p. 301. Also, see Rakocy and Jones, *Mogollon Diary, 1877–1977*.

12. T. M. Pearce, ed., *New Mexico Place Names: A Geographical Dictionary* (Albuquerque: University of New Mexico Press, 1965), pp. 8–9.

13. On farming and flooding in this area during the early 1900s, see Dale C. Maluy, "Boer Colonization in the Southwest," *New Mexico Historical Review* 52 (1977): 93–110. Also, see Ira G. Clark, "The Elephant Butte Controversy: A Chapter in the Emergence of Federal Water Law," *Journal of American History* 61 (1975): 1006–33; Paul A. Lester, "History of the Elephant Butte Irrigation District" (Master's thesis, New Mexico State University, 1977).

14. "In 1943, [Delano] photographed on as-

signment from the United States Office of War Information [formerly FSA] in New Mexico, concentrating on pictures of the Atchison, Topeka & Santa Fe Railroad locomotives, stations, yards, and shops. He was very active in Albuquerque at the large shop maintained there by the A.T.&S.F., in Gallup, and along the tracks in Clovis, Isleta, and Vaughn, New Mexico. His were directly recorded pictures full of information but without any special artistic character— just the type of pictures the government wanted for documentary purposes." Van Deren Coke, *Photography in New Mexico: From the Daguerreotype to the Present* (Albuquerque: University of New Mexico Press, 1979), p. 31.

15. See Agnes Morley Cleaveland, *Satan's Paradise: From Lucien Maxwell to Fred Lambert* (Boston: Houghton Mifflin, 1952).

16. Cleaveland, with Fitzpatrick, *The Morleys*, p. 29.

17. Ibid., p. 243. Also, see Agnes Morley Cleaveland on her brother Ray, "who was all-American and captained the Columbia football team in 1900–01 and who gained later fame as a New Mexico cattleman and practical joker," in "Titan of the Range," *New Mexico Magazine,* December 1941, pp. 16, 37.

18. Russell Lee, "Pie Town, New Mexico," *U.S. Camera,* October 1941, pp. 39–54, 88–89, 106–7. Also, see Toby Smith, "A Return to Pie Town," *Impact: Albuquerque Journal Magazine,* vol. 6, no. 14 (18 January 1983), pp. 4–8. According to Van Deren Coke, "Russell Lee ... had a degree in chemical engineering from Lehigh University and ... also studied art at the California School of Fine Arts before joining the FSA team. This background probably accounts for his ability to overcome technical problems as well as to place the elements in his photographs sensitively so as to produce pictures that were much more than mere documents.... He documented his subjects with an acute social consciousness, but the bleakness, to be believed, he felt, had to be recorded clearly and frontally. The results are photographs that are strong and unsmiling but also evoke feelings of sympathy and have distinct artistic qualities." Coke, *Photography in New Mexico,* pp. 30–31. Bill Ganzel interviewed and re-

photographed Pie Town residents, including Jack Keele and George Hutton in October 1980. Ganzel, *Dust Bowl Descent* (Lincoln: University of Nebraska Press, 1984), pp. 80–87.

19. Marian Meier, "Piñon Country," *New Mexico Magazine,* September 1977, p. 33. Also, see Arthur L. Campa, "Piñon as an Economic and Social Factor," *New Mexico Business Review* 1 (1932): 144–47.

20. On the Hispano approach to gathering piñons, see Reyes N. Martínez's NMFWP submission, "Piñon Picking," reprinted in Cleofas M. Jaramillo, *The Genuine New Mexico Tasty Recipes* (1942; reprint, Santa Fe: Ancient City Press, 1981), p. 31.

21. Ellis Arthur Davis, ed., *The Historical Encyclopedia of New Mexico* (Albuquerque: New Mexico Historical Association, 1945), p. 807.

22. Eleanor Davenport MacDonald and John Brown Arrington, *The San Juan Basin: My Kingdom Was a Country* (Denver, Colo.: Green Mountain Press, 1970), p. 79. Arrington also remembered that "the Markley family shipped in by wagon freight one of the first pianos in Farmington." Ibid. William Locke's reminiscences are in Agnes Miller Furman, *Tohta: An Early Day History of the Settlement of Farmington and San Juan County, New Mexico, 1875–1900* (Wichita Falls, Tex.: Nortex Press, 1977), pp. 61–64.

23. "Restoration of New Mexico Missions," *El Palacio* 17, 10 (November 15, 1924): 251–53. Those on the Committee are listed as Daeger, Hewett, Vierra, Mr. Paul A. F. Walter, Dr. and Mrs. Frank E. Mera, Mr. Frank Springer, Mr. Dan Kelly, Mrs. J. C. Robinson, Miss Ann [*sic*] Evans, and Miss Mary Williard, with Mr. Burnham Hoyt as architect and Meem as assistant architect.

24. Bainbridge Bunting, *John Gaw Meem: Southwestern Architect* (Albuquerque: University of New Mexico Press, 1983), pp. 15, 17. Bunting gives the dates as 1927–30, but B. A. Reuter's NMFWP submissions consistently indicate 1926–29.

25. "Acoma Pueblo," coll. B. A. Reuter from "investigation and personal experience"; 3,500 wds, 10 pp. typed, 16 January 1939 (A#62; handwritten, penciled original, 27 pp., LCms#5).

According to a "Correction to manuscript of March 10/39 by Bernhardt A. Reuter on Acoma Pueblo," "I was employed by the Society on August 17, 1926. I went to Acoma in company with Mr. Meem a few days later but can not give the exact date. My hand-bag was stolen from my car in Albuquerque containing all my records and therefore I have no records to consult" (7 April 1939, LCms#6).

26. "The Work [?] of Restoring the Acoma Mission," p. 1, coll. B. A. Reuter; 8 pp., n.d. (A#62). Bautisto Rey served as Pueblo Governor in 1926. Ward Alan Minge, *Acoma: Pueblo in the Sky* (Albuquerque: University of New Mexico Press, 1976), p. 144.

27. "Acoma Pueblo (Section II of manuscript of week ending Jan. 27, '39)," coll. B. A. Reuter from "Acoma Indians and personal experience"; 3,200 wds., 9 typed pp., 7 February 1939 (A#62; handwritten, penciled original, 25 pp., 3 February, LCms#5).

28. James H. Miller served as Pueblo Governor in 1924 and 1925. Minge, *Acoma*, p. 144.

29. HABS NM-5, Library of Congress. See Alicia Stamm, "The Checklist of Buildings, Structures, and Sites," in *Historic America: Buildings, Structures, and Sites* (Washington, D.C.: Library of Congress, 1983), p. 515. Also, see Peter Nabokov, *Architecture of Acoma Pueblo: The 1934 Historic American Buildings Survey Project* (Santa Fe: Ancient City Press, 1985). A 1934 drawing of a pueblo house by Paul Atwood, Stanley Kent and A. G. Longfellow appears in *Historic America*, p. 20.

Chapter Three:
Commerce and Cowboys:
The Northeast

1. NMSRC WPA-PWAP #5361. William Henry Spurlock, II, "Federal Support for the Visual Arts in the State of New Mexico: 1933–1943" (Master's thesis, University of New Mexico, 1974), p. 71. Chapman painted seven other oils of the same dimensions for Shuler Audito-

rium in 1934: "Maxwell Mansion—1865 A.D.";
"Wooton Toll Gate—1868 A.D."; "Cheyenne Village—1845 A.D."; "Clifton Station—1875 A.D."; "Blossburg Mine—1895 A.D."; "Raton's First Street—1893 A.D."; and "Elizabethtown—1885 A.D." According to an anonymous account, "Blazed Trails: Art and Artists in New Mexico" (probably by Ina Sizer Cassidy), "It seems to me a bit of poetic justice that this son of a pioneer [Chapman] should have been chosen to record the history of his fathers. Being, myself, the daughter of a pioneer, I can fully and deeply appreciate the emotion actuating Manville Chapman, and the work he has done for the generations to come who can know little or nothing of the real struggles of the early vanguard of civilization. . . . Thus in Shuler Auditorium, named for a famous pioneer physician, Dr. Shuler, is recorded for generations to come the exciting pioneer history of the Gateway to New Mexico. We of today and those of tomorrow should be grateful to the Public Works of Art Project and to Manville Chapman" (LCms#1, pp. 2–3, 4). Directions for locating both Willow Springs and Shuler Theater are in Marc Simmons, *Following the Santa Fe Trail: A Guide for Modern Travelers* (Santa Fe: Ancient City Press, 1984), pp. 136–37.

2. From "S 600—Willow Springs Ranch House," coll. Manville Chapman from research in books, Charles B. Thacker ("one time inhabitant of Willow Springs house"), and W. A. Chapman ("pioneer of Colfax County"); 2 pp., 13 May 1936 (A#115).

3. Simmons, *Following the Santa Fe Trail*, p. 207.

4. From "Historical: History of Cattle in the Southwest," coll. Kenneth Fordyce; 25 June 1938 (A#104), p. 9. Also see J. B. Jackson, "High Plains Country: A Sketch of the Geography, Physical and Human, of Union County, N.M.," *Landscape* 3, 3 (1954): 11–22.

5. See, for example: Van Deren Coke, *Taos and Santa Fe: The Artist's Environment, 1882–1942* (Albuquerque: University of New Mexico Press, 1963); Marta Weigle and Kyle Fiore, *Santa Fe and Taos: The Writer's Era, 1916–1941* (Santa Fe: Ancient City Press, 1982); idem, comps. and

eds., *New Mexico Artists and Writers: A Celebration, 1940* (Santa Fe: Ancient City Press, 1982); Robert R. White, ed. and annotator, *The Taos Society of Artists* (Albuquerque: University of New Mexico Press, 1983).

6. Patricia Janis Broder, *Taos: A Painter's Dream* (Boston: New York Graphics Society, 1980), p. 50, and illus., pp. 36, 55, 58.

7. "In 1936 [Rothstein] made his most famous single picture, a gritty view of a farmer and his boys rushing toward the shelter of a low, roughly finished wooden shed for protection from a swirling Oklahoma dust storm. From Oklahoma, Rothstein came to New Mexico, where he photographed Taos Pueblo and did some work around Las Cruces. None of his New Mexico pictures match in intensity his Dust Bowl photographs. There are even picturesque elements in some of his Taos pictures." Van Deren Coke, *Photography in New Mexico: From the Daguerreotype to the Present* (Albuquerque: University of New Mexico Press, 1979), p. 31.

8. F. Stanley, *The Des Moines New Mexico Story* (Pep, Texas: Author, 1965), pp. 3, 11. "When the Colorado & Southern Railroad extended its lines through New Mexico in 1887–88 a station was set at the foot of the Sierra Grande and named Des Moines. For 19 years there was no town at this site; but in 1907 two sites were surveyed and settled, one founded by R. M. Saavedra, the other by J. F. Branson. The former was named for its founder; the latter was called Des Moines. . . . In 1915–16, Saavedra took the lead in population. . . . Then the Townsite Company, assisted by railroad interests, bought 17 acres lying between Saavedra and Des Moines and this tract drew the two groups together [and] . . . the name Des Moines was adopted. . . . For a time the population grew so rapidly much of it was housed in hastily built shacks. An early settler named Rogers became known as the Shack Builder after constructing 75 of these shelters in 90 days." *New Mexico: A Guide to the Colorful State* (New York: Hastings House, 1940), p. 304.

9. Jesse James Swaggerty (b. Tennessee, 1890; mar. Kansas, 1909) ranched in Elida, New Mexico, before establishing the Swaggerty Lumber Company in Clayton in 1918. He was also an architect and contractor. By 1945, his son Ancil was married, with one child, and a lieutenant in the Navy Air Corps. See Ellis Arthur Davis, ed., *The Historical Encyclopedia of New Mexico* (Albuquerque: New Mexico Historical Association, 1945), p. 1626.

10. Clara Toombs Harvey, *Not So Wild, The Old West: A Collection of Facts, Fables and Fun* (Denver, Colo.: Golden Bell Press, 1961), pp. 335, 334.

11. On famous cowboy and later Clayton resident Col. Jack Potter (1864–1950), see Jean M. Burroughs, *On the Trail: The Life and Tales of "Lead Steer" Potter* (Santa Fe: Museum of New Mexico Press, 1980).

12. A 1937 ad for Raton's Swastika Hotel, "100 rooms—strictly modern—fireproof—garage," managed by Ainslee D. Embree, proclaims: "This Hotel is 'Run' to Suit YOU. Raton is the center of many interesting and scenic trips and the Swastika, with cafe connecting, offers every convenience and comfort to visitors. Many enjoy the attractive cocktail lounge and bar." Single rates ranged from $1.50 to $3.50. *Picturesque Southwest*, vol. 1, no. 1 (1937), p. 82.

13. On Sumpter's part in the capture of William Coe, who was lynched in Pueblo, Colorado, on July 21, 1868, see Marc Simmons, *Ranchers, Ramblers and Renegades: True Tales of Territorial New Mexico* (Santa Fe: Ancient City Press, 1984), pp. 33–34.

14. On Col. Jack Potter's view of McJunkin and other "Negro cowboys," see Burroughs, *On the Trail*, pp. 133–36.

15. See, for example, David Stuart, "The Folsom Site: A World-Class Discovery," *Glimpses of the Ancient Southwest* (Santa Fe: Ancient City Press, 1985), pp. 23–26; George A. Agogino, "Indians of Roosevelt County," *Rio Grande History*, no. 5, Summer 1975, pp. 20–23, with photo of McJunkin, p. 20.

16. *New Mexico: A Guide*, pp. xxxi, 232–33. Bean Day was established in 1911 to join area corn and bean farmers and ranchers in celebrating the harvest. It became an annual Labor Day event.

17. From "Unusual Industries," coll. Genevieve Chapin from Deam; 25 July 1936 (A#238;

LC47.1), pp. 3–4. Also, see Harvey, *Not So Wild,* p. 366.

Chapter Four:
The Literary Tularosa

1. NMSRC WPA-PWAP#5518. According to Mrs. W. C. Totty, "'The Round-Up' and 'The Chino Mines' murals were painted by Theodore Van Soelins [*sic*] who was hired by the Public Works of Art Project. These paintings were done in 1933 and 1934 and were accepted in a speech by John O'Leary for the county. Mr. Van Soelins is an adopted son of New Mexico. . . . Mr. Van Soelin's picture of the 'Round-Up' isn't painted from imagination of observation, but from actual experience having worked on one of the Fernandez Company ranches." Totty, "Points of Interest: The Courthouse Murals," 1 p., 19 June 1937; LCms#1.

2. John L. Sinclair, *New Mexico: The Shining Land* (Albuquerque: University of New Mexico Press, 1980), p. 109.

3. Harvey Fergusson, *Home in the West: An Inquiry into My Origins* (New York: Duell, Sloan and Pearce, 1944), p. 65.

4. Delbert E. Wylder, "Emerson Hough (1857–1923)," in *Fifty Western Writers,* ed. Fred Erisman and Richard W. Etulain (Westport, Conn.: Greenwood Press, 1982), p. 207.

5. Fergusson, *Home in the West,* p. 66.

6. Emerson Hough, *Heart's Desire* (New York: Macmillan, 1905; reprint, with introduction by Peter White, Lincoln: University of Nebraska Press, 1981).

7. N. Howard (Jack) Thorp, with Neil M. Clark, *Pardner of the Wind* (1941; reprint, Lincoln: University of Nebraska Press, 1977), p. 14.

8. Facsimile reprint and extensive discussion in N. Howard ("Jack") Thorp, *Songs of the Cowboys,* ed. Austin E. and Alta S. Fife (New York: Bramhall House, 1966).

9. Jim Bob Tinsley, *He Was Singin' This Song: A Collection of Forty-Eight Traditional Songs of the American Cowboy* (Orlando: University Presses of Florida, 1981), pp. 84–87.

10. Thorp, with Clark, *Pardner of the Wind,* p. 14.

11. C. L. Sonnichsen, *Tularosa: Last of the Frontier West* (1960; reprint, Albuquerque: University of New Mexico Press, 1980), pp. 202–27.

12. Eugene Manlove Rhodes, "Neglecting Fractions," reprinted in Marta Weigle and Kyle Fiore, *Santa Fe and Taos: The Writer's Era, 1916–1941* (Santa Fe: Ancient City Press, 1982), pp. 152–53.

13. Sonnichsen, *Tularosa,* p. 202.

14. C. L. Sonnichsen, ed., *Morris B. Parker's White Oaks: Life in a New Mexico Gold Camp, 1880–1900* (Tucson: University of Arizona Press, 1971), p. 5.

15. Ibid., p. 127.

16. In the late 1890s the South Homestake owners sold to the Wild Cat Leasing Company, which included miner Ed Queen. Ibid, p. 116.

17. Sinclair, *New Mexico: The Shining Land,* p. 113.

18. John L. Sinclair, *Cowboy Riding Country* (Albuquerque: University of New Mexico Press, 1982), p. 70.

19. Ibid., p. 105.

20. Betty Woods, "He Man's Town," *New Mexico Magazine,* April 1941, p. 37. A photo of the saloon appears on p. 13.

21. Edwin W. Gaston, Jr., "Eugene Manlove Rhodes (1869–1934)," in *Fifty Western Writers,* pp. 369–71.

22. On Colonel Albert Jennings Fountain and his young son Henry's mysterious 1896 murder, see, for example, Sonnichsen, *Tularosa,* pp. 115–30.

23. Thomas Casad helped found the Mesilla *Independent* in 1877. His son Humboldt went to the University of the Pacific, where Rhodes enrolled in 1888. Ibid., pp. 66, 209, 214.

24. Charles F. Lummis (1859–1928) wrote numerous books on the Southwest and entertained many western writers in his Los Angeles home, El Alisal. See, for example, Turbesé Lummis Fiske and Keith Lummis, *Charles F. Lummis: The Man and His West* (Norman: University of Oklahoma Press, 1975). Rhodes's first published work, the poem "Charlie Graham," appeared in

Lummis's magazine *Land of Sunshine* in April 1896. Gaston, "Eugene Manlove Rhodes," p. 370.

25. "Mrs. Heeman" may be Felicia Hemans.

26. According to Gaston, Alan Rhodes (b. June 12, 1901, in Tularosa) was named for Alan Breck in Robert Louis Stevenson's *Kidnapped*. Gaston, "Eugene Manlove Rhodes," p. 370.

27. Democrat Antonio Joseph was territorial delegate to Congress in 1884 and 1886. In 1888 he defeated Republican Mariano S. Otero, who was Thomas Benton Catron's (1840–1921) choice. Victor Westphall, *Thomas Benton Catron and His Era* (Tucson: University of Arizona Press, 1973), pp. 202–203.

Chapter Five:
Southeastern Scouts, Ranchers, and Homesteaders

1. The fresco secco "Sun and Rain" is flanked by smaller (51″ × 27″) panels entitled "Sorghum" and "Yucca," as illustrated in William Henry Spurlock, II, "Federal Support for the Visual Arts in the State of New Mexico: 1933–1943" (Master's thesis, University of New Mexico, 1974), p. 32. Hurd was commissioned to do the frescos and did not enter a competition as many Treasury Section artists did. According to Spurlock, he was paid in installments: "twenty-five per cent after the preliminary designs were accepted, twenty-five per cent for full size cartoons, twenty-five per cent when the mural was half completed, and the final installment when the murals were approved and photographed. Hurd . . . went to great lengths to make his subject matter as representative of and relevant to the community as possible." Ibid., pp. 27–28.

Hurd's letters show some of his negotiations with the Treasury Department, especially over the frescos in the Dallas Post Office Terminal Annex Building, which he did in 1940. Robert Metzger, ed., *My Land is the Southwest: Peter Hurd Letters and Journals* (College Station: Texas A & M University Press, 1983), pp. 217–25. His letters show him at work on the Alamogordo cartoon on June 25, 1941. Ibid., p. 247. On August 4, 1941, he wrote his wife, Henriette Wyeth

Hurd: "You ask what I am painting: only the tiniest part of the Cartoon for Alamogordo remains then Rodden of Roswell will come to photograph it to be sent to Washington for approval. They have already seen and approved photographs of the two supplementary end panels. Then the two landscapes I told you of in recent letters—'The Shower of the Plain'—and Landscape with Sheepherder." Ibid., p. 250. On October 31, he is planning to ask Edna Imhoff to pose and to return to work at Alamogordo in January 1942, having delayed the contract until May 1st. Ibid., p. 254. Hurd announces the frescos' completion in a letter dated April 21, 1942. Ibid., p. 259.

2. Paul Horgan, *Far From Cibola* (1936; reprint, Albuquerque: University of New Mexico Press, 1974), pp. 9–10.

3. May Price Mosley, *"Little Texas" Beginnings in Southeastern New Mexico,* ed. Martha Downer Ellis (Roswell, N.M.: Hall-Poorbaugh Press, 1973), p. 2. For a useful overview of the Staked Plains, see William B. Conroy, "The Llano Estacado in 1541: Spanish Perception of a Distinctive Physical Setting," *Journal of the West* 11 (1972): 573–81.

4. Mosley, *"Little Texas" Beginnings,* p. 6. According to Mosley, "chosey" is a "corruption of the Spanish *achosa,* meaning camp house." Ibid., p. 3. Also, see Jean M. Burroughs, "The Last of the Buffalo Hunters, George Causey: Hunter, Trader, Rancher," *El Palacio* 80, 4 (November 1974): 15–21.

5. Mosley, *"Little Texas" Beginnings,* p. 6. Mosley also described another subsurface resource—oil—which was drilled in the early 1920s in Lea County. Ibid., pp. 83–86. As with water, windmills were also important in oil. Holt Priddy, "Windmills and Petroleum," *El Palacio* 80, 4 (November 1974): 22–27.

6. James D. Shinkle, *Fifty Years of Roswell History—1867–1917* (Roswell, N.M.: Hall-Poorbaugh Press, 1964), p. 56.

7. See, for example, Paul Bonnifield, *The Dust Bowl: Men, Dirt, and Depression* (Albuquerque: University of New Mexico Press, 1979); Donald Worster, *Dust Bowl: The Southern Plains in the 1930s* (New York: Oxford University Press, 1979).

8. Katheryn L. Fambrough, "Depression Years in Lincoln County," *Rio Grande History,* no. 9, 1978, p. 10.

9. May Price Mosley, *"Little Texas" Beginnings,* a selection from her NMFWP submissions. Also, see Pen La Farge, "The Changes of a Plain: Lea County, New Mexico," *El Palacio* 80, 4 (November 1974): 1–14.

10. Ken Cobean, "Uncle Kit," *New Mexico Magazine,* June 1957, pp. 20–21; Elvis E. Fleming and Minor S. Huffman, eds., *Roundup on the Pecos* (Roswell, N.M.: Chaves County Historical Society, 1978), pp. 42, 88; Marc Simmons, "The Poet Scout," in idem, *Ranchers, Ramblers and Renegades: True Tales of Territorial New Mexico* (Santa Fe: Ancient City Press, 1984), pp. 15–17.

11. Redfield cites as her source for this account Ralph Emerson Twitchell, ed., *The Leading Facts of New Mexican History,* vol. 2 (Cedar Rapids, Iowa: Torch Press, 1912), p. 441. Also, see Simmons, "The Fate of Charlie McComas," in *Ranchers, Ramblers and Renegades,* pp. 61–63, where he gives various speculations, including the possibility that McComas survived to lead a band of free Apaches in northern Sonora as late as 1930.

12. According to Cobean, however, Carson was married "to a Taos Pueblo Indian girl named Little Wild Rose [and] says the marriage cost him seven good horses. Kit and his Indian wife were very happy together until her death in 1902. He was then left to bring up their little daughter, Nucki. She too died soon after being shut up in school all day long." Cobean, "Uncle Kit," p. 21.

13. John Sinclair, *Cowboy Riding Country* (Albuquerque: University of New Mexico Press, 1982), p. 10.

14. Martin Van Buren Corn is the subject of a short biographical monograph by James D. Shinkle, *Martin V. Corn, Early Roswell Pioneer* (Roswell, N.M.: Hall-Poorbaugh Press, n.d., but apparently 1972 or 1973). Among the valuable photographs is one of the family of Robert L. and Maggie B. Corn (p. 45), and a photo taken in 1914 or 1915 of Martin V. Corn and his twelve sons (p. 47). Also, see Georgia B. Redfield, "Martin V. B. Corn and His Descendants," in Fleming and Huffman, *Roundup on the Pecos,* pp. 182–88.

15. See Cecil Bonney, *Looking Over My Shoulder: Seventy-Five Years in the Pecos Valley* (Roswell, N.M.: Hall-Poorbaugh Press, 1971).

16. "Another invaluable source of information has been personal interviews [in 1970, 1971 and 1972] with Mrs. May Corn Marley and Waid H[ampton] Corn [?–1972], who were the second and third children of the second family of Martin V. Corn. In his later years Martin V. Corn probably told more about his early life to May Corn Marley than any other member of his second family." Shinkle, *Martin V. Corn,* p. 4. A photo of Mrs. May Corn Marley, second daughter of Martin V. Corn and Julia McVicker Corn, appears on p. 44. Another account of planting the Lover's Lane trees was given in 1927 by May Corn Marley's sister, Mrs. Mary E. Corn Hudson (1868–1941) of Roswell, and is reprinted in Shinkle, *Fifty Years of Roswell History,* p. 280; and in idem, *Reminiscences of Roswell Pioneers* (Roswell, N.M.: Hall-Poorbaugh, 1966), p. 71. Also, see Lovers' Lane photo and accounts in Fleming and Huffman, *Roundup on the Pecos,* pp. 11, 55, 184, 196, 412.

17. James Phelps White (1856–1934) was a noted cattleman and businessman who came to New Mexico in 1881 and purchased the Bosque Grande Ranch. Roswell's J. P. White Building is on the corner of Third and Main Streets. See Ellis Arthur Davis, ed., *The Historical Encyclopedia of New Mexico* (Albuquerque: New Mexico Historical Association, 1945), p. 1100. Also, see Gretchen Smith White, "James Phelps White Family," in Fleming and Huffman, *Roundup on the Pecos,* pp. 71–77.

18. Shinkle, *Fifty Years of Roswell History,* p. 174; Minor S. Huffman and Eve Ball, "Amonett Family," in Fleming and Huffman, *Roundup on the Pecos,* pp. 105–107.

19. John L. Sinclair mentions only Matt Brand as making cowboy boots in E. T. and Edd Amonett's saddle shop. Sinclair, *Cowboy Riding Country,* pp. 23–27.

20. Jean M. Burroughs, "Land of No Rivers: Curry and Roosevelt Counties," *El Palacio* 84, 1 (Spring 1978): 12. Also, see Don McAlavy, "Curry County: The Crafty Creation of Charles Scheurich," ibid.: 20–29.

21. For an account of Clayton Reed's part in early Clovis, see Tom Pendergrass, "Prodigy on the Plains: The Founding of Clovis, New Mexico, 1906–1908," *Rio Grande History,* 2, 1 and 2 (Summer 1974): 5–6.

22. An acutely infectious disease of the skin or mucous membranes manifesting itself by local inflammation and fever.

23. Maxwell also wrote in the same manuscript, "I'm glad I voted for the sales tax. I voted against the limit on mill levy. Sorry I lost. I have always voted for what I deemed for the interest of the schools. Should I live to vote one-hundred years longer, I'll still do this. I've taught 30 years in New Mexico. I feel I have earned every dollar I've drawn. There are so many teachers beside me who have helped lay the foundation of a good school system. Many present teachers [are] carrying on what we began. I makes me happy to view the present situation." "Schools and Teachers of Curry County," n.d., A#191.

24. James D. Shinkle reprints a news item of March 21, 1902, about the "First Automobile in the Pecos Valley": "Dr. W. E. Parkhurst received this week an 'Oldsmobile' from Lansing, Michigan. It is a handsome machine, lightly but strongly built, weighing 800 pounds, and is 'Strictly a runabout.' He set it up at the home of Mr. George E. Mabie, and as soon as he has learned to run it, will have it 'down town,' so that the public can see it on the streets. It is the first to be brought to the Pecos Valley, and the doctor deserves credit for his enterprise." Shinkle, *Fifty Years of Roswell History,* p. 225. A picture of this ten horsepower, single cylinder machine, which was "shipped packaged by express . . . assembled by Dr. Parkhurst [and] . . . later sold to John Gill," appears in Shinkle, *Reminiscences of Roswell Pioneers,* p. 235.

25. Van Deren Coke, *Photography in New Mexico: From the Daguerreotype to the Present* (Albuquerque: University of New Mexico Press, 1979), p. 30.

"And there are the WPA jobs, lifesavers for many. There are few private jobs for these people, and they have little chance to sell their services. People of the village [El Cerrito] have almost no land or livestock left, but their needs are greater than ever. They must earn money, and they earn it as best they can" (Irving Rusinow, *A Camera Report on El Cerrito, A Typical Spanish-American Community in New Mexico*, BAE, USDA, Misc. Pub. 479, January 1942, p. 82; neg. no. 83-G-37883, National Archives).

GLOSSARY

*of Pertinent
New Deal Projects*

Bureau of Agricultural Economics (BAE). Part of the U. S. Department of Agriculture. During 1940, BAE social scientists studied six typical rural American areas: the village of El Cerrito, New Mexico; Grafton County, New Hampshire; Lancaster County, Pennsylvania; Putnam County, Georgia; Haskell County, Kansas; and Shelby County, Iowa.

Civil Works Administration (CWA). Created by Executive Order on November 9, 1933, as a federal employment program. Administered by FERA administrator Harry Hopkins. Terminated on March 31, 1934.

Farm Security Administration (FSA). First established April 30, 1935, as the Resettlement Administration, an independent agency to provide short-term relief for impoverished farm families and long-term rural rebuilding. It became part of the U.S. Department of Agriculture on January 1, 1937, and the name was changed to the Farm Security Administration on September 1, 1937.

Roy Stryker officially joined the Resettlement Administration on July 10, 1935, as Chief of the Historical Section with a broad mandate to direct investigators, photographers, econ-

omists, sociologists, and statisticians. An Information Division to provide a unified photographic service was established in October 1935, initially with Stryker in charge. Among the photographers eventually employed by Stryker were Arthur Rothstein, Carl Mydans, Walker Evans, Ben Shahn, Dorothea Lange, Paul Carter, Theodor Jung, Russell Lee, John Vachon, Marion Post Wolcott, Jack Delano, and John Collier, Jr., while Gordon Parks became a trainee.

By March 1942 Stryker and his staff were doing work for the Office of War Information, no longer able to document the rural and urban poor but instead enlisted for war propaganda. Paul Vanderbilt began archiving the 130,000 FSA photographs in 1942, and they were transferred to the Library of Congress in 1944. Stryker resigned in September 1943 and went to work for Standard Oil, heading a team to document the oil industry's impact on New Jersey and eventually nationwide.

Federal Art Project (FAP). Part of Federal One. Established August 2, 1935, as a work relief program to employ artists and skilled and unskilled personnel associated with the arts to do mural painting, easel paintings, sculpture, applied arts like posters and signs, photography, lectures, criticism, and preparation of catalogues and pamphlets, circulating exhibitions of art, art teaching, and other such activities. Community art centers and the Index of American Design were initiated later. National director: Holger Cahill.

With Arizona, Colorado, Utah, and Wyoming, New Mexico was in FAP Region Five, headed by Donald Bear. Russell Vernon Hunter (1900–1955) directed the NMFAP throughout, from its inception in October 1935 to its close (as the N.M. Art Program) late in 1942. Hunter was assisted by Joy Yeck, and his first state advisory committee included Paul A. F. Walter (President, First National Bank, Santa Fe), Mrs. Mary R. Van Stone (Curator, Museum of New Mexico Fine Arts Museum, Santa Fe), Francis del Dosso (art instructor, University of New Mexico, Albuquerque), and three Santa Fe artists—Raymond Jonson, Gustave Baumann, and Randall Davey.

The NMFAP was considered exemplary, employing 206 persons between 1935 and 1939. Taos woodcarver Patrocinio Barela was among the native artists encouraged. The "Portfolio of Spanish Colonial Design," directed by E. Boyd Hall, containing fifty plates was handpainted and colored by August 1, 1938. New Mexico art teaching and exhibition centers were established at Melrose (directed by Martha Kennedy), at Roswell (directed by Roland Dickey), and at Las Vegas and Gallup (both directed by Toni Thoburn).

Federal Emergency Relief Administration (FERA). Established by Act of May 12, 1933, to provide five hundred million dollars for outright grants to the states for relief. National administrator Harry Hopkins set up direct relief, work relief, and special programs. Final state FERA grants were made at the end of 1935, and the Emergency Relief Appropriation Act of 1936 provided for the FERA's termination.

Federal One. Part of Works Progress Administration. Federal Project Number One, the first of six white-collar work relief projects, was officially announced on August 2, 1935. Its first four subprojects were: Art, directed by Holger Cahill; Music, directed by Nicolai Sokoloff; Theatre, directed by Hallie Flanagan; and Writers, directed by Henry G. Alsberg. The Emergency Relief Appropriation Act of 1939 marked the end of Federal One on August 31, 1939.

Federal Writers' Project (FWP). Part of Federal One. Established August 2, 1935, to employ writers, teachers, map draughtsmen, photographers, reporters, editors, journalists, librarians, and research workers. The major, basic program, which underwent many changes, was to produce an American Guide Book. Some creative work was encouraged, but most writing involved was nonfiction. In addition to the guides, there were projects in social-ethnic studies, Negro studies, various encyclopedias, and the collection of folklore and slave narratives. National director: Henry G. Alsberg.

Ina Sizer Cassidy (1869–1956) was hired to direct the NMFWP on October 1, 1935. She was demoted in January 1939 and replaced by Aileen Nusbaum, who served from February 1 until August 31, 1939. Four districts were set up: One (Taos, Colfax, Union, Harding, Quay, Guadalupe, San Miguel, and Mora counties), Two (Curry, Roosevelt, Lea, Eddy, Eddy, Otero, Lincoln, De Baca, and Chaves counties), Three (Santa Fe, Rio Arriba, San Juan, McKinley, Valencia, Bernalillo, and Sandoval counties), and Four (Socorro, Doña Ana, Luna, Hidalgo, Grant, Catron, and Sierra counties). They were responsible to editors and the director in Santa Fe, who, in turn, were responsible to state and federal officials.

At various times between November 1935 and August 1939, the NMFWP subprojects included: Coordinating (editorial work at Santa Fe), Reporting, Folklore, and the American Guide. A *Calendar of Events* (1937), two issues of a mimeographed periodical, *Over the Turquoise Trail* (1937), and a mimeographed literary magazine by the same title (1938) were published, but all the other work remained in the growing files in Santa Fe and Washington.

Historic American Buildings Survey (HABS). Initially part of CWA, November 1933 to May

1934, the program was to provide employment for architects and draftsmen to survey, document, and assemble a national archives on historic American architecture. Thomas C. Vint directed the work in 1933, and a national advisory committee, which included John Gaw Meem of Santa Fe, was convened in January 1934. A tripartite Memorandum of Agreement was signed on July 23, 1934, among the National Park Service, the American Institute of Architects, and the Library of Congress. It established HABS as permanently responsible for documenting historic American buildings, with the Library's Division of Prints and Photographs the depository and the AIA the professional counsel. Legislative mandate was provided by the Historic Sites, Buildings, and Antiquities Act of 1935 and reaffirmed in the Historic Preservation Act of 1980. Active recording stopped in 1941, but was reactivated in 1957. As of 1983, HABS and the Historic American Engineering Record (HAER) were administered under the National Architectural and Engineering Record of the National Park Service, United States Department of the Interior.

In New Mexico, John Gaw Meem served as HABS regional advisor from 1934 to 1955.

Historical Records Survey (HRS). Part of Federal One. Luther H. Evans was officially appointed director, October 1, 1935. At first HRS was subordinate to the Writers' Project, so field workers on both were urged to cooperate with each other. First state project unit was organized and the *Manual of the Survey of Historical Records* completed in January 1936. HRS became an independent unit on October 15, 1936. The national office was technically defunct after August 31, 1939, but was nominally continued. Evans resigned in 1939 and was replaced by Sargent D. Child in 1940, who was succeeded in 1942 by Lillian Kessler. In the fall of 1942, Cyril E. Paquin oversaw the task of liquidation.

George P. Hammond served as state director in New Mexico and was succeeded by Herbert O. Brayer and then G. Robert Massey. According to the "Inventory of the Records of the Historical Records Survey of New Mexico as of July 1, 1942,"

The project in New Mexico was called upon to "Prepare and duplicate inventories of Federal, State, County, municipal, and other public archives; prepare and duplicate inventories, guides, and calendars of manuscript collections, including church archives; prepare and duplicate inventories of books, pamphlets, and broadsides printed in the United States and its territorial possessions prior to January 1, 1891, and of newspapers located in the United States; transcribe older and more important archives and manuscripts as a measure of preservation; file, assemble, classify, index, transcribe, map and photograph data to be used in the preparation of essay upon historical sites in New Mexico, arrange records and other archives, manuscripts, and printed materials as a preliminary step to preparing inventories, guides and calendars; prepare and make available inventories of civilian organization; make descriptive inventories of housing and storage facilities for records, and museum treasures; and assist curators and custodians in preparing priority lists of such materials." (Record Group 69, National Archives)

A directory of churches and religious organizations came out in 1940; an index to Bandelier's final report on his investigations among Southwestern Indians and a guide to public vital statistics appeared in 1942. Inventories of county archives were finished, 1937–42, and inventories of state archives, 1940–41.

Public Works of Art Project (PWAP). Established by a grant from CWA to the Treasury Department in December 1933. Directed by Edward Bruce. In all, 3,600 artists on work relief produced more than 16,000 works in various media until the PWAP closed in June 1934.

New Mexico was with Arizona in Region 13, directed by Jesse Nusbaum (1877–1975). Gustave Bauman (1881–1971) coordinated work in New Mexico. According to his 1934 report, "A Retrospect of Work and the Artists Employed in the Thirteenth Region under the Public Works of Art Project" (A#155), the following artists worked on the PWAP: from

Taos—Kenneth Adams, Charles T. Berninghaus, Emil Bisttram, Laverne Nelson Black, Herbert Dunton, Joseph A. Fleck, Blanche C. Grant, Gordon K. Grant, Martin Hennings, Victor Higgins, Gene Kloss, Ward Lockwood, Ila Mcafee Turner, Walter Ufer, and Carl Woolsey; from Santa Fe—Charles Barrows and James S. Morris (boys), William Emmett Burk, Jr., Gerald Cassidy, Randall Davey, Fremont Ellis, Irene Emery, William Penhallow Henderson, Wendell Cooley Jones, Raymond Jonson, Paul Lantz, Tom Lea, Hannah Mecklem, Willard Nash, B. J. O. Nordfeldt, Sheldon Parsons, Bert Phillips, Hubert Rogers, Olive Rush, Bruce Wilder Saville, Will Shuster, Theodore Van Soelen, Francisco Delgado, and Emilio Padilla; from Raton—Manville Chapman; from Las Vegas—Omar W. Hearn; from Albuquerque—Nils Hogner, Bill Lumpkins, J. T. McMurdoo, Carl Redin, Esquipula Romero de Romero, Stuart Walker, and Paul Brooks Willis; from Texico—Vernon Hunter; from Farmington—Warren E. Rollins; and from Cordova—José Dolores López.

Treasury Relief Art Project (TRAP). Established by a grant from the WPA to the Treasury Department in July 1935. Directed by Olin Dows. Up to 356 artists produced work for old and new federal buildings. When TRAP was closed on June 30, 1938, 85 murals, 39 sculptures, and 10,215 easels had been completed.

New Mexico and Arizona, Region 13, were directed by Jesse Nusbaum, who was also Southern New Mexico Supervisor, with Emil Bisttram (1895–1975) as Northern New Mexico Supervisor. Among the commissions were William P. Henderson's six paintings for Santa Fe's Federal Building, begun under the PWAP, and paintings by Joseph Fleck (1893–?) and Paul Lantz (1908–   ) for post offices in Raton and Clovis respectively.

Treasury Section of Painting and Sculpture (Section). Established by Departmental Order of the Secretary of the Treasury, October 1934. Directed by Edward Bruce. It was not a relief measure but a national program to secure art for public buildings by anonymous competi-

tions. By December 1942, 13,033 artists had submitted 36,009 designs for 193 competitions resulting in murals and sculpture for 1,101 cities.

New Mexican artists won some of the competitions. Emil Bisttram did a mural for the Justice Department in Washington, while Theodore Van Soelen painted a mural for the Portales post office and Peter Hurd did frescoes for the Alamogordo post office.

Work Projects Administration (WPA). The Emergency Relief Appropriation Act of 1939 provided for reorganization of the Works Progress Administration effective July 1, 1939. Colonel Francis G. Harrington became national WPA Commissioner, subordinate to Federal Works Administrator John M. Carmody. Control of the various projects was to be returned to the states. James J. Connelly was New Mexico's state administrator. WPA terminated in 1943, by which time most work was war related.

Works Progress Administration (WPA). Established by Executive Order No. 7034 on May 6, 1935, to coordinate and implement "the work relief programs as a whole" and to develop "small useful projects designed to assure a maximum employment in all areas." National administrator: Harry Hopkins. New Mexico state administrator: Lea Rowland.

Writers' Program (WP). Part of Work Projects Administration. Reorganized FWP effective September 1, 1939, with fewer workers and state and locally supported projects. National director: John D. Newsom.

Charles Ethrige Minton (1893–1976) directed the NMWP. Three books were published: *New Mexico: A Guide to the Colorful State* (New York: Hastings House, 1940); *New Mexico,* American Recreational Series, No. 30 (Northport, N.Y.: Bacon & Wieck, 1941), and *The Spanish-American Song and Game Book* (New York: Barnes, 1942). A number of publications were in progress by the late 1942 termination, among them a history of grazing, a health almanac, studies of Las Placitas, Cordova, and Taos County religious practices, and Annette H. Thorp's "Some New Mexico Grandmothers."

SELECTED BIBLIOGRAPHY

National and New Mexico
New Deal Sources
Subsequent to 1933–1943

Baldwin, Sidney. *Poverty and Politics: The Rise and Decline of the FSA.* Chapel Hill: University of North Carolina Press, 1968.

Banks, Ann, ed. *First Person America.* New York: Alfred A. Knopf, 1980.

Bermingham, Peter. *The New Deal in the Southwest: Arizona and New Mexico.* Tucson: The University of Arizona Museum of Art, n.d. [1980].

Bloxom, Marguerite D., comp. *Pickaxe and Pencil: References for the Study of the WPA.* Washington, D.C.: Library of Congress, 1982.

Braeman, John, Robert H. Bremner, and David Brody, eds. *The New Deal,* vol. 2: *The State and Local Levels.* 2 vols. Columbus: Ohio State University Press, 1975.

Brown, James Seay, Jr., ed. *Up Before Daylight: Life Histories from the Alabama Writers' Project, 1938–1939.* University: University of Alabama Press, 1982.

Brown, Lorin W., with Charles L. Briggs and Marta Weigle. *Hispano Folklife of New Mexico: The Lorin W. Brown Federal Writers' Project Manuscripts.* Albuquerque: University of New Mexico Press, 1978.

Contreras, Belisario R. *Tradition and Innovation in New Deal Art.* Lewisburg: Becknell University Press; London and Toronto: Associated University Press, 1983.

Córdova, Gilberto Benito, comp. *Bibliography of Unpublished Materials Pertaining to Hispanic Culture in the New Mexico WPA Writers' Files.* Santa Fe: New Mexico State Department of Education, December 1972.

Davidson, Katherine H., comp. *Preliminary Inventory of the Records of the Federal Writers' Project, Work Projects Administration, 1935–44.* National Archives Pub. No. 54-2; Preliminary Inventories No. 57. Washington, D.C., 1953.

Dwyer-Shick, Susan. "Review Essay: Folklore and Government Support." *Journal of American Folklore* 89 (1976): 476–86.

Federal One: A Newsletter of 1930's Culture. Institute on the Federal Theatre Project and New Deal Culture, George Mason University, 4400 University Drive, Fairfax, Virginia 22030.

Gabriel, Bertram. "WPA Murals—Fine Art from Hard Times." *New Mexico Magazine,* November 1982, pp. 16–22.

Ganzel, Bill. *Dust Bowl Descent*. Lincoln: University of Nebraska Press, 1984.

Hefner, Loretta L., comp. *The W.P.A. Historical Records Survey: A Guide to the Unpublished Inventories, Indexes and Transcripts*. Chicago: Society of American Archivists, 1980.

Historic America: Buildings, Structures, and Sites. Recorded by The Historic American Buildings Survey and the Historic American Engineering Record. Checklist compiled by Alicia Stamm. Essays edited by C. Ford Peatross. Washington, D.C.: Library of Congress, 1983.

Howard, Donald S. *The WPA and Federal Relief Policy*. New York: Russell Sage Foundation, 1943.

Hurley, F. Jack. *Portrait of a Decade: Roy Stryker and the Development of Documentary Photography in the Thirties*. Baton Rouge: Lousiana State University Press, 1972.

Leuchtenburg, William E. *Franklin D. Roosevelt and the New Deal, 1932–1940*. New York: Harper & Row, 1963.

Loomis, Ormond H., coordinator. *Cultural Conservation: The Protection of Cultural Heritage in the United States*. A study by the American Folklife Center, Library of Congress, carried out in cooperation with the National Park Service, Department of the Interior. Washington, D.C.: Library of Congress, 1983.

Lowitt, Richard. *The New Deal and the West*. Bloomington: Indiana University Press, 1984.

Mangione, Jerre. *The Dream and the Deal: The Federal Writers' Project, 1935–1943*. Boston: Little, Brown, 1972.

Marling, Karal Ann. *Wall-to-Wall America: A Cultural History of Post-Office Murals in the Great Depression*. Minneapolis: University of Minnesota Press, 1982.

McDonald, William F. *Federal Relief Administration and the Arts: The Origins and Administrative History of the Arts Projects of the Works Progress Administration*. Columbus: Ohio State University Press, 1969.

McElvaine, Robert S. *The Great Depression: America, 1929–1941*. New York: Times Books, 1984.

McKinzie, Richard D. *The New Deal for Artists*. Princeton, N.J.: Princeton University Press, 1973.

Nabokov, Peter. *Architecture of Acoma Pueblo: The 1934 Historic American Buildings Survey Project*. Santa Fe: Ancient City Press, 1985.

Noggle, Burl. *Working with History: The Historical Records Survey in Louisiana and the Nation, 1936–1942*. Baton Rouge: Louisiana State University Press, 1981.

O'Connor, Francis V. *Federal Support for the Visual Arts: The New Deal and Now*. Greenwich, Conn.: New York Graphic Society, 1969.

———, ed. *Art for the Millions: Essays from the 1930s by Artists and Administrators of the WPA Federal Art Project*. Boston: New York Graphic Society, 1973.

———, ed. *The New Deal Art Projects: An Anthology of Memoirs*. Washington, D.C.: Smithsonian Institution Press, 1972.

O'Neal, Hank. *A Vision Shared: A Classic Portrait of America and Its People, 1935–1943*. New York: St. Martin's Press, 1976.

Park, Marlene, and Gerald E. Markowitz, *Democratic Vistas: Post Offices and Public Art in the New Deal*. Philadelphia: Temple University Press, 1984.

Patterson, James T. *The New Deal and the States: Federalism in Transition*. Princeton, N.J.: Princeton University Press, 1969.

Pearce, T. M., ed., assisted by Ina Sizer Cassidy and Helen S. Pearce. *New Mexico Place Names: A Geographical Dictionary*. Albuquerque: University of New Mexico Press, 1965.

Pells, Richard H. *Radical Visions and American Dreams: Culture and Social Thought in the Depression Years*. New York: Harper & Row, 1973.

Penkower, Monty Noam. *The Federal Writers' Project: A Study in Government Patronage of the Arts*. Urbana: University of Illinois Press, 1977.

Rapport, Leonard. "How Valid Are the Federal Writers' Project Life Stories: An Iconoclast Among the True Believers." *Oral History Review*, 1979, pp. 6–17.

Romasco, Albert U. *The Politics of Recovery: Roosevelt's New Deal*. New York: Oxford University Press, 1983.

Schlesinger, Arthur M., Jr. *The Age of Roosevelt.* 3 vols. Boston: Houghton Mifflin, 1957–60.

Slade, Thomas M., ed. *Historic American Buildings Survey in Indiana.* Bloomington: Indiana University Press, 1983.

Spurlock, William Henry, II. "Federal Support for the Visual Arts in the State of New Mexico: 1933–1943." Master's thesis, University of New Mexico, 1974.

Stark, Richard B., ed. *Juegos Infantiles Cantados en Nuevo México.* Santa Fe: Museum of New Mexico Press, 1973.

Steichen, Edward, ed. *The Bitter Years, 1935–1941: Rural America As Seen by the Photographers of the Farm Security Administration.* New York, 1962.

Stott, William. *Documentary Expression and Thirties America.* New York: Oxford University Press, 1973.

Stryker, Roy Emerson, and Nancy Wood. *In This Proud Land: America 1935–1943 as Seen in the FSA Photographs.* Boston: New York Graphic Society, 1973.

Terrill, Tom E., and Jerrold Hirsch, eds. *Such As Us: Southern Voices of the Thirties.* Chapel Hill: University of North Carolina Press, 1978.

Weigle, Marta, with Mary Powell. "From Alice Corbin's 'Lines Mumbled in Sleep' to 'Eufemia's Sopapillas': Women and the Federal Writers' Project in New Mexico." *New America: A Journal of American and Southwestern Culture* 4, 3 (1982): 54–76.

Weigle, Marta, ed. *Hispanic Villages of Northern New Mexico: A Reprint of Volume II of The 1935 Tewa Basin Study, with Supplementary Materials.* Santa Fe: The Lightning Tree, Jene Lyon, Publisher, 1975.

White, George Abbott. "Vernacular Photography: FSA Images of Depression Leisure." *Studies in Visual Communication* 9, 1 (Winter 1983): 53–75.

Wroth, William, ed. *Russell Lee's FSA Photographs of Chamisal and Peñasco, New Mexico.* Santa Fe: Ancient City Press; Colorado Springs: Taylor Museum of the Colorado Springs Fine Arts Center, 1985.

INDEX

223